MAKE AMERICA FIRST AGAIN

MAKE AMERICA FIRST AGAIN

Grand Strategy Analysis and the Trump Administration

Jacob Shively

Rapid Communications in Conflict and Security Series
General Editor: Geoffrey R.H. Burn

CAMBRIA PRESS

Amherst, New York

Requests for permission should be directed to
permissions@cambriapress.com, or mailed to:
Cambria Press
100 Corporate Parkway, Suite 128
Amherst, New York 14226, USA

Library of Congress Cataloging-in-Publication Data on file.

ISBN: 9781621965404

TABLE OF CONTENTS

List of Tables

Acknowledgements

I am indebted to a number of colleagues, students, friends, and family members. I particularly want to thank Nina Silove, Christopher Fettweis, and Ionut Popescu, whose insights on key portions of this text were extremely helpful and deeply appreciated. The book's peer reviewers also gave me exceptional feedback, the impact of which is felt in the following chapters. My fellow grand strategy panelists at the 2019 ISSS-IS conference—Dan Caldwell, Paul Viotti, William James, and Julie Thompson-Gomez—also helped to solidify the project's final stages. Colin Dueck commented on an earlier project on which this work is based, and his trenchant insights helped shape this work. Thanks, also, to the Honorable Jerry Maygarden, Brigadier General John Adams, U.S. Army (Retired), and Dr. Ken Ford of IHMC for their candid insights into applied strategy. My colleagues at the University of West Florida's Reubin O'D. Askew Department of Government, Michelle Williams, Al Cuzán, David Ramsey, Adam Cayton, and Brian Crisher continue to inspire with their commitment to serious scholarship and teaching. Of course, none of this would be possible without Geoffrey R. H. Burn, whose editorial insights and guidance breathed life into the project, as well as the team members at Cambria Press, who are serious professionals doing impressive work.

Profound appreciation goes to my graduate students and assistants, whose hard work and insights helped lay the foundations for the case narratives. These include Kim Budnick, Kelly Dutton, Joe Haber, Bobby Lint, Dylan Mortensen, Evelyn VanDerbeck, and John Link. I'd also like to thank Oscar Griffin for his truly impressive efforts on earlier, related projects as well as on building a formidable timeline.

As I developed this manuscript, my cousin Guy Jason Shively passed away suddenly and unexpectedly. In the preceding year, we tangled and debated over politics. We both wanted to learn from each other, and we both wanted a better world. I wish we could have kept up that discussion. I'll miss you, cousin.

None of this would be possible without folks closer to home, as well. Good neighbors make life a little saner and sweeter, and I am grateful that the Bradleys, the Barnes, the Halls, and the Ballows are some of the best. Dad and mom: your love and support continue to have profound impact across many generations. Elam, Jude, Eve, and Aver: I love you deeply. My wife, Gen, has borne with me throughout this project and my career. I deeply value her insights, her mind, and her perspective. Thank you.

MAKE AMERICA FIRST AGAIN

CHAPTER 1

A STRATEGIC RIDDLE

INTRODUCTION

Donald Trump insisted that he held a secret plan to defeat the Islamic State (ISIS). Under a black flag, the Islamist insurgency had torn across Syria and Iraq with brutal violence.[1] Its leaders had an uncompromisingly apocalyptic ideology. Through 2014 and 2015, images of systemically murdered prisoners of war and stories of women forced into marriages or slavery shocked the world. The group grew from seeds planted by earlier Iraqi extremists and now emerged as a well-organized, conventional military force that seized and held territory. President Obama's administration responded slowly. Officials feared falling into a quagmire. Nevertheless, when ISIS threatened genocide and murdered two American journalists, US officials ramped up a strategy to slowly strangle the organization. Many saw ISIS as one of the globe's most critical security threats. Pressed by reporters about how he would respond, then-candidate Trump declared that he wanted to be unpredictable. He said his political opponents in the Republican primary were giving away victory plans with public, detailed policy positions. What kind of strategist gives away his plans? Unpredictability, Trump pronounced at energized rallies across the country, had always been crucial to his success.[2]

Establishment Republicans replied that Trump was utterly ignorant about foreign affairs. Unimpressed, Trump elevated his approach. In spring 2016, he talked about a "doctrine of unpredictability."[3] Americans, he said, had given too much away with their unoriginal policies. Trump assured victory over the terrorist threat. Yet he also offered no tactical or strategic details. Incredulous, critics complained that Trump the reality television star still had no strategy and no foreign policy. His unpredictability with governments like North Korea, they told him, is dangerous. Trump doubled down and said he would even be unpredictable with American allies. Republican voters vindicated Trump's approach as he slowly picked off his presidential primary challengers.

That fall, the general election pitted Trump against Hillary Clinton, an establishment powerhouse with extensive, almost unparalleled political and foreign policy experience. Trump said NATO was obsolete, suggested dissolving and renegotiating dozens of established trade deals, and floated the prospect of using nuclear weapons against ISIS.[4] Clinton outpaced Trump during their televised debates. She showed her grasp of policy and baited Trump into angry retorts regarding his relationship with Russia. On the campaign trail, she said Trump's grand strategy—his approach to national security and foreign affairs—was "dangerously incoherent" and did not even rise to the level of ideas. He offered "just a series of bizarre rants, personal feuds, and outright lies."[5] Nearly every poll predicted a Clinton win. Nearly every senior foreign policy figure, Democrat and Republican, endorsed Clinton.

And then, something unexpected: Donald Trump won the election. Vindicated, many of his supporters looked forward to a foreign policy defined by both tough confrontations and limited international entanglements. Trade protection and economic expansion. Perhaps most of all, they expected renewed respect for the United States on the world stage and security at home.

Two years later, President Trump released an official White House statement. "America First! The world is a very dangerous place!" it proclaimed.[6] Earlier that month, the 2018 midterm election saw Republicans suffer a national rout and lose control of the House of Representatives. Over two years in office, Trump's approval ratings had hovered at the same levels: around 40%. On foreign policy, he remained dogged by Russia's attempt to shape the 2016 election, raging fights over immigration, discontent over his growing "trade war" with China, frustration and fear among allies regarding his reliability, and his own ever-shifting official statements. Now, Turkish officials were releasing evidence that Saudi journalist and US resident Jamal Khashoggi had walked into his country's Istanbul consulate for marriage papers only to be murdered and dismembered. Later, leaks revealed that US Central Intelligence Agency (CIA) officials believed Saudi Arabia's ruler, Crown Prince Mohammed bin Salman, had ordered the murder.[7] Many Americans and foreign leaders demanded some response to this act. The assassination also renewed questions about indirect US support for bin Salman's ongoing war in Yemen, with its tens of thousands of civilian casualties and images of child starvation.[8]

Trump, however, was fully committed to his existing approach. His White House statement said Khashoggi's murder was "terrible" but, in a verbal shrug, "we may never know all of the facts surrounding the murder." Crown Prince Salman might have had knowledge of "this tragic event—maybe he did and maybe he didn't!" The statement observed that the United States conducted extensive business with Saudi Arabia, was enjoying low oil prices, and shared a mutual adversary in Iran. The United States would "remain a steadfast partner of Saudi Arabia to ensure the interests of our country." More generally, "America is pursuing its national interests and vigorously contesting countries that wish to do us harm. Very simply it is called America First!"

Trump's strategic approach to the world had proven relatively unchanged since 2016. Perhaps more confident in what "America first" looks like in action, Trump still offered few details and demonstrated little interest in spreading American values. Most observers now agreed that the president's basic approach to other governments was transactional. Many of those observers, just as in 2016, were also groping for a clear Trump grand strategy. Trump and his team plowed forward. They managed an ever-changing mix of the president's general principles and his idiosyncratic decisions and behaviors toward major issues and international leaders. "America first" remained their basic standard. However, without a defining crisis, success, or failure, both Trump's critics and his supporters remained deeply convinced that the Trump administration fostered either strategic calamity or strategic genius.

Agenda

This book examines US grand strategy between two moments, the 2016 presidential election and the 2018 midterm election. It is an early history and an assessment of the Trump administration's grand strategy, but it is also a study of much larger questions. Like US presidents and other heads of government, Donald Trump provokes a wide range of debates. For grand strategy, the debates are familiar but profound: what exactly is the administration's approach to the world and national security? In addition, can one administration or even one individual change a state's grand strategy? Trump's temperament is notoriously public. Is it also uniquely influential? Perhaps Trump the man fundamentally changed US grand strategy during this period. Or, perhaps, he and his administration were constrained by existing strategic commitments. To answer these questions, the following pages unfold the story of Trump's early grand strategy.

As a concept, grand strategy itself remains contested. Scholars disagree about whether such strategies are easily changed based upon one leader's prerogatives. They also debate whether and to what degree grand strategies are, in fact, a set of ideas and practices whose direction—like that of an oil tanker in a narrow channel—is unlikely to change. To study this concept itself, the book applies an innovative "grand strategy analysis" framework. Scholars and professionals have traditionally talked past one another on this topic, yet their work is converging. This project draws these strands together, and it uses them to help us understand Trump's grand strategy. It aims to learn whether Trump is indeed a true strategist. It seeks to determine whether one man alone can revise his government's grand strategy.

Readers may disagree with the final analyses in this book, but hopefully they will find the claims unignorable, grand strategy analysis (GSA) a vital innovation, and the case history invaluable. To date, work on the Trump administration's grand strategy, though extensive, has been journalistic, partial, or scattered. This book offers a more complete and systematic picture of Trump's grand strategy over its first two years. For students, practitioners and scholars, such substantive, concrete work is foundational. The book also engages live and ongoing debates about how to characterize and assess grand strategy. Its grand strategy analysis proposal is an essential consideration for anyone studying or working in this field. Finally, the book sets the stage for ongoing debates. It offers insight for policy makers and a revised analytical framework for scholars.

Do Leaders Matter?

The riddle of Trump's grand strategy is how the man and the outcomes interact. But finding the answer will tell us something about all grand strategies. Donald Trump improvises, confronts, and exaggerates. He is unpredictable, and he challenges all accepted wisdom about US foreign policy. During his first two years in the White House, he also presided over a government that had maintained global leadership for decades. "America first" appeared to guide his strategic thinking, yet the United States remained enmeshed politically, economically, and strategically in a complex world. How exactly can observers define Trump's approach to the world, and what exactly drives that approach?

I teach a graduate survey course on international relations. Students select a few articles to review for their classmates. Inevitably, one title gains the most requests: "Do Leaders Matter and How Would We Know?" Humans seem predisposed to believe that individuals—particularly the most visible individuals—make a difference to outcomes. Consider the classic counterfactual, *Would World War II in Europe have occurred without Adolph Hitler?* Now, imagine presenting that question to a random collection of people. They might debate for hours. Similarly, imagining the success of the American Civil Rights movement without Martin Luther King Jr. is not impossible, but it is difficult. Yet those examples also demonstrate constraints upon individuals. Each leader emerged from large, historical forces. World War II and the Civil Rights movement both unfolded for a host of reasons divorced from any one person. Appointing the world's most effective CEO to run a carriage business in 1900 does not change the reality that the business model is doomed. Do leaders matter, and how would we know?

Robert Jervis, one of the great US foreign policy scholars, penned "Do Leaders Matter?" Jervis was particularly interested in American presidents. He observed several strong arguments against the relevance of individual leaders. For example, no leader rises to the top of a system like the US government without already embodying or espousing at least some core precepts of that society.[9] Alternatively, he said, leaders may be socialized into a given role or set of prerogatives once in office, or they simply may be constrained by existing frameworks, expectations, sunk costs, and so forth. For international relations in general, scholars tend to defer to incentive structures, constraining environments, and other types of material factors to account for state behavior. Individuals matter, but they matter only at the margins. Any one decision or leadership style may seem impactful, but on balance, ran the argument, states tend to conform to a median set of expected behaviors and outcomes. Stated differently, leaders matter, but the weight one places on them should give way to other factors, such as the international balance of power or domestic economic interests. Leaders may matter in the immediate but not the long term.

As an analytical problem, studying the effect of leaders is a serious challenge. Because observers cannot run history twice with different individuals in different roles, they often use counterfactuals to study leader impacts. The impulse is simple. For example, analysts often assume that if a particular president had not won an election, then most decisions and policies would have turned out very differently. To be more precise, Jervis points to turning points or windows of opportunity.[10] At these moments, the individual sitting in the Oval Office can make a difference. That George W. Bush rather than Al Gore was president on 9/11 would seem to matter to US grand strategy as it developed over the next decade. Jervis takes this a step further. By what mechanisms might individual leaders make a difference during key moments? He lists four: 1) the president's "outlooks, values, and beliefs;" 2) personality and leadership style; 3) "political style and skill, which in turn influences their ability to mobilize support;" and 4) how others, domestically and internationally, respond to a given president. Jervis then evaluates two decisions to use violence, one by Harry Truman and one by G.W. Bush. He concludes that "Presidents are not mere pawns, but neither are they masters of their countries' fate."[11]

Jervis' article is preliminary. It restates a long-standing question in the light of more recent events and research, but it is not definitive. This book will add to that same line of questions. I argue that grand strategy is well-positioned as a phenomenon as well as a field of study to carry this type of question forward.

Answering the Riddle

To answer these questions, the following chapters seek to create an early history of the Trump administration's grand strategy for students, scholars, and professionals. They also propose grand strategy analysis (GSA) as a newly emerging framework and apply it to the Trump administration. To do all this, the book will develop four narrative case histories running from Trump's inauguration to the 2018 midterm elections. The final chapter compares theoretical predictions against the book's findings. This is an essential contribution for practioners, who often rely on systematic case studies to understand how presidential administrations unfold. It will also contribute to the early scholarship and theorizing on Trump's grand strategy as well as remain an enduring piece of contemporary analysis for future observers.

Questions

Raging debate over grand strategy is not unusual. The stakes are high, and grand strategy itself remains difficult to define. During Trump's early tenure, three questions prove particularly contested. In the first, "What is Trump's grand strategy?", broad consensus appears to have emerged. Trump seemed to be transactional and explicitly nationalistic. He was willing to risk some economic backlash to get better "deals" on trade relationships, but he was far more interested in talking about military power than using it. This conventional wisdom is helpful, but it is limited. For example, by what standard can observers say Trump is "transactional"? More generally, any sustained observation of the administration reveals ongoing internal debates and disagreements, and over the time studied in this book, Trump himself threw out contradictory tweets and vague official statements. A key goal of this book is to observe systematically the Trump administration's grand strategy. Conventional wisdom may not be wrong, but observers cannot know for certain until it is rigorously examined.

In the second question, Trump's temperament and management challenge common theories of strategy and foreign policy. Do leaders matter? Scholars continue to debate the degree to which specific individuals or individual characteristics affect actual strategy. Psychology and individual preferences seem to matter to foreign policy, but so do material interests, long-established priorities, and rational calculation. Ionut Popescu's recent study of "emergent strategy," for example, argued that effective strategy actually involves constant learning and short-term adaptation.[12] Popescu cites two of America's great Cold War foreign policy leaders, Dean Acheson and Henry Kissinger, who admitted that, in effect, their strategies were really just a pattern of short term decisions. If this is accurate, is the mind of the president or prime minister the only variable observers need to know to predict "strategy"? Many observers argue that Donald Trump's temperament is particularly voluble and visible. Do they need to know his personality traits to understand American grand strategy during his time in office?

Skeptics of grand strategy argue that, rather than imagining and implementing long-term plans, leaders hold only enough focus and resources to respond to crises. Psychological frames, personal impulses, group dynamics, immediate threats, bureaucratic interests, and political constraints seem to matter to national security strategy far more than long-term threat assessment and planning. Ronald Reagan, they might insist, wound down the Cold War not through careful strategic manipulation but by creating political space and seizing a personal opportunity with Mikhail Gorbechev.[13] Other observers insist that grand strategy is possible, real, and necessary. It sets priorities and offers direction for immense power. The problem, they often find, is not that grand strategy is an illusion, but that any given administration is pursuing the wrong strategy. George W. Bush relied too much on unilateral power and overextended US resources. Barack Obama failed to project a coherent, strong strategy. With the Trump administration, one critic complains that, amidst all the roiling debate and personality politics, observers "cannot be blamed for missing the grand strategy in it all."[14] Others have worried that Trump's "unpredictability" is really just erratic and counterproductive behavior, whereas scholars with a longer view suspect that Trump himself—or most presidents, for that matter—will have little fundamentally positive or negative impact on US grand strategy.

In a third question, observers wrangle over a strategy's success or failure. In Trump's first two years, was American grand strategy successful? For most students, professionals, and scholars, this question is the bottom line for studying grand strategy. The answer, however, is often more difficult to than most commentators will admit. For one thing, timeframes matter. A sort-term success, like the early 2003 invasion of Iraq or expansion of NATO in the 1990s, may prove hard to sustain in the long run. Conversely, any good strategic thinker tries to shape the long-term environment, yet a long-term strategic success like Cold War containment may look like compromise and failure for years before it bears fruit. Further, professionals often hold different ideas about strategic goals and how to define "success." A fully developed framework for this question deserves extensive treatment. It would also make for a very long book with even more moving parts. Instead, the final chapter will address this issue with a narrower analytical question: Was the early Trump grand strategy successful in comparison to the administration's *own* standards? In other words, did Trump achieve his own strategic goals, or did he at least set up the groundwork to achieve them?

Approach

To engage all these questions, the book offers an early and, as much as possible, honest overview of the Trump administration's approach to strategy. Many grand strategy analyses are driven by an ideological, political, or theoretical position. Though important, such work can obscure the case itself and the actors' logic and agendas as events unfolded. By contrast, this book's core is a set of case histories that allow the reader to observe and assess Trump's grand strategy its own terms. To do this, the cases draw upon the array of reports, statements, and policies emerging from and around this administration. Chapter 2 details the book's framework and methodology. The focus is grand strategy itself and how it unfolded. Often, these types of projects will focus on a subset of the most strategically salient issues or regions. They are topical rather than general. Though valuable, such work can lose sight of the overarching grand strategy itself. To avoid that, the cases seek to build a general history across four consecutive time periods. This type of systematic overview is skilled yeoman's work that most early reports and studies bypass. As such, it is uniquely valuable.

Still, analytically, the book takes sides. It argues that research on grand strategy has evolved over the last generation. Observers can now reliably study grand strategy the same way they study interstate wars or diplomatic crises or trade deals. Grand strategy, in other words, is a social phenomenon. It can exist on its own independent of any one leader or administration. The following pages dub this emerging field *grand strategy analysis*.[15] The book then uses that framework to highlight and assess the most prominent approaches to Trump's grand strategy. It concludes with arguments about personal versus impersonal forces as well as ongoing disagreements about how to characterize or categorize Trump's grand strategy. Takeaways appear in two basic categories. First, I will apply a simple three-dimensional framework to characterize the administration's grand strategy. Second, the conclusion draws upon the book's core case histories to determine which, if any, approaches best explain grand strategy in the Trump administration. The book ends with an assessment of the strategy's success or failure.

What is Grand Strategy?

We should pause to define the core concept: grand strategy. In short, this book uses the term to refer to a state's overarching plan to secure its international interests. Grand strategies are the ways that governments define their goals and then organize and deploy their capabilities to serve that goal. To be more concise, grand strategy is *a state's plan to determine and to achieve its national interests, especially security.* This is my own definition, though it significantly overlaps with many mainstream definitions, which are reviewed in Chapter 2.

That, however, is a working definition. What the book really advances is far more ambitious. Its GSA framework holds that however researchers and analysts define grand strategy, they increasingly agree that it is a distinct, observable phenomenon. "Grand strategy" often refers to an intellectual vision of state interests and how the state should operate in relation to other states and the international system. From a different angle, though, grand strategy might be defined as a pattern of behavior, a pattern that runs independently of any one leader or group. Interestingly, some scholars argue that grand strategies are inevitable. Historian Hal Brands argued that "all leaders—consciously or unconsciously, on the basis of reasoned analysis, pure ideology or intuition, or something in between—make judgements about which goals are most important, which threats most deserving of attention, and how resources should be deployed to meet them."[16] In other words, he concludes, "These sorts of grand strategic choices are inherent in the process of governing." However one approaches it empirically, this book argues that grand strategy is a phenomenon that can be studied on its own terms and may have a life of its own outside any one leader or administration.

Strategy itself typically refers to a means-ends calculation. Strategies answer a simple question: "How do we achieve our goal with the resources at hand?" For instance, strategies are famously common among business professionals, who must analyze a market and seek profit within it. Strategies are also integral to thinking about war, sports, and elections. In each of those cases, the goal is discrete and clear: victory. In international relations, goals can be more amorphous. States usually want security first, but security might be relative. Accepting proxy violence, threats of nuclear destruction, and military spending in the Cold War, for example, were considered by the United States and the Soviet Union necessary to avoid direct warfare. Similarly, state leaders usually want to ensure prosperity. This might involve protecting free trade or, at another extreme, directly conquering resources and markets. Some states also may want global political cooperation on pervasive issues like climate change. Whatever the goals, larger and more powerful states tend to display the characteristics of a grand strategy. They have more resources and a wider set of regional and global interests, so their leaders are more likely to seek or identify a broad, unifying approach to national interests. Still, strictly defined, grand strategy is not limited to any one type of state. There is no reason to think less powerful governments are not also interested in a large, coherent approach to the world. Indeed, leaders in small states may have far greater incentives to develop an efficient, unified strategy. By not maximizing their own strengths or clearly ordering their priorities, they run the risk of having their interests and terms dictated by others.

States live far longer than any one leadership regime. National leaders must constantly respond to immediate problems and crises. Consequently, a coherent, long-term grand strategy is difficult to build and maintain. Some critics even insist that grand strategy is really an illusion. Where a business or military leader can conceive a strategy and follow it coherently, national leaders inherit pieces of old strategies and, at the same time, implement elements of their own new strategies. Along the way, they are constantly reacting to changing circumstances. These critics argue that observers imagine strategic patterns exist when, in reality, decision makers are simply constrained by domestic interests, ideological beliefs and/or external forces.[17] Basically, leaders are making things up as they go, and later, practitioners call it a "strategy." This is a serious concern. It is also based on a potentially false or oversimplified concept of grand strategy. The critique assumes that grand strategy must be like architectural plans or business approaches: a fully developed, detailed and concrete set of ideas and actions. In politics and international relations, such an approach indeed would be an illusion or catastrophically brittle. As Chapter 2 will posit, however, grand strategies can be far more flexible and varied than this critique assumes.

For these reasons, dozens of plausible definitions of grand strategy exist. This book's contribution, however, is focused not on definitions but on *how grand strategy is studied and analyzed.* Rather than circling around semantics, it argues that the study of grand strategy across fields is converging. "Grand strategy" is a distinct topic that can be and is studied in different ways. The reason many definitions exist is that scholars, like the blind men trying to identify an elephant based upon its different parts, have focused on distinct parts of grand strategy. Chapter 2 makes this case, and it includes an extensive evaluation of existing approaches. It argues that by treating grand strategy as a distinct field and treating individual decision makers as the units of analysis, the blind men can finally start talking with one another and putting the pieces together into a more complex whole.

DEBATING TRUMP AND HIS STRATEGY

On January 20, 2017, Donald J. Trump strode with a group of the country's highest elected leaders under the Capitol Dome and down a flight of stairs. Outside, thousands awaited his inauguration. When the doors opened, he gave a thumbs-up and slowly walked forward, nodding to the crowd. On the balcony, surrounded by officials and vanquished opponents, Trump repeated the presidential oath of office. It was an unexpected moment. The new president had no formal political experience. He had, instead, built his rise on a mix of rhetorical bombast, media savvy, and conservative frustration. America's electoral system transformed Trump the media character into Trump the president. That transformation, however, did little to calm pitched battles about what Trump meant for the United States and the world, battles persisting unabated during the period covered by this book.

The following year, a White House official bracingly summarized the Trump grand strategic stance: "We're America, bitch."[18] Foreign policy commentator Jeffrey Goldberg interviewed Trump appointees and friends in summer 2018. "Obama apologized to everyone for everything," explained this official, "He felt bad about everything … [whereas Trump] doesn't feel like he has to apologize for anything America does." As rhetoric, this approach was a direct counterpoint to Barack Obama's self-described doctrine of "don't do stupid shit."[19] For years, many Obama officials argued that whatever the failings of their foreign policy, at least they were not replicating mistakes from the George W. Bush administration. Now, a Trump friend argued, "we're justified in canceling out [Obama's] policies" after eight years of dissipating American power. Outbidding Obama officials, this friend explained that "there's the Obama Doctrine, and the 'Fuck Obama' Doctrine. We're the 'Fuck Obama' Doctrine." For Goldberg, such bombast served as Rorschach test. One could see it as a defiant statement from strength or as self-defeating delusion. Goldberg himself argued the latter, that Trump's strategic approach would make the United States weaker and would "undermine the Western alliance, empower Russia and China, and demoralize freedom-seeking people around the world." Still, by summer 2018, Goldberg also suspected that after a year of experience, Donald Trump would be "acting on his beliefs in a more urgent, and focused, way than he did in the first year of his presidency."

At base, these debates are about grand strategy. They are about how the United States will define and pursue its interests and security. Despite challenges, in early 2017, the United States remained the lead state in a world order it had maintained for decades. Trump, by contrast, was an unconventional candidate with nationalist-tinted rhetoric about foreign affairs. Would these seemingly divergent elements fuse to generate new, productive energy? They might just as easily fissure, either exploding into war or imploding under their own weight. Trump's own personal style and psychology became targets for analysis. Where temperament might play a role in shaping grand strategy for someone like George W. Bush or Barack Obama, many analysts now wondered if Trump's temperament might be the *only* relevant factor. Of course, others focused on Trump's stated nationalist views and those of his advisors. Others believed that, barring major systemic shocks, grand strategy is unlikely to change significantly from one year to the next.

Skeptics United

Temperament over Character

For months surrounding Trump's inauguration, skeptical cartoonists imagined the new president in versions of the same scene: sitting in the Oval Office impulsively deciding to hit one of two giant red buttons: "tweet" or "nuke." To many policy observers across the planet, strategy seemed less relevant than psychology to understand Trump's approach to the world. In one unsparing analysis, psychologist Dan P. McAdams characterized Trump as a "primal leader."[20] "Like the alpha male of a chimpanzee colony," McAdams wrote, "Trump leads (and inspires) through intimidation, bluster, and threat, and through the establishment of short-term, opportunistic relationships with other high-status agents." McAdams continued,

> Trump's leadership style derives readily from his personality makeup, which entails a combustible temperament mixture of high extraversion and low agreeableness, a motivational agenda centered on extreme narcissism, and an internalized life story that tracks the exploits of an intrepid warrior who must forever fight to win in a Hobbesian world of carnage. ... Donald Trump's inimitable personality profile appears tailor-made for assuming the dominant role in the authoritarian dynamic.

Journalist Michael Wolff characterizes Trump's personality in more approachable terms. According to those around him, Trump proved charming, even gentle, in person but also constantly playing the role of "a rebel, a disruptor, and, living outside the rules, contemptuous of them." Wolff summarizes that Trump "simply had no scruples."[21] Wolff cites Roger Ailes, a longtime political operative and original force behind the Fox News television network. He considered Trump a "rebel without a cause" who lacked any serious capacity for planning beyond immediate personal aggrandizement.[22] Still, Trump also seemed to seek affirmation and approval. After two years in office, academics and reporters had observed that "the White House and Fox [News] interact so seamlessly that it can be hard to determine, during a particular news cycle, which one is following the other's lead."[23] For his part, runs this thesis, Trump watched hours of the network daily. He relied on it to keep track of his base supporters, to gather information about the world, and even to directly seek affirmation on contested issues by calling in to favored shows like "Fox and Friends."

Apparently reaching similar conclusions about Trump's temperament, many governments started to push their agendas with the United States by working Trump's ego and personal preferences. France's president Emanuel Macron impressed Trump with a traditional military parade, and during Trump's Asia trip, Chinese officials feted the American president with imperial splendor. Poland's president Andrzej Duda took these efforts a step further. In a White House visit, he raised a long-standing request for a permanent US military presence in his country. He promised to pay two billion dollars and name the new base "Fort Trump."[24]

Back in the United States, foreign policy elites united in alarm over Trump's foreign policy approach. They feared his temperament, leadership style, and foreign policy beliefs. The new president seemed to create internal chaos and communicate inconsistent policy views. Eliot Cohen, a Republican and former George W. Bush Department of State official, compared Trump to Captain Ahab. He is a leader who lets his fractious team battle below decks, whereas the man commanding the wheel drops contradictory orders and pursues "whatever Moby Dick his imagination has just conjured up." Observing Trump's first months in office, conservative scholar Kori Schake agreed. Trump was undermining his own national security agenda. "Policy processes produce sensible policies," she pointed out, "that are then upended by the president's decisions."[25] For its partners, the United States had become "an unreliable ally." Even from a realist perspective, argued commentator Robert Kaplan, Trump demonstrated no sense of the "tragic," or of what can go wrong in a given situation or relationship.[26] Keren Yarhi-Milo writing in *Foreign Affairs* called this problem a "credibility gap."[27] Leaders require broad support, yet public opinion polls in the United States and elsewhere showed that most people found Trump untrustworthy. Yarhi-Milo suspected that Trump's weak approval might force the United States to take "more costly and extreme actions" to communicate seriousness. Daniel W. Drezner, a professor at Tufts University and a frequent commentator, made similar arguments. As a kind of perverse strength, he wrote, Trump's "complete lack of shame and awkwardness can give him an advantage in one-on-one negotiations."[28] In fact, says Drezner, "Trump is unburdened by awareness of failure, or really any knowledge at all about world politics."

Brookings Institution fellow Benjamin Wittes invoked "Hanlon's razor" to take this characterization a step further: "Never attribute to malice that which can be adequately explained by stupidity."[29] Fortunately, Wittes observed, even in cases of malice, the administration displayed "malevolence tempered by incompetence." According to Drezner, the real Trump agenda was about dominating news cycles and fighting domestic opponents. And with a smaller than normal foreign policy team, Trump's administration "lacks the bandwidth to handle all the myriad crises this president has triggered." For Trump's senior officials, this means they must make hard choices. As professionals, they could disagree with the president and risk losing personal influence, or they could superficially agree with the president but then head back to their agencies and "correct" Trump's ill-informed or impetuous decisions.[30]

Peril Over Promise

Trump skeptics also worried about a deeper, systemic challenge: collapse of the international liberal order. In its first 2017 issue, the influential *Foreign Affairs* magazine hosted a set of articles penned by prominent experts. They were worried. Trump and his team appeared to be disavowing the postwar order orchestrated by the United States in the 1940s. Prominent scholar Joseph Nye insisted that American leadership could persist, but the principle of an open, internationalist world order was now under siege. Michael Mazarr suspected that Washington would fail to adjust properly to changing geopolitical conditions. Schake argued that Trump was likely to ignore good advice and, instead, "retrench further: moving away from defense alliances and trade agreements, allowing China and Russia to increase their influence in their neighborhoods, disengaging from nation building, and scaling back efforts to influence the domestic policies of other countries." Eighteen months later, in summer 2018, longtime foreign policy commentator Josef Joffe concluded unambiguously, "Yes, Donald Trump really does want to demolish the international order the United States had built, financed, and guarded since World War II."[31] In the staunchly conservative *Weekly*

Standard, Thomas Donnelly and William Kristol pulled Trump's predecessor, Barack Obama, into this failure. Both presidents, they argued, had
pushed the United States away from "its previous global responsibilities."[32]
Projecting forward, Rebecca Friedman Lissner and Mira Rapp-Hooper
found that Trump's "defiant nationalism and ruthless transactionalism,
is a decidedly radical departure from the strategic mainstream."[33] As
a muted silver lining to these storm clouds, Lissner and Rapp-Hooper
argued that Trump's leadership remained too chaotic to seriously change
US foreign policy. Unfortunately, they wrote, there is a deeper problem.
"At best," they explained, "the next president stands to inherit a liberal
international order on life support, with some pieces, like the global free-
trade system—significantly weakened, and others—like U.S. alliances—
damaged but not defunct."[34] As scholar Hal Brands summarized, "Trump's
initiatives and mannerisms are serving primarily to diminish the American superpower, and to intensify the stresses on a system that has served
Washington and so many others so well for so long."[35]

Some voices over these two years gave Trump credit for isolating
serious issues or raising real concerns. Yet even many of these found
the president and his administration faltering on implementation. For
instance, Stephen Sestanovich, a longtime government official and fellow
on the Council of Foreign Relations, wrote that candidate Trump had
been savvy. "He sensed," explained Sestanovich, "that the public wanted
relief from the burdens of global leadership without losing the thrill
of nationalist self-assertion."[36] As a strategy, this meant that Trump
embraced both more aggressive activism and broader disengagement.
The new president managed to combine global sheriff with self-sufficient
rancher. Unfortunately, those agendas are incompatible without active,
informed management. "No president with any knowledge of government
at all," Sestanovich concluded, "would have bungled these matters as
Trump has." Well-known realist scholar Stephen Walt was slightly
more forgiving. In the Middle East, for instance, Trump—"in his own ill-
informed, impulsive, and erratic way"—was trying to restore America's
offshore balancing strategy that it had pursued throughout the Cold

War.[37] This would allow the United States to place a finger on the scale in favor of allies. Of course, Walt surmises that the administration was bungling offshore balancing because its approach was partial. It was committing to a few friendly regimes rather than diplomatically engaging all players.

Walt also raised a broader concern after a remarkable press conference with Russian president Vladimir Putin. Trump appeared to side with Putin *against American officials* on his interpretation of international affairs. Mainstream foreign policy officials were stunned and outraged yet impotent. Why? Walt concluded that whatever Trump's faults, a "bipartisan caste of national security managers" (called "the blob" several years prior by Barack Obama's exasperated foreign policy advisor, Ben Rhodes) had run US foreign policy for decades but never suffered accountability for its many failures.[38] He later observed that, despite Trump nation's conviction that a liberal "deep state" existed in the government, most of these foreign policy elites do their work in plain daylight, are serious professionals, and "genuine patriots."[39] The real concern is that "they've been marinating in a bipartisan worldview that sees the United States as the last best hope for mankind and in a political system that rewards conformity and penalizes even relatively mild acts of dissent." Stated simply: Trump may be ineffective with grand strategy, but the experts had never grappled with their own failures. In fact, "if these elites had done a better job over the past 25 years or so, Trump would probably not have become president."

Defending Trump's Strategic Approach

Draining the Swamp

Of course, Trump and his supporters insisted that no person rockets to the presidency without strategic prowess or a vision for America in the world. For them, early fears were naturally overblown. Trump was an unconventional candidate challenging the Washington establishment, "the swamp" as some called it. Indeed, in 2016, dozens of foreign policy insiders signed a letter refusing to serve a Trump administration. The president's supporters argued that after these experts failed to impact the election, they now spun impotent, frustrated commentary. Of course, lacking access to these personnel also created holes in the administration's professional support staffing. Political appointments at the assistant director level and below simply sat unfilled at the Department of State, National Security Council, and other agencies. These gaps likely contributed to the administration's turnover and a series of failed or revised policies during its first months.

Still, Trump officials projected confidence, and their candidate's message had been clear: The United States was bound by terrible trade deals and paid too much for security institutions like NATO. It was internally menaced by poorly controlled immigration and should spend more on its military. In his March 2017 address to Congress, Trump delivered a simple message, "My job is not to represent the world. My job is to represent the United States of America." And this meant spending less on foreign adventures, renegotiating trade, threatening intransigent governments like Iran, and curtailing immigration. These are priorities set by a basic idea of national interest: protection from the outside world and trade that creates jobs.

Strong Dealing
In one early assessment, Brookings Institution fellow Thomas Wright placed candidate Trump's "remarkably coherent and consistent worldview" in a larger context.[40] Where others worried that Trump wanted to break the postwar internationalist order, Trump and many of his key advisors welcomed it. Since the 1980s, Trump the real estate mogul and celebrity had aired his nationalist grievances. Though never explicit, he seemed to liken great power politics and world order to real estate franchising. A global brand providing benefits, the United States should be receiving literal payments from partners (rather than merely enjoying the more diffuse benefits of setting global economic rules and security arrangements). On military alliances and trade, he believed that

Americans "were laughed at around the world for losing a hundred and fifty billion dollars year after year, for defending wealthy nations for nothing." On leadership, he admired strongmen. Watching the Soviet Union collapse under Mikhail Gorbachev, he commented in a 1990 Playboy interview, "When the students poured into Tiananmen Square, the Chinese government almost blew it. Then they were vicious, they were horrible, but they put it down with strength. That shows you," he continued, "the power of strength. Our country is right now perceived as weak...as being spit on by the rest of the world."

Wright traced how Trump's grand strategic instincts fit certain strains in the history of the Republican Party. In particular, through the Franklin Roosevelt and Harry Truman years, Senator (and sometime presidential candidate) Robert Taft defended isolationism, criticized aggressive efforts to expand trade, and even opposed containment as expensive and provocative. Before Trump, says Wright, "Taft's speeches are the last time a major American politician has offered a substantive and comprehensive critique of America's alliances." Scholar Henry Nau, at George Washington University, endorsed this basic approach. Making the case for *conservative internationalism*, he argued, "Conservatives have always favored a different world order than liberals do, one based on nationalism."[41] When Trump claims that "I'm a nationalist and a globalist," he means it. For him, Americans can share values of individual freedom, rule of law, family, and so forth with friendly states without actively pushing US prerogatives on others. Rather, governments can negotiate and partner to find mutually beneficial deals. In a similar vein, former national security analyst turned scholar Matthew Kroenig and, separately, former diplomat Elliot Abrams argued that Trump's early team represented a serious commitment to professionalism and to extending established trends in US foreign policy.[42] In turn, the administration displayed positions on nuclear weapons, alliances, the Middle East, military power, human rights, and other areas that basically fit long-standing US policies. "The Trump strategy represents a significant accomplishment," summarized Walter Russell Mead, a well-established voice in the foreign policy establishment, "It reconciles the instincts of an unconventional president with the views of a more seasoned and conventional national security team."[43] By contrast, academic and former diplomat Philip Zelikow was less convinced that, aside from anti-Communism, a traditional Republican foreign policy even existed.[44] Instead, Trump was simply "using foreign policy as a vehicle to align with factions in America's culture wars." Despite Zelikow's skepticism, Nau and others remained optimistic that, as a Republican, Trump could marry nationalism and internationalism.

Clashing Visions

In and around the administration, however, officials and commentators wrangled over defining and pursuing Trump's strategic priorities. Over the first year in particular, they typically broke into two camps. On one side, Trump's personal supporters endorsed the president's nationalist instincts and brash, unpredictable style. On the other side, Trump's more mainstream supporters saw the man as a vessel for standard Republican policies and strategies. Trump advisor and self-described "anti-globalist" Stephen Bannon, for instance, espoused nationalism or even mercantilism. Though Bannon was ousted in the administration's first year, he helped shape Trump's early view that China is a serious competitor on trade and power, that a version of the "clash of civilizations," particularly with the Muslim world, represents an existential threat, and that zero-sum competition defines international affairs. By contrast, Trump's Secretary of Defense, James Mattis, spent many meetings during Trump's first year quietly reassuring US allies and partners around the world that, yes, the administration represented a change in tone and emphasis; however, the United States would also remain stable and reliable. Diplomacy, he insisted, mattered as much as military power.

Outside the administration, friendly observers also disagreed about Trump's ability to helm US grand strategy. In one remarkable act of conceptual framing, commentator Jerry Hendrix warmly praised Donald Trump's "strategic ambiguity."[45] The president's rhetoric, he argued, remained consistently *in*consistent, an approach that raises doubt and uncertainty among friends and foes alike. This may parallel President Richard Nixon's "madman theory" (discussed further in the conclusion). In the space created by uncertainty, new dialogue and negotiation is possible. "Solid predictability," explained Hendrix, "is not a winning strategy." By contrast, another conservative commentator, Fred Barnes, saw Trump's ever-changing positions and rhetoric not a deliberate strategy but, rather, as evidence of personal growth and acceptance of more mainstream Republican strategic views. "Trump has changed his policies in his first 100 days in office more than any president in the post-World War II era," he explained, "And for the most part the changes have been for the better."[46] For Barnes, Trump's low initial knowledge and reliance on advisors simply set the stage for growth toward consistent strategic positions on trade, immigration, Russia, and so forth. Trump might still emerge as a mainstream Republican foreign policy president.

In Congress, meanwhile, most Republican members sought to support Trump's national security positions when those coincided with their own positions. They also parted with the president and pushed mainstream policies when Trump diverged from standard GOP priorities. For instance, in summer 2018, Congress easily passed a spending bill expanding funds for the military, something Trump strongly prioritized, as well. The previous year, however, Republicans passed legislation imposing sanctions on Russia as a response to that government's interference in the 2016 election. They did this despite Trump's personal affinity for Vladimir Putin, and despite the uncomfortable implications that such legislation implied about their president's electoral performance. Similarly, as Trump loudly announced plans to cut foreign aid, "even the most hawkish of lawmakers" quietly defied the president.[47] In their committees and bills, they protected funds for aid and other soft power tools. Worried that the administration might abandon Washington's traditional support for Taiwan, Senators like Marco Rubio (R-FL) and Cory Gardner (R-CO) introduced a bill with Democrats that would downgrade relations with governments revising their own relations with Taiwan and in favor of China.[48]

This project will analyze the core debates over grand strategy prompted by the Trump administration. In building case histories of Trump's early grand strategy, it will explore their parameters and merit. Based upon that evidence, it will also make preliminary claims about which approaches get their claims right and whether the administration set out and implemented a successful strategy during its first two years.

CONTRIBUTION

This book fills a gap between several categories, and it does this with its substantive focus, contemporaneous timing, and analytical innovation. Recent work on US grand strategy tends to fall into several categories. These include broad overviews, scholarly research on a specific administration or grand strategy type, case studies and broad reviews for scholars and students, and "first takes" combining current events with long-term trends and my own policy recommendations. As a set of case narratives, this book aims be both an approachable history as well as an assessment of the Trump administration's early grand strategy. It offers a first cut at the Trump grand strategy carefully sourced in a systematic review of statements, journalism, and government documents. It is a text for students and practitioners as well as grand strategy and foreign policy scholars. For both the near and long term, it is designed to help set scholarly and policy discussion as well as remain a go-to reference.

John Lewis Gaddis' *On Grand Strategy* exemplifies the widest category of recent grand strategy writing.[49] Here, authors like Gaddis seek to categorize and explain grand strategy as a phenomenon and then offer their own assessments of effective implementation. Chapter 2 precisely analyzes and categorizes these and other approaches to grand strategy, but a brief overview here is helpful to place this book in a larger context. Other recent examples include Lukas Milevski's *The Evolution of Grand*

Strategic Thought and William C. Martel's *Grand Strategy in Theory and Practice: The Need for an Effective American Foreign Policy.*[50] Finally, Hal Brands' *What Good is Grand Strategy?* is a good model of this subgenre that has also proven highly visible across audiences and in the press. Rather than compete with such books, this project will draw upon them to help contextualize its use and application of grand strategy.[51]

Another strong tradition observes US grand strategy across administrations and then offers prescriptive recommendations. It is assessment and advice. Some of it is partisan. Recent examples include Barry Posen's *Restraint: A New Foundation for US Grand Strategy*, Stephen Sestanovich's *Maximalist: America in the World from Truman to Obama*, and Paul Miller's *American Power and Liberal Order: A Conservative Internationalist Grand Strategy.*[52] Finally, Colin Dueck's *The Obama Doctrine: American Grand Strategy Today* and *Age of Iron: On Conservative Nationalism* are perhaps the closest examples of texts similar to the current project. They assess and diagnose presidents' grand strategy approaches. Dueck devotes a significant portion to the political implications of Obama's and Trump's grand strategies for Republicans and conservatives. By contrast, this book will observe the general environment rather than highlight one side of these partisan debates.

Of course, in every presidential election cycle, more holistic reviews and analyses appear. For the 2012 election year, for instance, former government officials at the Brookings Institution, Martin S. Indyk, Kenneth G. Lieberthal, and Michael E. O'Hanlon published *Bending History: Barack Obama's Foreign Policy*, which presented a broad overview of key debates and moments along with observation and analysis of specific issues and decisions.[53] This is a valuable overview with a set of policy diagnoses and prescriptions; however, it proves far thinner regarding systematic theory or scholarly frameworks. Finally, Hal Brands' *American Grand Strategy in the Age of Trump* exemplifies a hybrid approach by integrating some preliminary observations of the administration with a far more substantial scholarly overview and assessment of U.S. grand strategy trajectories.[54]

ANALYZING TRUMP'S GRAND STRATEGY

There are two interweaving debates throughout this chapter. First, what is the administration's grand strategy? Second, why does it take the shape that it does? The first is a contentious but common question for all presidencies. It is a question about definition and categorization. This book will apply a simple diagnostic framework to identify Trump's grand strategy and its basic content. The second question is harder to study, but it is essential. It is a question about the sources of that grand strategy, and it is about the possibilities for grand strategy change. Trump's approach to governing makes it inescapable: does the leader and his temperament fundamentally shape or change grand strategy? Did individual perceptions and shared ideas set US grand strategy during Trump's first two years? By the end of 2018, US grand strategy had moved in new directions under the Trump administration. This book will examine how and why it moved, and it will seek to define that strategy.

Much Ado about Nothing?

A classic illustration of these questions, as with many Trump imbroglios, began with a tweet. It occurred as a postscript to the period covered in this book. On 19 December 2018, the president announced that "we have defeated ISIS in Syria, my only reason for being there."[55] For his part, Trump had long wanted to get the United States out of most long-standing military commitments, including Afghanistan. Despite that impulse, based on advice from his generals and national security team, he had agreed to several extensions.[56] After the midterm election, Trump seemed to want some action and a win.

In a follow-up to his tweet, the White House confirmed that the United States military would withdraw from Syria within 30 days. Most observers were shocked at the abrupt decision. In a rare and remarkable move in American politics, Secretary of Defense James Mattis, citing differences in guiding principles, effectively resigned in protest.[57] The Department of Defense and others had developed contingency plans for such a move over previous months; nevertheless, the decision appeared to have been sudden and unexpected. Indeed, later reporting revealed that Trump apparently finalized his decision extemporaneously during a phone call with Turkish president Recep Tayyip Erdogan. Erdogan assured him that Turkey could finish the job as the United States withdrew. The decision contradicted assurances from Secretary of State Pompeo and Secretary of Defense Mattis that war would have to be carefully wound down rather than summarily ended.[58] Even many of Trump's Republican supporters, such as Senator Lindsey Graham (R-SC), sharply criticized the move and the manner in which it was announced. Not only would an abrupt withdrawal potentially undermine regional stability, but it would also leave the Kurds, a steadfast but stateless regional ally, at the mercy of the Turkish government, which considered the possibility of an independent Kurdish state to be a threat to Turkish sovereignty. Within two weeks, Trump shifted the pullout to four months and then later said he did not necessarily support that timeframe, either. Trump's National Security Advisor, John Bolton, who wanted to keep up pressure on Iran and had never approved of precipitous withdrawal, used a Middle East trip to insist that "there are objectives that we want to accomplish that condition the withdrawal."[59] The withdrawal was still happening. So was the *status quo ante*. Debate and uncertainty persisted for months. Every initial Trump position had been reversed or modified.

This example displays all the key dynamics of grand strategy formation and change. Specifically, Trump attempted to implement a highly visible change in US grand strategy, and it was a change based upon his ideological and personal preferences. Unfortunately for Trump, a host of factors pushed the administration's position back toward a median or standard position. These factors included larger commitments to a strategically important region, responses from allies and adversaries, domestic politics, and bureaucratic pushback. In short, Trump's personal preference affected US strategy, but the effect was muted or constrained.

Plan of the Book

The burden of this book is to provide a framework to help us disentangle these interacting variables. To that end, it divides the first two years of the Trump administration into four narrative case studies. Then it will use those case studies to evaluate the administration's grand strategy with two frameworks. The first framework is a simple diagnostic tool. It will help us identify and name Trump's grand strategy. This is a rubric that distills dozens of grand strategy categorization schemes into three basic dimensions: *scope, substance,* and *assertiveness.* These refer to, respectively, a grand strategy's geographic extent, its definitions of interests and goals, and its balance of force versus other means. (Chapter 2 defines this rubric in more detail.) These dimensions are by design open-ended. There is no fixed set of possible grand strategies. Simple comparison or generalizability is more challenging with this approach, but the benefit is that it provides a set of standards that could be applied to any case at any point in history. It also allows us to faithfully represent a grand strategy as it was practiced and understood by those involved.

That precision is crucial, because this book's other goal is to evaluate how that strategy formed and changed. To do this, Chapter 2 offers a novel and ambitious second framework: *grand strategy analysis* (GSA). Specifically, I propose foreign policy analysis (FPA) as a useful guide for the interdisciplinary and cumulative study of grand strategy. Several distinct traditions study grand strategy, yet they rarely engage one another. I argue that this has not prevented them from unwittingly converging. "Grand strategy" has emerged in recent decades as something more than a vague organizing concept or ideal. For many scholars and professionals, grand strategy is a distinct, observable phenomenon. It is increasingly treated as a term of art. In a similar fashion, foreign policy analysis emerged from several decades of scholarship that revolved around an overlapping set of questions and approaches. FPA is actor-centric and emphasizes decision making as the "ground" of international relations. In turn, GSA emphasizes individual decision makers as units of analysis. By using such an approach, scholars from different disciplines and methodological approaches can "talk" to one another across studies.

In Chapters 3 through 6, GSA guides the empirical focus. The case histories will observe key decision makers and build a narrative of the grand strategy as a whole (as opposed to focusing on a discrete set of issues). Grand strategy itself is identified by evaluating the overlap between words, policies, and decisions or actions. Since the US system allows presidents to wield outsized influence over foreign affairs, Trump's national security impulses and his strategic positions will remain the baseline focus. Many grand strategy studies only observe a select set of strategy issues, such as wars or regions. This allows the researcher to trace out familiar topics in detail, but it risks losing the larger grand strategy picture. Other analyses set out a strategic or theoretical position and build a case around it. Though necessary to evaluate those frameworks, the possible selection bias is clear. By contrast, case histories in this book will seek to portray the grand strategy as a whole, as it emerged across a range of domains from statements and decisions made in the White House and among other foreign policy principals.

Chapter 7 returns to the book's basic questions: what was Trump's grand strategy, what effect did Trump as an individual have on US grand strategy, and was Trump's strategy successful? It returns to the *scope, substance,* and *assertiveness* rubric, and it argues that despite efforts among his more mainstream advisors and appointees, Trump maintained a consistently nationalist approach to grand strategy. The chapter unpacks exactly what this means and its policy implications. Still, though potentially radical, this approach remained constrained, in no small part *because* of those contrary efforts from his team. The rest of the chapter applies a set of analytical questions set out in Chapter 2. It evaluates Trump's impact on US grand strategy. I will argue that, fundamentally, grand strategies are defined by a host of contextual factors and only interpreted by individuals. Leaders matter at the margins, and their individual beliefs and personal psychologies matter to their grand strategy positions. However, leaders are constrained within many existing geopolitical, economic, policy, and other parameters. Radical change will be rare. In his first two years as president, Donald Trump floated many radical changes to US grand strategy. His "America first" approach was indeed a specific, nationalist grand strategy change. Nevertheless, in nearly every case of major attempted change, Trump was met with sufficient resistance, domestic and external, that he tended to return to a median position. That Donald Trump was president affected US grand strategy, but his presence alone was not sufficient to fundamentally change US grand strategy.

Overall, *Make America First Again* provides a necessary service and crucial insight. Where scholarly work remains broad and often, for many, inaccessible, this project is focused and approachable. Where scholarly texts divide grand strategies into issues or doctrines, this project presents it holistically. Where many fresh takes focus on content over analysis (or on the context rather than the administration), this project combines the case itself with a clear analytical framework: *grand strategy analysis.*

NOTES

1. Due to translation as well as political disagreements, official English names for this Islamist insurgency varied. For simplicity, this book will use terms commonly used in the contemporary media: Islamic State and ISIS.
2. William Saletan, "How Trump's 'Unpredictability' Dodge Became the Dumbest Doctrine in Politics." *Slate* 3, May 2016, https://slate.com/news-and-politics/2016/05/trumps-moronic-unpredictability-doctrine.html. See also William Gallo, "Trump Embraces Unpredictability as Foreign Policy Strategy," *Voice of America* (VOA), November 25, 2016, https://www.voanews.com/a/trump-foreign-policy-unpredictability/3610582.html.
3. Michael H. Fuchs, "Donald Trump's doctrine of unpredictability has the world on edge," *The Guardian* Opinion: Trump administration, February 13, 2017, https://www.theguardian.com/commentisfree/2017/feb/13/donald-trumps-doctrine-unpredictability-world-edge.
4. Max Fisher, "What is Donald Trump's Foreign Policy?" *The New York Times*, The Interpreter, November 11, 2016, https://www.nytimes.com/2016/11/12/world/what-is-donald-trumps-foreign-policy.html.
5. James Carden, "The Problem with Hillary Clinton's Attack on Trump's Foreign Policy Is...Hillary Clinton," *The Nation Foreign Policy*, June 3, 2016, https://www.thenation.com/article/the-problem-with-hillary-clintons-attack-on-trumps-foreign-policy-ishillary-clinton/.
6. The White House, *Statement from President Donald J. Trump on Standing with Saudi Arabia*, Washington, DC, November 20, 2018, https://www.whitehouse.gov/briefings-statements/statement-president-donald-j-trump-standing-saudi-arabia/.
7. Shane Harris, Greg Miller, and Josh Dawsey, "CIA Concludes Saudi Crown Prince ordered Jamal Khashoggi's assassination," *The Washington Post*, November 16, 2018, https://www.washingtonpost.com/world/national-security/cia-concludes-saudi-crown-prince-ordered-jamal-khashoggis-assassination/2018/11/16/98c89fe6-e9b2-11e8-a939-9469f1166f9d_story.html?utm_term=.9b5c5aa26552.
8. Greg Myre, "Lawmakers Reassess U.S.-Saudi Alliance In Yemen After Killing of Jamal Khashoggi," *All Things Considered*, National Public Radio, November 28, 2018, https://www.npr.org/2018/11/28/671675682/

lawmakers-reassess-u-s-saudi-alliance-in-yemen-after-killing-of-jamal-khashoggi.

9. Robert Jervis. "Do Leaders Matter and How Would We Know?" *Security Studies* 22 (2013): 153–159.

10. Ibid., 159–161.

11. Ibid., 178

12. Ionut Popescu, *Emergent Strategy and Grand Strategy: How American Presidents Succeed in Foreign Policy* (Baltimore: Johns Hopkins University Press, 2017).

13. James Graham Wilson, *The Triumph of Improvisation: Gorbachev's Adaptability, Reagan's Engagement, and the End of the Cold War* (Ithaca, NY: Cornell University Press, 2014).

14. Fuchs, "Donald Trump's doctrine of unpredictability has the world on edge."

15. A similar claim with a different framework appears in Thierry Balzacq, Peter Dombrowski, and Simon Reich, *Comparative Grand Strategy: A Framework and Cases* (New York: Oxford University Press, 2019).

16. Hal Brands, *What Good is Grand Strategy? Power and Purpose in American Statecraft from Harry S. Truman to George W. Bush* (Ithaca, NY: Cornell University Press, 2014), 6.

17. Stephen Krasner, for example, argues for "orienting principles" rather than grand strategy. Stephen Krasner "An Orienting Principle for Foreign Policy." *Policy Review* 1 (October 1, 2010), https://www.hoover.org/research/orienting-principle-foreign-policy.

18. Jeffrey Goldberg, "A Senior White House Official Defines the Trump Doctrine: 'We're America, Bitch,'" *The Atlantic*, June 11, 2018, https://www.theatlantic.com/politics/archive/2018/06/a-senior-white-house-official-defines-the-trump-doctrine-were-america-bitch/562511/.

19. Jeffrey Goldberg, "The Obama Doctrine," *The Atlantic*, (April 2018), https://www.theatlantic.com/magazine/archive/2016/04/the-obama-doctrine/471525/.

20. Dan P. McAdams, "The Appeal of the Primal Leader: Human Evolution and Donald J. Trump," *Evolutionary Studies in Imaginative Culture* 1, no. 2 (2017): 1–13.

21. Michael Wolff, *Fire and Fury: Inside the Trump White House* (New York: Henry Holt and Company, 2018), 23.

22. Ibid., 3.

23. Jane Mayer, "The Making of the Fox News White House," *The New Yorker,* March 11, 2019, https://www.newyorker.com/magazine/2019/03/11/the-making-of-the-fox-news-white-house.

24. Alan Cowell, "Fort Trump? Poland Makes a Play for a U.S. Military Base," *The New York Times,* September 19, 2018, https://www.nytimes.com/20 18/09/19/world/europe/poland-fort-trump.html.

25. Kori Schake, "Trump is Destroying His Own Administration's Policies," *The Atlantic,* June 10, 2017, https://www.theatlantic.com/international/ archive/2017/06/trump-foreign-policy/529800/.

26. Robert Kaplan, "On Foreign Policy, Donald Trump is no Realist," *Washington Post* Opinions, November 11, 2016.

27. Keren Yarhi-Milo, "After Credibility: American Foreign Policy in the Trump Era," *Foreign Affairs* 97, no. 1 (Jan/Feb 2018): 68–77.

28. "The deep confusion of Trump's foreign policy." PostEverything: Perspective. *The Washington Post,* May 14, 2018, https://www. washingtonpost.com/news/posteverything/wp/2018/05/14/the-deep-confusion-of-trumps-foreign-policy/?utm_term=.44307ab3730c.

29. Benjamin Wittes, "Malevolence Tempered by Incompetence: Trump's Horrifying Executive Order on Refugees and Visas," Refugees: Blog post, *Lawfare,* January 28, 2017, https://www.lawfareblog.com/malevolence-tempered-incompetence-trumps-horrifying-executive-order-refugees-and-visas.

30. "Why you will always be disappointed with Trump's foreign policy team," PostEverything: Perspective, *The Washington Post,* March 22, 2018, https://www.washingtonpost.com/news/posteverything/wp/2018/03/2 2/why-you-will-always-be-disappointed-with-trumps-foreign-policy-team/?utm_term=.5dd00934f58d.

31. Josef Joffe, "The Great Unraveling, Cont'd," *The American Interest,* July 6, 2018, https://www.the-american-interest.com/2018/07/06/the-great-unraveling-contd/.

32. Thomas Donnelly and William Kristol, "The Obama-Trump Foreign Policy," *The Weekly Standard,* February 9, 2018, https://www. weeklystandard.com/the-obama-trump-foreign-policy/article/2011526 . See also Thomas Donnelly, "Retreat from Reliability." *The Weekly Standard* 2, no. 38 (2017): 27–29.

33. Rebecca Friedman Lissner and Mira Rapp-Hooper, "The Day After Trump: American Strategy for a New International Order," *The Washington Quarterly* 41, no. 1 (2018): 7–25.

34. For other examples, see, Patrick J. Deneen, *Why Liberalism Failed* (New Haven: Yale University Press, 2018); Francis Fukuyama, *Identity: The Demand for Dignity and the Politics of Resentment* (New York: Farrar, Straus and Giroux, 2018); Robert Kagan, *The Jungle Grows Back: America and Our Imperiled World* (New York: Penguin, 2018); Edward Luce, *The Retreat of Western Liberalism* (New York: Atlantic Monthly Press, 2017); and John Mearsheimer, *Great Delusion: Liberal Dreams and International Realities* (New Haven: Yale University Press, 2018).

35. Hal Brands, *American Grand Strategy in the Age of Trump* (Washington, D.C.: Brookings Institution Press, 2018), 154.

36. Stephen Sestanovich, "The Brilliant Incoherence of Trump's Foreign Policy," *The Atlantic* 319, no. 4 (2017): 92–96, 98, 100–102.

37. Stephen Walt, "Has Trump Become a Realist?" Voice: *Foreign Policy*, April 17, 2018, https://foreignpolicy.com/2018/04/17/has-trump-become-a-realist/.

38. Stephen Walt, "Why Trump is Getting Away with Foreign-Policy Insanity," Voice: *Foreign Policy*, July 18, 2018, https://foreignpolicy.com/2018/07/18/why-trump-is-getting-away-with-foreign-policy-insanity/. See also Stephen M. Walt, *The Hell of Good Intentions: America's Foreign Policy Elite and the Decline of U.S. Primacy* (New York: Farrar, Straus and Giroux, 2018).

39. Stephen M. Walt, "The Battle for Crazytown," Voice: *Foreign Policy*, September 7, 2018, https://foreignpolicy.com/2018/09/07/the-battle-for-crazytown/.

40. Thomas Wright, "Trump's 19th Century Foreign Policy," *Politico Magazine*, January 20, 2016, https://www.politico.com/magazine/story/2016/01/donald-trump-foreign-policy-213546.

41. Henry R. Nau, "Trump's Conservative Internationalism," *National Review Online*, August 28, 2017, https://www.nationalreview.com/magazine/2017/08/28/donald-trump-foreign-policy-nationalism/. Paul Miller also constructs a "conservative internationalist" grand strategy, but his version counters Nau's. "American security and liberal order," he found, "are mutually constitutive: Liberal order is the outer perimeter of American security, and American power upholds liberal order." Paul D. Miller, *American Power and Liberal Order: A Conservative Internationalist Grand Strategy* (Washington, DC: Georgetown University Press, 2016), 17.

42. Matthew Kroenig, "The Case for Trump's Foreign Policy: The Right People, the Right Positions," *Foreign Affairs* 96, no. 3 (2017): 30–34. Elliott

Abrams, "Trump the Traditionalist: A Surprisingly Standard Foreign Policy," *Foreign Affairs* 96, no. 4 (2017), 10–16.

43. Walter Russell Mead, "Trump's 'Blue Water' Foreign Policy," (Opinion: Commentary) *The Wall Street Journal*, December 25, 2017.

44. Philip Zelikow, "There's No Such Thing as 'Traditional' Republican Foreign Policy," Voice: *Foreign Policy*, July 24, 2018, https://foreignpolicy.com/2018/07/24/theres-no-such-thing-as-traditional-republican-foreign-policy/.

45. Jerry Hendrix, "Donald Trump and the Art of Strategic Ambiguity," (Politics and Policy) *National Review Online*, March 21, 2018, https://www.nationalreview.com/2018/03/donald-trump-foreign-policy-strategic-ambiguity-american-interests/.

46. Fred Barnes, "Trump Unbound," *The Weekly Standard* 22, no. 32 (2017), 18–19.

47. Jenna Lifhits, "Trump's Democracy Man," *The Weekly Standard* 43, no. 22 (2017), 9–10.

48. Zhenhua Lu, "US senators introduce legislation to punish Taiwan allies who switch sides, accusing Beijing of 'bullying,'" *South China Morning Post*, Updated September 6, 2018, https://www.scmp.com/news/china/article/2162961/us-senators-introduce-legislation-discourage-taiwan-allies-switching.

49. John Lewis Gaddis, *On Grand Strategy* (New York: Penguin Press, 2018).

50. Lukas Milevski, *The Evolution of Modern Strategic Thought* (New York: Oxford, 2016); and William C. Martel *Grand Strategy in Theory and Practice: The Need for An Effective American Foreign Policy* (New York: Cambridge University Press, 2015).

51. See Brands, *What Good is Grand Strategy?*

52. Barry R. Posen, *Restraint: A New Foundation for U.S. Grand Strategy* (Ithaca, NY: Cornell University Press, 2014). Stephen Sestanovich, *Maximalist: America in the World From Truman to Obama* (New York: Vintage Books, 2014); Colin Dueck, *The Obama Doctrine: American Grand Strategy Today* (New York: Oxford University Press, 2015); and Colin Cueck, *Age of Iron: On Conservative Nationalism* (New York: Oxford University Press, 2019).

53. Martin S. Indyk, Kenneth G. Lieberthal, and Michael O'Hanlon, *Bending History: Barack Obama's Foreign Policy* (Washington, D.C.: Brookings Institution Press, 2012).

54. Brands, *American Grand Strategy in the Age of Trump.*

55. Adam Taylor, "Trump's Syria withdrawal (if there is one), explained," *The Washington Post*, January 7, 2019, https://www.washingtonpost.com/world/2019/01/07/trumps-syria-withdrawal-if-there-is-one-explained/?utm_term=.3766a1a69b16.

56. Mark Landler, "Trump Unites Left and Right Against Troop Plans, but Puts off Debate on War Aims," *The New York Times*, December 27, 2018, https://www.nytimes.com/2018/12/27/us/politics/trump-syria-afghanistan-withdraw.html.

57. Daniel Bush, "Read James Mattis' full resignation letter," *PBS NewsHour*, December 20, 2018, https://www.pbs.org/newshour/politics/read-james-mattis-full-resignation-letter.

58. Missy Ryan and Josh Dawsey, "U.S. troops to be pulled out of Syria quickly, White House says," *The Washington Post*, December 19, 2018, https://www.washingtonpost.com/world/national-security/trump-administration-plans-to-pull-us-troops-from-syria-immediately-defense-official-says/2018/12/19/4fcf188e-0397-11e9-b5df-5d3874f1ac36_story.html?utm_term=.bcdeb40cce87.

59. Zeke Miller, "Bolton Puts Conditions on Plan for Withdrawal From Syria," *RealClear Politics*, January 7, 2019, https://www.realclearpolitics.com/articles/2019/01/07/bolton_puts_conditions_on_plan_for_withdrawal_from_syria_139108.html.

CHAPTER 2

GRAND STRATEGY ANALYSIS

A NEW FRAMEWORK

"There never is a strategy because he's not a strategic thinker." Trump biographer Tim O'Brien was blunt when asked about a fresh batch of domestic challenges facing the president: "Two things motivate almost 100 percent of his behavior: self-preservation or self-aggrandizement."[1] Trump himself, more than one adviser confirmed later, liked to quote the 1980s boxing champ, Mike Tyson: "Everybody has a plan until they get punched in the mouth."[2] Many around the president characterized their boss as someone who likes to talk about having plans without seriously developing them. The president personally preferred, as one reporter summarized, "to wing it." For grand strategy scholars, this is a problem. Skeptics argue that an overarching strategy in foreign affairs is impossible. Leaders, they say, are universally focused on immediate crises and challenges. Decision makers may pursue general approaches or hold to certain principles, but the notion of a master plan over domestic or foreign affairs seems incredible. Grand strategy is an illusion. Maybe scholars should pack everything up and study psychology and incentive structures.

Yet even Trump and his supporters used the language of strategy. His unpredictable policy positions and rhetoric, they say, were designed to keep adversaries and allies alike off balance. "America first" was to be a set of long-term priorities that, just as importantly, were designed to offset a prior, "globalist" strategy. American military commitments around the world cannot be reversed easily even if Trump wants to stop paying for them. In debating the administration, experts are concerned not just about defining but also assessing the effectiveness of Trump's strategic approach.

More to the point, as this chapter will show, grand strategy is a distinct phenomenon. It may exist in the minds of a few leaders, or it may exist as a set of behaviors beyond any one group's control. It may change frequently or rarely. It may be intentional or implied. Whatever grand strategy's specific characteristics, it does affect foreign policy decisions, and it shapes long-term behavior. For those of us trying to understand grand strategy, this fact raises a set of familiar questions. Who—if anyone —shapes it? What is its content? When does it change? Why is it that way? How does work? As this chapter shows, there already exists a growing set of answers to these questions. What scholars lack is a way to organize this research or to allow different approaches to "talk" to one another. The following pages set out this framework and how it fits into existing professional and scholarly frameworks. At the end, the chapter also sets out the book's thesis and theoretical predictions as they are applied to the Trump administration. GSA is a large framework with many possible applications. This study explores and tests a subset of them.

One other note on this chapter. Readers new to scholarly debates on grand strategy may wish to jump to the final section "GSA and the Trump Administration," read the case histories, and then return here to understand the background of the analysis. I have tried to avoid the "inside baseball" jargon common (but often necessary) among professionals. Still, this chapter engages long-running debates about the concept of grand strategy itself. In turn, it makes novel proposals to address shortcomings in existing approaches. That said, this chapter is also designed to serve as a primer on the concept and study of grand strategy. It should be valuable for both old hands and new students.

GSA

I argue that foreign policy analysis (FPA) provides a sensible framework to unify grand strategy scholars, students, and practitioners. FPA scholars focus on agents—policy makers, government elites—making decisions. For international relations, this is crucial because, as Valerie Hudson observes, "all that occurs between nations and across nations is grounded in human decision makers acting singly or in groups." For Hudson and many others, the FPA approach pays handsome dividends because it allows the scholar to directly evaluate "the point of theoretical intersection between the most important determinants of state behavior: material and ideational factors." FPA focuses on decision makers. It allows us to observe how both human minds and impersonal factors affect international outcomes. By its nature, an FPA analysis will include many variables and may include multiple levels of analysis. It may also be interdisciplinary, and it is open to theoretical integration. Of course, it is also agent-oriented and actor-specific. Finally, "theoretical *integration*," or integration across levels and types of analysis, is FPA's most general benefit.[3] It allows the scholar to integrate many different types of variables and explanations. Admittedly, this can be difficult. Any one level of analysis, for example, includes many variables. Integrating different types of approaches can further multiply those relevant variables. Stated plainly: FPA can be complex. Nevertheless, by focusing on decision makers or decision groups discrete and specific units, FPA allows great analytical flexibility without losing focus or rigor.

For grand strategy, the FPA approach is a natural fit. Hudson and others study individual and group decision making as a foundational phenomenon. For GSA, the phenomenon is a *pattern of thought and policy*. Strategies may be classified on a spectrum with full individual control on one end and, on the other, a set of priorities and approaches that persist for decades. Grand strategy scholars themselves disagree about the true nature of strategy and where on this spectrum strategy is most pure; nevertheless, in all cases, what they seek to observe or produce is a consistent set of priorities and options that leaders and other decision makers apply over time. Again: a pattern of thought and policy. The simplest way to observe such patterns is to evaluate individual leaders and leader groups as they set priorities, make decisions, and respond to crises. With this focus, GSA allows the scholar to integrate international structures, decision processes, and ideas. As an approach, grand strategy analysis (GSA) makes no commitments about how to define grand strategy or the specific variables that may matter in any given case. Rather, it provides an organizing framework in which, for example, scholars from strategic and security studies can evaluate their different analyses. GSA provides a shared analytical framework to historians, policy professionals, political scientists and others.

Specifically, GSA

- treats grand strategy as a unit of analysis (rather than a byproduct of domestic or international politics);
- is agent-oriented and actor-specific. This focuses empirical analysis on people without excluding systems and structures. Crucially, it also allows for human psychology, perceptions, and so forth;
- allows flexibility on how one defines grand strategy, which may include plans, principles, or behavior. Scholars can observe, respectively, what policy makers *do*, their *stated beliefs*, and whether all of that fits *existing patterns*;
- is multifactorial, multilevel, and integrative, as described in the FPA overview;
- assumes that both ideas and material factors *can* matter equally to grand strategy. Claiming that ideas and material factors both matter may seem noncontroversial. After all, in any given social or political situation, is this not what most of us assume? In fact, many political scientists have grown skeptical that scholars can

observe and analyze ideas and beliefs. By contrast, many historians and policy makers tend to assume that ideas matter, but they often fail to rigorously separate the nature and effects of ideas and beliefs from other factors. GSA provides a vocabulary and a framework to do this;

- holds that grand strategy is distinct from, but intertwined with, foreign policy. Foreign policy might be characterized as all facets of a state that interact with and set behavior toward other states. By contrast, grand strategy is typically described as a specific plan or set of actions and positions to achieve high-order foreign policy goals.

In short, GSA is a framework to study grand strategy. GSA scholars assume that grand strategy can and does exist as a real phenomenon, and that grand strategy is best observed through the statements and actions of policy makers. Grand strategy may be a mode of thinking or a pattern of policy. Either way, it can be shaped and changed by many different factors. A GSA approach allows the historian, political scientist, professional strategist, or student to compare these different factors by observing how they interact with relevant policy makers. In turn, GSA also gives these different types of analysts a shared vocabulary. Even if the outcome of this shared vocabulary is disagreement about the nature and practice of grand strategy, that disagreement can be sensible to all sides.

The following pages review different approaches to studying grand strategy before turning to how these approaches are converging. As international relations scholarship in particular has evolved, the study of grand strategy has emerged as a distinct phenomenon studied by scholars across fields and disciplines. The chapter further explains the notion of GSA itself, and then it turns to more recent and ongoing work that fits this category. It concludes with a return to the Trump administration and GSA's relevance in understanding and analyzing this case.

THE PROBLEM AND PROMISE OF STUDYING GRAND STRATEGY

In 2017, the American economist Richard Thaler won a Nobel Prize. The award committee lauded Thaler for applying "psychologically realistic assumptions into analyses of economic decision-making."[4] In other words, he and other economists assumed that humans are less than fully rational and behave accordingly. "He has shown," the press release explained, "how these human traits systematically affect individual decisions as well as market outcomes."

Thaler had joined a revolution. For decades, economists led a wave in the social sciences that valued abstract models of human behavior. Historians, theorists, and informed observers for centuries had drawn inconsistent lessons about human nature or causes of war or monetary systems. By the twentieth century, social scientists were attempting to clean up the clutter. They developed testable hypotheses tied to clear theories, and they worked to narrow possible explanations for given phenomena. Thus, for example, rather than "fanaticism" explaining extreme ideologies, specialists could point to economic conditions or to individual disaffection or to "us versus them" preferences. Though powerful, these approaches demanded a major tradeoff. They required specialization and narrow questions. General theories and unifying frameworks became harder to maintain. Even psychology veered into narrow, testable question sets. More importantly, these fields communicated with one another less and less even as their own, internal research silos subdivided into narrower specializations. Critics today delight in showing how far the social sciences and humanities have spiraled into irrelevance. This charge is not unfair, but it is partial. In fact, much insight and knowledge has flowed from these theories and the debates they have inspired. This social science has also cycled upwards most common understandings of human behavior. For example, vague ideas about "honor" leading to war have been discarded, but the notion of honor still exists in more precise formulations. Perceptions and other psychological phenomena scholars might have traditionally called honor may make war more likely, though in slightly different ways than traditionally understood. By breaking big questions into pieces, social scientists can provide more precise analysis. Thoughtful scholars can also use these pieces to refine big questions and observe familiar phenomena in new ways.

Grand strategy is ripe for this kind of update. Models to explain human affairs always oversimplify. Nevertheless, they often interact with old wisdom, and new theories can more effectively explain well-established knowledge. Hindsight bias, for example, was a familiar experience long before modern psychology; however, systematic study and tested theories help observers understand more precisely how this experience affects peoples' thinking. Thus, what emerges from new theories may be a more complete, precise understanding of a given phenomenon.

In a similar way, grand strategy is a mature concept. Scholars and practitioners have studied and applied it along parallel tracks. This book divides these approaches to grand strategy into three rough categories. What I will call *traditionalists*, *theorists*, and *professionals*. Understanding these categories is important to see how the concept of "grand strategy" is evolving and how it has been both useful and limited. It is also helpful to understand how and why there are actually several cross-cutting discussions about this topic, discussions that do not always prove mutually comprehensible. It also reveals their shared weakness. This book argues that these tracks remain fruitful, but like a braided river, they are evidence that a more coherent, single stream exists.

The *traditionalist* approach—often associated with "strategic studies"—relies upon classic texts to frame historical analysis. Scholars working in this tradition are often historians or political scientists who focus on texts and historical methods. They draw upon writers like Thucydides or Clausewitz as frameworks. This approach allows a certain level of subjective interpretation and a freedom to draw lessons for current challenges.

Theorists, by contrast, are often political scientists—frequently in "security studies"—seeking to break down human behavior into observable variables. In turn, these variables work within larger theories or schools of thought. This approach allows insight into the specific agents of grand strategy and offers a more precise and testable set of hypotheses than the classics of strategy. Some theorists may focus on foreign policy outcomes and decision making whereas others emphasize international systemic variables or bargaining models. They may even debate whether a premeditated strategy is possible and argue that a host of individual, domestic, and international variables drive strategic behavior.

In the third category, *professionals*, military and other policy planners are specifically focused on national security success. They draw upon insights from traditionalists and theorists—as well as their own training, intuition, and experience—as they find them useful. Practitioners and professional strategists focus on identifying goals and optimizing outcomes. They are concerned about scholarship to the degree that it provides actionable insights into creating strategic priorities and projecting success. Here, strategy is not an object of analysis but a policy agenda. The goal is a "good" strategy.

Notably, this professional approach almost always affects analysis among traditionalists and theorists. I argue that traditionalists, theorists, and professionals muddy the very concept they are studying by mixing factual observation of *how grand strategy works* with prescriptions about *how to make grand strategy work effectively*. After all, why study grand strategy if you don't want to understand and help implement an effective grand strategy? Theorists in particular are famous for working in a "basic research" vein. Their job, like a physicist or geologist, is to understand how the world works. Let others find the applications. In fact, though, theorists typically include extensive discussions about what constitutes an effective grand strategy. They may hope to make the world either a better or at least a more stable place. Perhaps they hope to join the professionals—or they themselves have been professionals—who directly shape government policy. And under scrutiny from a skeptical public and funding agencies, they also wish to make their work relevant. These are all worthy and understandable motivations. However, these traditions fail to treat grand strategy as a stand-alone phenomenon. A phenomenon one can empirically observe separately from what one wants it to be. To make this case, the book references behavioral economics as a model to illustrate its agenda. It then argues for grand strategy as a distinct, complex empirical phenomenon.

The Art and Science of Strategy

Studies of war, peace, and strategy are the research areas most proximate to this study of grand strategy. Really, this scholarship breaks into two areas: *strategic studies* and *security studies*. Scholar Joshua Rovner maintains footing in both areas, and he characterizes their shared agenda as "two approaches to the study of war and peace."[5] Imagine you are tasked with analyzing World War I, and you have free reign to set your questions and approaches. What do you do? Do you focus on specific details to learn lessons, or do you try to apply and test abstract theories? Your answer likely tips you into one camp or the other.

The field of strategic studies is perhaps the older sibling, or at least the sibling steeped in history and the classics. Writers in this tradition often reference the ancient Chinese general Sun Tzu or the classical Greek historian Thucydides or the Prussian cavalry officer Clausewitz. More pointedly, work in strategic studies is historical. It seeks to observe the interaction of war technique and political agendas, and it uses those to draw lessons about effective strategy. Professional military strategists and academic historians most often work in this tradition. Their backgrounds and approaches allow them to draw insights about psychology and leadership as well as about broad historical trends and technological change. As historian Williamson Murray observers, "those who have been most successful at [practicing grand strategy] ... have been willing to adapt to political, economic, and military conditions as they are rather than as they wish them to be."[6] Crucially, Williams continues, "Perhaps the most important factor in the development and execution of successful grand strategy has been leadership at the top."[7] Examples of other work in this area include Paul Kennedy's *Rise and Fall of the Great Powers*, Lawrence Freedman's *Strategy*, John Lewis Gaddis' *On Grand Strategy*, Russell Weigley's *The American Way of War*, and Colin S. Gray's *The Strategy Bridge*.[8] To its detriment, however, strategic studies is also primarily focused on war, and as a field, it lacks central organizing theories or frameworks. In other words, it is not quite grand strategy, and its insights are not quite portable to other cases or categories. The midcentury strategic thinker Bernard Brodie recognized this limitation. In a 1949 article, he argued that "classical principles of strategy" are "too insubstantial."[9] Inspired by the social sciences, he called for a science of strategy, one studying how a state can maximize its resources for military preparedness and war.

Brodie was riding a wave from whose crest he saw the wider landscape. The general outlines of human behavior, studied for centuries from the trough between waves, could now be surveyed more clearly and systematically from the peak. Ever since, strategic studies scholars and professionals have wavered uncomfortably between strategy as wisdom or art and the modern demand for precision and underlying principles. They realize that policy makers require simplified takeaways and actionable points. For that reason, a "science of strategy" remains appealing. Indeed, business researchers and game theorists argue that they have isolated (quite different) versions of such a science.[10] However, these approaches either tend to study business firms, which have a limited profit objective, or treat human motivation as a rational abstraction. For strategic studies scholars, these approaches are fatally limited because they dismiss the rich weight of history. Knowledge from careful study of history can serve as a guide to action and as a constraint upon policy makers. Freedman closes his massive review of strategy deeply aware of these tensions. His conclusion, however, is firm: "Strategy is art and not a science."[11] Done well, it involves developing a sense of next steps as events unfold. Freedman also warns his readers to be wary of stylized "stories," or narratives that conveniently draw together clear cause-effect relationships. Yet in his parting discussion, he also describes how humans rely on psychological scripts and narratives to frame the actions. As I will argue, this is not surprising. Even if one rejects strategy as science, a theory or framework of how strategies emerge and how people interact with them is simply a matter of empirical observation.

Security studies, by contrast, is typically associated with political scientists. If not the younger sibling, it is at least more comfortable with more recent analytical techniques and streamlined theoretical models. Examples are extensive and cited throughout this text, but some of the more general classic texts include Thomas Schelling's *The Strategy of Conflict*, Kenneth Waltz's *Theory of International Politics*, Robert Axelrod's *The Evolution of Cooperation* and Bruce Bueno de Mesquita and David Lalman's *War and Reason*.[12] What these and other works share is a concern for understanding the causes and outcomes (as well as the prevention) of war as determined by a wide range of observable variables. For instance, in explaining Britain's pre-World War I changing security, Steven E. Lobell found that psychological framing effects and prospect theory created the conditions for Britain's ability and willingness to escalate its military commitments to the continent.[13] Such studies also extend to deterrence and diplomatic strategies, both of which, notably, occur far more frequently than war. Lantis, for example, demonstrates how a "culturist turn" in security studies "provides a bridge between material and ideational explanation of state behavior."[14] He observes several studies of Australia, China, and several other Pacific Rim countries. In those cases, security policies emerged from an interaction effect. The international structure and the state's cultural predispositions were interpreted within the framework of long-standing historical narratives and political-military cultures. Of course, some approaches in this field oversimplify strategy by focusing narrowly upon rational calculation, military capacity and war motivations.

Now, reconsider the question at the top of this discussion: how to study World War I. If your impulse is to dig into documents, details of tactics and strategies, and leaders themselves, you are thinking like a strategic studies scholar. If your impulse is to develop a theory, isolate the key variables, and draw findings that apply across cases and between wars, you may be doing security studies.

As argued throughout this chapter, these approaches tend to study grand strategy as the byproduct of other phenomena, such as foreign policy decision making or international systems. Or they do little to separate actual grand strategy behavior from desired outcomes. They display no coherent study of grand strategy as a distinct phenomenon. There is no "grand strategy analysis." Yet as I argue, such a research agenda is emerging.

An Emerging Research Program

The late scholar and former national security official William C. Martel penned one of the more comprehensive analyses of grand strategy. His major work canvassed ancient and modern texts on foreign policy. It exhaustively cited major definitions. Martel argued that "grand strategy" represents a "broad consensus on the state's goals and the means by which to put them into practice."[15] Grand strategy is a consensus about state interests and how to achieve them. Martel then traced this concept across the history of American foreign policy. His conclusion? "Only grand strategy provides the broad vision that helps policy makers conduct foreign policy." Unfortunately, his argument continued, after the Cold War, the United States lacked a single vision or adversary. It "has been dangerously adrift for more than two decades."[16] Like most others in this grand strategy genre, it set out definitions and priorities, worked up a case study, and drew both diagnoses and prescriptions. The study ends with a set of recommendations for policy makers.

This is *strategic studies* developed to its fullest limits on grand strategy. Martel based his analysis in classic writings and then drew those insights forward in an historical case. The book focuses on policy makers who are free to shape and change grand strategy. Martel uses the word "theory" to describe the patterns of behavior that he observes. In reality, as a set of lessons rather than formal propositions and predictions, what he developed is not quite theory the way most social scientists use the term. Martel's approach was both too broad and too narrow. To simultaneously isolate a grand strategy, diagnose its problems, and build recommendations for leaders is necessary work. It is also general work. Actual policy makers may find that grand strategy raises an endless series of questions about target timeframes or domestic political sacrifices or military tradeoffs. In other words, even if it is thoroughly researched and defined, "grand strategy" may still leave observers with no clear idea about either the phenomenon or its application. The approach is also too narrow. It merely seeks recommendations for effective grand strategy. Perhaps, for example, grand strategies are a phenomenon that can evolve a life of their own, a life outside any one set of leaders. Certainly, US and Soviet strategies through the Cold War lived far longer than any one ruling administration. It also may be that leaders often cannot rationally or simply change grand strategy to make it better.

I highlight Martel's work not because it is poorly done. In fact, it is quite thorough. Rather, I highlight it because even in the case of a former professional turned academic armed with extensive historical study and an encyclopedic review of grand strategy, the underlying approach has reached its limits. This is not unique to strategic studies or what I call the *classic* approach. As seen earlier, the theoretical and professional approaches also continue to produce real insights; yet, they are inherently limited. In the case of *theory*, grand strategy is rarely developed on its own terms as a phenomenon. Instead, it is often treated as the output of other variables, such as individual decision frameworks or international systemic constraints. Meanwhile, under time pressures, those working in the *professional* category often run with "what works," which can easily shift from one crisis or policy or report or duty assignment to the next.

Diagnosis vs. Observation

Among those attempting to bridge these approaches, Ionut Popescu's work stands out. *Emergent Strategy and Grand Strategy: How American*

Presidents Succeed in Foreign Policy focused on, and made recommendations for, the process of forming grand strategy.[17] It argued that work
on grand strategy tends to fall into either (a) grand strategy as a fully
formed and stable plan, or (b) grand strategy as conduct or process. The
first approach is perhaps the most common and traditional. Empirically,
it treats grand strategy as a fixed set of goals and a relatively stable
plan to achieve them. As a set of prescriptions, it holds that success is
mostly likely when policy makers hold closely to that overarching plan.
A related, intermediary approach also holds that goals and means should
be largely stable, but to achieve success, policy makers need to focus
on evaluating the strategic environment and effectively applying the
state's capabilities. The second approach championed by Popescu but
also hinted by others (such as Freedman) focuses on process. Here, policy
makers who slavishly follow a preordained strategy are as likely as not
to fail because the approach is hidebound. As an empirical theory, this
approach seems to suggest that strategies themselves are rarely fixed
but, rather, flexible as policy makers respond to events as well as their
own preexisting beliefs and worldviews.

These approaches offer real value to scholars and policy makers;
however, they risk falling into a conceptual trap. They tend to combine
grand strategy as a behavior with *grand strategy as an agenda for success.*
Stated more academically, they conflate grand strategy as an empirical
phenomenon with grand strategy as a set of policy prescriptions. Naturally, scholars and practitioners want to answer two simple questions:
Is grand strategy real? If so, what is a good grand strategy? In turn,
they study both at the same time. Such questions are essential, but by
attempting to answer both with one framework, scholars risk allowing
the goal of diagnosing "good grand strategy" to define their empirical
study of grand strategy. For instance, any mechanic's or physician's
primary job is diagnosis and treatment, but before either of these is
possible, the engineer or the researcher will have either created or identified the system in question. Again, in the academic language of political

science, empirical observation and theory are separate functions from prescription and policy.

A Converging Body of Work

Still, new work like this illustrates how "grand strategy analysis" is emerging as a distinct field. It also demonstrates how grand strategy observers can work within that field to make progress and talk with rather than past one another. Realism, foreign policy analysis, constructivism, strategic and security studies, among other contributions, all shape grand strategy analysis. What emerges is a research agenda that looks something like behavioral economics, with its mix of classic theory and human psychology. Methodologically (in other words, how to study the topic), grand strategy analysis is patterned after foreign policy analysis.

Today, grand strategy scholarship bears the hallmarks of an independent research program. Academics and practitioners across different fields seek to understand it. They are producing an extensive and growing body of works focused primarily on grand strategy. They study and analyze grand strategy as a distinct phenomenon, one that can be defined and identified separately from other phenomena. They may even interact professionally, yet this work remains tracked into silos. The *traditionalists*, *theorists*, and *professionals*, as described earlier, have different agendas and different analytical frameworks. Their work is not quite cumulative beyond their own research streams. Thierry Balzacq, Peter Dombrowski, and Simon Reich made much the same case in their proposal for "comparative grand strategy."[18] They argued that traditional approaches to grand strategy, though concise, rely too much upon rationalist theorizing and the specific case of the United States. Instead, Balzacq and his collaborators proposed a broad comparative framework, one that unites general IR approaches with specialized area studies. Researchers can evaluate any given state's grand strategy in terms of its external context in conjunction with a set of domestic factors, ranging from collective memories to political actors. Overall, then, a grand strategy research program is forming but has not quite coalesced.

Too often, scholar Nina Silove has argued, scholars use the grand strategy concept loosely. They invoke it as a familiar concept, but they are not actually testing it as a dependent variable or as a distinctive phenomenon.[19] Rather, they are focused on defining the term in ways that suit some other analytical agenda. Most debate about the concept itself, she says, "can be described as semantic." Is grand strategy a fixed plan or a blind process? Is it an illusion or an empirical reality? Citing the well-known political scientist Gary Goertz, Silove observed that debates about defining grand strategy prove sterile because they circle around who defines the language and how they define it rather than how to study the phenomenon itself. Imagine, for example, members of a police department debating how to define a street riot. Some insist that a riot cannot exist without ringleaders or at least a clear agenda. Others are more worried about the difference between civil disobedience and a riot. Beat cops, meanwhile, just want to know how to stay safe and clear the street. Can they define members of the riot as violent criminals? You may notice, however, that actual riot formation and evolution of riots themselves is lost in this debate. Everyone agrees that riots exist. Yet this understaffed police department is debating definitions rather than the phenomenon itself.

In a similar way, the grand strategy phenomenon seems to exist. Trying to observe it on its own terms, however, is challenging. Grand strategies are seen as shorthand for other issues, such as a framework for specific historical analysis (i.e., why did *that particular* grand strategy emerge) or a set of prescriptions for national security (i.e., how to shape *the next grand strategy*). These are important questions, but a well-rounded research program will also include studies of the phenomenon itself and how it behaves as an empirical or ideational phenomenon (i.e., *why do grand strategies emerge in a certain form* and *how do they behave* once under way). Just as the imagined police department appears to lack a specialist devoted primarily to riots, the nascent grand strategy field involves observers from different traditions with cross-cutting agendas; however, they have yet to articulate a single or coherent common ground.

Silove was seeking to begin the process of "develop[ing] a theory of the concept of grand strategy." She found that grand strategy typically refers to one of three different types of phenomena. The first is *grand plans*. These are "deliberate, detailed plan[s] devised by individuals." It is the scenario in which leaders devise a specific set of goals and steps to reach them, and then they basically follow that plan.[20] Second, *grand principles* are an underlying set of ideas. Here, the scholar assumes that grand strategy is held in peoples' minds but is really about a general set of priorities and goals rather than a limited plan. Third, *grand behavior* is simply a pattern of state activity. Here, whether policy makers choose a grand strategy or explicitly hold one in their minds is not important. What matters is that, like the Roman or Han Empires or any other historical or current polity, the state displays a consistent set of strategic behaviors. Scholar Rebecca Friedman Lissner breaks the grand strategy research agenda into slightly different pieces. "Grand strategy as variable" refers to state behavior, structures and agency. This is basically similar to this book's argument for treating grand strategy as an empirical phenomenon in the tradition of social science. "Grand strategy as process" and "as blueprint," meanwhile, respectively refer to processes of developing and, second, agendas to shape future governmental behavior.[21] What Silove and Lissner—as well as Balzacq, Dombrowski, and Reich—suggest is that, taken together, these approaches represent a proto-research program. They are different aspects of a single phenomenon.

Current Research
Other recent works exemplify these treatments of grand strategy. They also demonstrate how a "grand strategy analysis" research program is possible. Each advances understandings of how grand strategies emerge, function, or change. On their own, however, with no ties to a general grand strategy theory or research program, these works represent a circular debate. Applying slightly different definitions, slightly different theories, and weighing priorities for a "good" grand strategy in slightly different ways, they make arguments that the reader cannot directly

compare with alternatives. They also vary regarding agency and structure. Who actually makes grand strategy? Are leaders free to shape and change it as they see fit? Or does grand strategy emerge from domestic and international factors no matter the intentions and positions of individual policy makers?

A Distinct Phenomenon

Barry Posen, a political scientist at the Massachusetts Institute of Technology, created one of the most enduring definitions of grand strategy: it is a means/ends calculation, or a "state's theory about how to produce security for itself."[22] When done effectively, grand strategy subjects military power to "the discipline of political analysis."[23] More recently, in his book *Restraint*, he argued that for decades the United States has pursued a grand strategy of "liberal hegemony." Unfortunately, he argued, liberal hegemony is inherently expansionist and therefore unsustainable and unstable.[24] Grand strategy, under this framework, is the output of policy maker calculations, national politics, and military conditions.[25] It also can assume a life of its own and persist, in Posen's view, even when it has grown ineffective and self-destructive. In another example, Patrick Porter writing in the journal *International Security* found that US grand strategy has remained relatively stable for decades. Why? Porter pointed to what he calls "habit." He said foreign policy elites after World War II conformed to professional and social pressure. There emerged among these leaders only one acceptable strategy—primacy—and all debates happened within its parameters.[26] This created self-reinforcing norms and self-censorship. Porter argued that this consensus has led to US overextension and should be reconsidered. The takeaway is that—perhaps in the vein of Silove's "grand principles"—both Posen and Porter find that grand strategy ideas persisted on their own separate from any one individual's or group's control. Grand strategy exists as a distinct phenomenon.

In his 2014 book *What Good is Grand Strategy*, historian Hal Brands studied this same period with a view of grand strategy as a "conceptual logic."[27] For Brands, grand strategy sets fixed priorities that guide decision makers. Brands extended this work in 2018 by arguing that US grand strategy has actually remained consistent for decades.[28] He objected to arguments like Porter's and Posen's that call for US retrenchment or offshore balancing. Instead, Brands said that the raw facts of US power, alliance systems, economic investments, and military experience mean that US internationalism will remain robust. Again, Brands' agenda was to draw lessons about effective grand strategy, and his approach assumed grand strategy itself as a phenomenon. Finally, in his ambitious book *On Grand Strategy*, John Lewis Gaddis flipped this approach. Gaddis is a Cold War historian and foundational figure in Yale's well-known Brady-Johnson Program in Grand Strategy. His goal was to study grand strategy as "common sense."[29] At first glance, this approach appears to completely negate grand strategy as a concept. After all, why study grand strategy if it is indistinguishable from informed opinion? What Gaddis means, though, is that effective grand strategy requires a reservoir of knowledge, knowledge that will help decision makers confront specific challenges with general strategies. It is a mode of thinking about a specific topic. At its best, it is wisdom. This is probably the least empirical formulation of grand strategy possible. Still, it recognized the phenomenon on its own terms. Grand strategy is something that leaders of polities do. They may do it poorly or well, but the moment they devise beliefs or make decisions or respond to existing conditions that involve expansive or long-term implications, they are doing grand strategy.

A Social Scientific Phenomenon
Perhaps true to form, political scientists prove far more comfortable than historians with explicitly studying grand strategy as a phenomenon. In *Harmony and War*, for instance, Yuan-Kang Wang applied a structural realist framework to the Song and Ming grand strategies.[30] Not surprisingly, he found that despite highly visible Confucian antimilitarist values, these empires displayed consistent grand strategies driven by traditional realpolitik calculations. Scholars studying strategic culture disagree with this realist framing. For them, security policies emerge from the opposite

direction. Domestic historical narratives about a country's role in the world shape how elites and the public interpret outside threats.[31] Meanwhile, still other scholarship continues the long tradition of evaluating how policy makers can or should shape strategy. Should the United States pursue deep engagement or offshore balancing? Why do governments like Iran and Russia espouse strategies that both challenge and engage the existing international system? What lessons can a rising China learn from earlier German and US grand strategies?[32] In one exemplary study, Julian Germann studied West German grand strategy in the 1970s. He found that leaders developed an economic approach that addressed domestic political challenges while integrating with the US-led economic order.[33] Elsewhere, Christopher J. Fettweis argued that—despite arguments to the contrary—America's post-Cold War allies are not passively freeriding on US security guarantees. Rather, they have developed "active, coherent, logical, rational grand strategies" to match a world with few serious threats.[34] Again, overall, such work tends to emphasize grand strategy as fixed and seeks to probe its origins and effectiveness. Whatever their disagreements, these studies demonstrate the plausibility and substance of a grand strategy research program.

Another research area emphasizes how and when grand strategy changes. After 9/11 and particularly the 2003 US invasion of Iraq, the post-Cold War world was jolted. The George W. Bush administration's aggressive "war on terror" appeared to many observers to be breaking with long-standing US grand strategy. There emerged a wave of studies on grand strategy change. Is such dramatic change possible? When *is* grand strategy change likely? For instance, Jeffrey Legro's 2005 book *Rethinking the World* focused on widely held foreign policy ideas. He argued that overarching strategic consensus only changes in rare situations. Specifically, when (1) an old idea is widely considered to have failed and (2) a single new idea pushed by an effective policy entrepreneur is available.[35] With a more psychological focus, David Welch found that major changes are rare because leaders, like all people, are motivated in part by loss aversion.[36] By contrast, Kevin Narizny emphasized domestic economic interests. Grand strategies shift, he says, depending upon the party or regime that holds office.[37] Colin Dueck also maintained that grand strategies can and often are "adjusted." However, rather than economic interest, strategic culture shapes the options available to decision makers.[38] More recently, William R. Thompson argued that all this research struggles to balance "the interaction among ideas, external structures and developments, and domestic politics."[39] He proposed a solution. In his theory, major strategic changes grow more likely and more durable as certain variables—such as shocks and political entrepreneurship—themselves experience change. Finally, at the individual level, Popescu made the case for "emergent strategy." As discussed earlier, this framework returns us to the psychological insights of behavioral economics and the actor-centric focus of FPA. Popescu held that many of the most effective strategies rely upon "emergent learning" rather than fixed plans. Under this framework, grand strategy change is incremental and is derived from a small group of elite decision makers.[40]

An Observable Phenomenon

Historically, governments seem to hold relatively stable grand strategies for long periods, yet they also demonstrate regular adaptation. Popescu joined many others to observe that the Roman and Byzantine empires appear to have adopted and held a set of strategic practices that persisted for centuries. Yet at any given point in time, leaders in these polities were as likely as not to be adapting to deal with imminent threats rather than focusing on a fixed strategic ideal. Working exclusively from either of these frameworks, then, sets up a paradox. If the ideal type is a fixed and unchanging grand strategy, one might expect such strategies to grow stale and ineffective very quickly as events accelerate beyond the conditions the strategy was designed to address. If adaptive strategy is the ideal type, observers might expect strategies to constantly fluctuate like a kaleidoscope. I argue that treating grand strategy as a distinct empirical phenomenon helps resolve this apparent contradiction. In fact, grand strategy is neither completely stable nor completely adaptive because at any point in time, it may be both. A grand strategy can exist as a set of parameters outside any one leadership cohort's prerogatives. When responding to events, effective leaders adapt (Popescu's emergent strategy), but they are also likely to be constrained within long-standing strategic parameters. This is likely a noncontroversial claim for many grand strategy observers, yet little scholarship specifically asserts and tests it. Clearly, scholars disagree about how easily or how frequently grand strategy can change, but they agree that the project of studying grand strategy change is vital.

Table 1. Traditions studying strategy compared.

	Phenomenon	*Unit of Analysis*	*Prescriptive Agenda?*	*Epistemology*
FPA	Decisions & Decision making	Individual policy makers & groups	No	Perceptions, ideas, material interests
GSA	Grand strategy: pattern of thought & policy	Individual policy makers & groups	No	Perceptions, ideas, material interests
Traditionalists (Strategic Studies)	War	Undefined	Yes	Perceptions, ideas, material interests, contingency, wisdom/insight
Theorists (Security Studies)	State & institutional behavior	States, institutions, decision makers	Mix	Material interests
Professionals	Strategic Planning	Organizations, Leaders	Yes	Material outcomes, "What works"

Note: Research traditions that typically study grand strategy as a distinct phenomenon and compared with GSA and FPA. These are broad tendencies. Exceptions exist. "Prescriptive Agenda?" refers to whether or not researchers in that tradition typically seek to make policy recommendations alongside empirical analysis.

In sum, scholarship on grand strategy is converging. It shows a distinct phenomenon that can be coherently and systematically studied. Specifically, this phenomenon is a *pattern of thought and policy* shaping how a state defines and seeks its interests. This pattern may be set or constrained by external factors like geography or relative power, or it may be set by domestic interests and culture. However it is formed, scholars and professionals can study individuals and groups, particularly the content of their decision making—to observe it. Still, approaches to studying and understanding grand strategy vary widely. Different fields and traditions struggle to communicate with one another or develop sustained or cumulative mutual growth. Grand Strategy Analysis offers a simple framework to draw these approaches together. It focuses on the individuals and groups who make and implement grand strategy, but it is agnostic about whether individual-, state-, or system-level factors drive grand strategy. It is also agnostic about whether grand strategies should be understood primarily as plans, principles or behaviors. Rather, it allows analysis and comparison amongst these understandings.

GSA and the Trump Administration

GSA is a vital tool to analyze Donald Trump and his presidential administration. Throughout the two years this book covers, Trump himself displayed every indication that he wanted to break old patterns. Critics claimed that he was mercurial and lacked focus, to say nothing of implementing coherent strategic thought. Raw psychological needs, they said, drove all his decisions. Supporters pointed to Trump's unexpected successes. Clearly, they countered, he is a rational dealmaker. Meanwhile, journalists highlighted an increasing tendency for Trump's senior officials to publicly commit to conventional foreign policy positions even as Trump himself picked fights with allies like Canada and praised the good sense of leaders like Russia's Vladimir Putin. Players like Secretary of Defense James Mattis or UN Ambassador Nikki Haley appeared to make calls from a traditional Republican playbook rather than jump with Trump's every tweet. In the international system, meanwhile, most leaders remained coy about their views of Trump and American grand strategy. Major issues like nonproliferation or the civil war in Syria or international trade continued to churn; yet no major realignments or crises emerged. Was US grand strategy basically stable and consistent despite Trump's confrontational demeanor? How can observers assess the relationship between individual psychology, bureaucratic priorities, national politics, and international structures?

Hudson argues that the real questions in foreign policy analysis should be "when do leaders matter" and "which leaders matter?"[41] She observes that a number of variables are relevant: regime type; the leader's interest in foreign policy; presence of a crisis situation; ambiguous or uncertain situations; degree of diplomatic training; leadership style; and group dynamics. In another influential study, political psychologists found that personality mattered to foreign policy outcomes. That influence depended on several conditions: the actor's location in the political system; a situation that includes many elements open to restructuring; a delicate balance between internal and external forces; and an issue that requires active effort rather than routine role performance.[42]

Studying grand strategy based on the impacts of individuals or domestic systems or international structures is important and offers insights. However, any one of those approaches can also skew the answer to the simple question, "What matters the most to the shape of grand strategy?" In contrast, GSA analyzes individuals and their decision making, but as a framework, it does not assume that those individuals alone drive grand strategy. Rather, individuals articulate and implement grand strategy. They are the agents of grand strategy. They are the basic units of analysis to understand grand strategy. A researcher may find, for example, that though individuals may believe that they alone drive a government's security strategy, they are in fact profoundly constrained by prior strategic commitments, national bureaucracies and the current balance of power. Thus, GSA at its best is not prejudiced against either stability or change, structures or agents. Rather, it allows us to evaluate a number of possible variables and their different impacts.

Studying Trump

All this is useful to study the Trump administration. Trump himself seems to scramble usual expectations about grand strategy. Where strategists might be careful and forward-thinking, Trump spent his first two years rushing into immediate, actionable issues. Where strategists might think about the world as a set of interlocking systems, Trump remained focused on one-off deals and individual state sovereignty. Where strategy must be executed in the context of an international structure, Trump's temperament and loose management style kept his own personality close to the center of all policy planning. Is grand strategy really a viable concept under these conditions? Perhaps Trump's first two years in office put the lie to a desire to see overarching order in foreign affairs.

In addition, public and professional debate over Trump's first two years generated an important set of substantive questions.

- Was Trump trying to collapse the liberal internationalist, postwar order?
- Is nationalism a viable alternative as a grand strategy?
- Is he—or any head of government—alone sufficient to achieve such a change?
- Is "strategic ambiguity" (as one Trump supporter dubbed the president's approach) Trump's actual, carefully considered approach?
- Is grand strategy, in any administration, relatively stable or ever-changing?

To untangle this braided set of topics, I propose two, simple analytical questions for Trump's first two White House years. Each is derived from a simple causal question: why did US grand strategy take the shape that it did during 2017–2018?

Q1: What was the Trump administration's grand strategy?

Q2: How much did Trump himself shape that grand strategy?

This study is a "proof of concept" for GSA. It will apply the actor-centric approach to explain grand strategy outcomes and answer those two analytical questions. Such study will then allow us to return to the general questions about Trump's overall effect on grand strategy. The observations will be four case narratives. They are chronological (rather than thematic) and divide the administration's first two years of development into roughly equal time periods. In each, I will focus on the most significant foreign policy, security, and strategic questions that the president and his senior officials are deliberating and on which they stake out policy positions. Picture a Venn diagram with three circles: statements and debate, actions taken, and policy positions. This book will be seeking their overlap. This allows us to include all three of *grand plans*, *grand principles*, and *grand behavior*.

Identifying Grand Strategy

The methods will be simple. To answer Q1, this study will apply a diagnostic rubric with three characteristics. This book has set aside the all-important question of "what *should be* US grand strategy?" in favor of another, more fundamental question: "What *is* US grand strategy?" This is a framework developed elsewhere. Sufficient to say here is that it is distilled from the extensive scholarship that seeks to define and then assess grand strategy. It is a summation of the most common characteristics used to identify a grand strategy. For the case studies, the study will seek to observe the administration's position on each dimension.

These dimensions can be applied to periods of time within an administration as well as between administrations, governments, and eras. They allow us to observe and compare grand strategies within and across cases. This is an open-ended framework, which means that there is no fixed set of grand strategy types that emerge when these dimensions are combined. They allow the observer to define the strategy in context as its practitioners understood and practiced it. Of course, any categorization scheme like this one includes possible biases and space for individual interpretation; however, this approach allows the observer to portray the strategy on its own terms, as it is understood and applied by decision makers. The tradeoff is less parsimony but greater precision. *Scope, substance,* and *assertiveness* do not shoehorn or distort the strategy to fit a preexisting set of expectations.

Table 2. The empirical elements of grand strategy.

Dimensions	Characteristics
SCOPE	Geographic Extent
	Allies
	Adversaries
SUBSTANCE	Core Interests
	Nature of System
	Role
ASSERTIVENESS	Force Level
	Security Strategies

Source. *Hope, Change, Pragmatism: Analyzing Obama's Grand Strategy* by Jacob Shively (New York: Palgrave, 2016).

Briefly, these dimensions are defined by the following specific characteristics:

- *Scope*: The strategy's geographic and relational parameters.[43] What are the areas relevant to national security? What threats are perceived? Who are partners and who are adversaries?
- *Substance*: The strategy's "operating system." What national interests do policy makers espouse, and how do they say the world works? This includes their ideologies and mental frameworks. What is the role of the United States in the world?

- *Assertiveness*: The strategy's aggression and force level. Is the strategy proactive or reactive? What types of coercion and force are applied? Secondly, what security strategies, if any, are articulated?

This categorization scheme allows observers to systematically observe and define a grand strategy. Rather than forcing evidence into preexisting categories, it allows the strategy itself, as its practitioners understand it, to emerge. However, this is only a categorization scheme. It is necessary to begin analysis and comparison, but it does not engage causal theories or whether the strategy is effective. In other words, *why* the strategy takes the form that it does and whether it achieves its goals are addressed once this categorization is in place.

Studying Individual Impact

This book's second major analytical question is also simple: How did Donald Trump shape US grand strategy? To answer Q2, the study will observe grand strategy decisions, statements and changes at and just below the presidential level. This will compare the president's statements and claims with the actual policies and actions of US government officials. The goal is to observe the responsiveness of overall US grand strategy relative to the president himself. As a secondary goal, it can shed light on just how constrained or free the overall administration was with regard to changing grand strategy.

On its face, Trump's larger-than-life persona and untethered style seem like a recipe for unique influence. After two terms of Barack Obama's measured internationalism, "America first" in and of itself would be a notable change. While campaigning in 2015 and 2016, Trump insisted that he would be unpredictable. That he was a brilliant negotiator and under-stood most situations better than anyone else and would solve intractable problems, ranging from trade to immigration to nonproliferation. "The swamp" in Washington, D.C. had failed, and he would bring something new. Trump's strategy was himself, and his incidental strategic agenda was nationalism. To what degree can an individual's prerogatives and temperament shape grand strategy? Did Trump's nationalism become US grand strategy? This book contends that grand strategy is a phenomenon as much as a choice. Scholars taking a long view argue that grand strategy is bigger than one person and difficult for anyone to move. Trump, argued scholar Stephen Walt, "ended up in the same places his predecessors did."[44]

In order to systematically probe the cases and evaluate the president's individual influence on the strategy, the book presents a set of questions. The approach follows the "structured, focused comparison" method set out by George and Bennett.[45] Here, researchers apply a standard set of analytical questions to a specific class of cases. "The method," they explain, "was devised to study historical experience in ways that would yield useful generic knowledge of important foreign policy problems." Observers can test or develop a theoretical framework by probing whether a set of cases display predicted characteristics. In this book, the cases are a series of periods within a larger case: the Trump administration's first two years. Each is broadly defined by time spans in which the administration's senior personnel was relatively stable and, in turn, internal debates and approaches likewise relatively consistent. Each of these cases is presented as an historical narrative. This narrative approach allows the observer to cast a wide net for empirical observation. Rather than focus on preselected variables, it explores debates and decisions across an array of topics.

To assess the Trump administration, the study will observe three correlations:

1. Presidential statements versus actual policy actions and agency statements.

2. The consistency between the United States' official policy before heading into a change and the US policy after the change. In other words, when the administration publicly articulates an adjustment to existing foreign policy, regardless of whose positions prevailed, did the grand strategic policy change, and how much did it change?

3. Trump's positions versus those of his foreign policy principals and Republican Party leaders. For example, on contentious issues, did Trump regularly overrule or ignore his National Security Council principals or party leaders?

As seen in table 3, the questions are designed to evaluate whether and to what degree the stated preferences and policies of the foreign policy executive—in this case, the US president—correlate with other domestic grand strategy players. This is a rough measure designed to uncover general trends. These questions help to isolate individual influence. The first two questions seek to determine whether the president's own prerogatives are directly reflected in policy and action. They evaluate how closely state behavior matches the president's words. The second category, meanwhile, seeks to determine whether the president holds an outlier position among senior foreign policy officials. Such a situation would suggest that his influence or prerogatives may be limited, at least during that period.

For each period, each question is assigned a simple ranking: Low (L), Medium (M), or High (H). High consistency indicates that the president's positions and those of other actors are effectively identical. Low consistency, then, indicates that they disagree in nearly every respect. A high gap between official policy before and after a foreign policy change indicates that the policy has been completely or fundamentally revised. A low gap indicates the adjustment is basically rhetorical or superficial, and it indicates that the policy or behavior of the US government is largely indistinguishable from before the putative change.

All three question assessments are probing for the patterns of thought and policy that characterize grand strategy analysis. As correlations, the findings indicate likely causes, but correlations alone cannot definitively isolate cause-effect relationships. For example, an executive may start out with outlier views that diverge with his foreign policy principals and government's policies. Over time, he may grow more synchronized with both. In that scenario, it may be that either (1) the president pulled others toward his position *or* (2) he is has been pulled toward the median position. Strictly speaking, then, the observed correlations are ambiguous. Fortunately, the content of the case histories provides two types of information. The first type answers the assessment questions with L, M, H designations. The second is the connective tissue among decisions and actions. Each chapter, in other words, is an overarching narrative of its time period. This second set of information, similar to process tracing, allows us to observe the direction and substance of the correlations.

Table 3. Assessment questions. Findings presented in Chapter 7, "Analyzing Trump's Grand Strategy."

Executive vs Other Actors	*Candidacy and Early 2017*	*Spring and Summer 2017*	*Fall 2017 to Spring 2018*	*Summer and Fall 2018*
Consistency between president's statements and administration policy, agency actions?				
Gap between an official US foreign policies before and after a change?				
Consistency between president's and principals' statements?				

This approach is a first cut at applying grand strategy analysis (GSA). GSA, like the field of foreign policy analysis (FPA), evaluates individuals within their larger policy contexts. The phenomenon FPA seeks to observe is individual and group decision making. GSA, by contrast, seeks to observe a *pattern of thought and policy*. By definition, a grand strategy must be larger than any one leader. At the least, it must be either held or applied by others in the leader's regime to be active. GSA assumes that grand strategy is indeed an observable phenomenon. It is also actor-centric. This allows the researcher to observe both personal decision-making as well as impersonal systems that might constrain individuals. Using this framework, observers can then evaluate both the impact of individuals on grand strategy as well as, potentially, the impact of a grand strategy upon individuals.

Predictions

"Do leaders matter?" is an old debate. For millennia, informed observers assumed that, yes, of course they do. But in the spirit of skepticism, nineteenth and twentieth century thinkers questioned conventional wisdom. After all, governments and practices like war persist for far longer than any one leader or group. Skeptics will concede that leaders may matter but only within clear parameters, or maybe even not at all. From that vantage, systems and institutions and cultures constrain or shape individual prerogatives. Individual decisions are the byproducts of larger structures. But just as assuming that individuals are the only units that matter to grand strategy, assuming that only structures matter can also bias one's analysis.

GSA is well positioned to evaluate these competing accounts. GSA itself is a framework for analysis. It helps us evaluate and compare both grand strategies and the theories used to explain them. Based on existing research, one possible grand strategy prediction is that Trump would have little impact on US grand strategy. After all, like ocean liners, grand strategies are hard to change course. They are determined by a mix of external and internal conditions. They are also held in the minds of many more people in and outside a given government. In other words, they take on a life beyond the control of any one president. In Silove's parlance, this is *grand principles* or—perhaps more likely—*grand behavior*. Based on a different set of assumptions, we could also predict the opposite. Because they are held in people's minds, grand strategies can change with the individuals in power. As Hudson herself emphasized, the "ground" of international relations is the people making foreign policy decisions. In the US system, presidents wield extensive executive power to change policies and use the "bully pulpit" to shape public and political opinion. In this approach, grand strategy is what policy leaders make of it. For the Trump administration, the president's unique psychology itself may overwhelm others' planning. Again, using Silove's categories, this is *grand plans* or—possibly—*grand principles*.

Overall, one can posit two sets of predictions based upon the analytical questions in table 3. Under the first set of theories, systemic, social, institutional, and other impersonal factors largely set grand strategy. If this approach is true, then the framework predicts low (L) or moderate (M) scores for all three questions. On balance, particularly early in the administration, there will be little or at most moderate consistency between the president's statements and those of his principals as well as his administration's policies and actions. Unless the president naturally agrees with all aspects of existing US grand strategy, his positions are likely to diverge regularly from official policy and, at least sometimes, the positions of his appointees. In turn, there will be little difference in US grand strategy before and after the president attempts to push a major policy change.

Under the second set of theories, grand strategies are pliable because they are mental plans and will change along with whoever may be the lead decision makers. If this approach is true, then this study predicts a pattern of high (H) scores across all three questions. On balance, US policies and agencies will reflect the president's stated preferences as well as those of the president's top appointees. In turn, the framework predicts that grand strategic policies will closely follow the president's lead as the administration officially implements its updated vision. Strategic policy will be responsive to individual preferences. Overall, the first set of predictions assumes that impersonal structures constrain leaders, so it anticipates low or moderate correlations between the president's preferences and the state's grand strategy. Under the second set of predictions, individuals are the foundation of all grand strategy and, as the primary agents, they will display high correlation between their positions and the state's grand strategy.

In Sum

Behavioral economics proved transformative, but its basic insight was to unite idealized models with observed human behavior. It modified theory with observation. In a similar fashion, grand strategy has long existed as an ideal type for academics and professionals. More recently, a growing body of scholarship puts flesh on these ideals and modifies them. Among those who study the topic, there is no question: grand strategy is real and observable. To date, those researchers cannot decide whether what they are observing is a form of classic wisdom, a theoretical and empirical phenomenon, or an actionable policy agenda. Does it exist only in the minds of policy makers or does it take on a life of its own?

Rather than directly tackle these debates, this chapter proposed a simple framework that allows these traditions to interact with one another. Grand strategy analysis (GSA) draws upon foreign policy analysis to construct this analytical approach. At base, this approach is "actor-centric." It assumes that individuals and small groups are the baseline units of analysis to understand a state's grand strategy at any given point in time. This focus allows a wide range of inputs or causal variables, including psychology, ideas, institutions, domestic politics, and international structures. Rather than preference one over the others, it provides a shared language and analytical focus that researchers from, say, security studies and strategic studies can apply for mutual comprehension.

The chapter ends with a research proposal. Donald Trump seems to pose a serious challenge to the notion of grand strategy. He is brash and his pronouncements are often contradictory. He also promised a fundamental break with existing American approaches to the world. This case poses an ideal challenge for GSA. It raises the possibility that grand strategies are really just illusions of order observers impose on a stream of events, but it also raises the possibility that a given leader is, in fact, unable to fundamentally change his state's grand strategy. I propose dividing Trump's first two years into four narrative cases that are focused on statements and policies around the most salient security issues that have emerged from Trump and his senior officials. Scholars can then interrogate what is the grand strategy as well as the relative impact of the president himself. Again, the GSA approach does not necessarily bias these inquiries. Rather, it helps organize them around the actors involved. This approach will also be accessible to political scientists and historians, policy makers and students. In whatever form Trump's grand strategy may emerge from this study, the analysis itself will demonstrate the utility—and necessity—of GSA.

Notes

1. Christopher Cadelago, "'There never is a strategy': Trump confronts twin Manafort and Kavanaugh crises," *Politico*, September 14, 2018, https://www.politico.com/story/2018/09/14/donald-trump-hurricane-florence-brett-kavanaugh-manafort-825300.
2. Jonathan Swan, "Trump's strategic planning inspiration: Mike Tyson," *Axios*, January 16, 2019, https://www.axios.com/donald-trump-mike-tyson-planning-strategy-bc799c7f-d1f2-432e-96e9-9e87d08a01ef.html.
3. Valerie Hudson, *Foreign Policy Analysis: Classic and Contemporary Theory* (New York: Rowman and Littlefield, 2007), 6-7 and 165 respectively.
4. "The Prize in Economic Sciences," Press Release, The Royal Swedish Academy of Sciences, October 9, 2017, https://www.nobelprize.org/prizes/economics/2017/press-release/.
5. Joshua Rovner, "Warring Tribes Studying War and Peace," (Special Series–The Schoolhouse) *War on the Rocks*, April 12, 2016, https://warontherocks.com/2016/04/warring-tribes-studying-war-and-peace/.
6. Williamson Murray, "Thoughts on Grand Strategy" in *The Shaping of Grand Strategy: Policy, Diplomacy, and War*, edited by Williamson Murray, Richard Hart Sinnreich, and James Lacey (New York: Cambridge University Press, 2011).
7. Ibid., 21
8. Paul Kennedy, *The Rise and Fall of the Great Powers: Economic Change and Military Conflict from 1500 to 2000* (New York: Random House, 1987); Gaddis, *On Grand Strategy*; Lawrence Freedman, *Strategy: A History* (New York: Oxford University Press, 2013); Russell F. Weigley, *The American Way of War: A History of United States Military Strategy and Policy* (Bloomington, IN: Indiana University Press, 1960); and Colin S. Gray, *The Strategy Bridge: Theory for Practice* (New York: Oxford University Press, 2010).
9. Bernard Brodie, "Strategy as a Science," *World Politics* 1, no. 4 (1949): 467–488.
10. On game theory and international relations, see Barry O'Neill, *Honor, Symbols, and War* (Ann Arbor: University of Michigan Press, 2001); and Robert Powell, *In the Shadow of Power: States and Strategies in International Politics* (Princeton, NJ: Princeton University Press, 1999). On business strategy, see especially Henry Mintzberg *Tracking Strategies:*

Towards a General Theory of Strategy Formation (New York: Oxford University Press, 2008).

11. Freedman, *Strategy,* 612

12. Thomas Schelling, *The Strategy of Conflict* (Cambridge, MA: Harvard University Press, 1960); Kenneth N. Waltz *Theory of International Politics* (New York: Random House, 1979); Robert Axelrod, *The Evolution of Cooperation* (New York: Basic Books, 1984); and Bruce Bueno de Mesquita and David Lalman, *War and Reason: Domestic and International Imperatives* (New Haven: Yale University Press, 1992).

13. Steven E. Lobell, "The International Realm, Framing Effects, and Security Strategies: Britain in Peace and War," *International Interactions* 32 (2006): 27–48.

14. Jeffrey S. Lantis, "Strategic Cultures and Security Policies in the Asia-Pacific." *Contemporary Security Policy* 35, ,no. 2 (2014): 166–186.

15. William Martel, *Grand Strategy in Theory and Practice: The Need for An Effective American Foreign Policy* (New York: Cambridge University Press, 2015), 339.

16. Ibid., 351–352.

17. Ionut Popescu, *Emergent Strategy and Grand Strategy: How American Presidents Succeed in Foreign Policy* (Baltimore: Johns Hopkins University Press, 2017).

18. Thierry Balzacq, Peter Dombrowski, and Simon Reich. "Introduction: Comparing Grand Strategies in the Modern World." In *Comparative Grand Strategy: A Framework and Cases* (New York: Oxford University Press, 2019).

19. Nina Silove, "Beyond the Buzzword: The Three Meanings of 'Grand Strategy,'" *Security Studies* 27, no. 1 (2018): 27–57.

20. For details on these concepts, see Silove, "Beyond the Buzzword," 29–44 and 49. Her summaries of each are quoted here. *Grand plans*: "the detailed product of the deliberate efforts of individuals to translate a state's interests into specific long-term goals, establish orders of priority between those goals, and consider all spheres of statecraft (military, diplomatic, and economic) in the process of identifying the means by which to achieve them. Given their level of detail, grand plans are likely to be—but are not necessarily—set down in written documents." *Grand principles*: "overarching ideas that are consciously held by individuals about the long-term goals that the state should prioritize and the military, diplomatic, and/or economic means that ought to be mobilized in pursuit of those goals. They tend to be expressed in single words or short

phrases." *Grand Behavior:* "long-term pattern in a state's distribution and employment of its military, diplomatic, and economic resources toward ends. In this context, the ends that receive the greatest relative resources can be deemed to be priorities, but the concept implies no inference that those ends were necessarily prioritized as a result of a grand plan, a grand principle, or any other factor."

21. Rebecca Friedman Lissner, "What is Grand Strategy? Sweeping a Conceptual Minefield," *Texas National Security Review* 2, no. 1 (2018).

22. Barry R. Posen, *The Sources of Military Doctrine: France, Britain and Germany between the World Wars* (Ithaca, NY: Cornell University Press, 1984): 13.

23. Barry R. Posen, *Restraint: A New Foundation for U.S. Grand Strategy* (Ithaca NY: Cornell University Press, 2014): xii.

24. Ibid., 44

25. Posen (*Restraint,* 22) specifically cites four driving causes or theories for the book: realism, nuclear weapons, nationalism and identity politics, and the "costly and not easily controlled" prospect of war.

26. Patrick Porter, "Why America's Grand Strategy Has Not Changed." *International Security* 42, no. 4 (2018): 9–46. Notably, Legro develops a more nuanced theory of foreign policy idea change that also explains long-term strategic stability. Jeffrey W. Legro, *Rethinking the World: Great Power Strategies and International Order* (Ithaca, NY: Cornell University Press, 2005).

27. Brands, *What Good is Grand Strategy?* 3.

28. Brands, *American Grand Strategy in the Age of Trump,*16.

29. Gaddis, *On Grand Strategy,* 27.

30. Yuan-Kang Wang, *Harmony and War: Confucian Culture and Chinese Power Politics* (New York: Columbia University Press, 2010).

31. For an introduction to this topic, see Jeffrey S. Lantis, "Strategic Cultures and Security Policies in the Asia-Pacific," *Contemporary Security Policy* 35, no. 2 (2014): 166–186. For another example, see David Brewster, "Indian Strategic Thinking about Asia," *The Journal of Strategic Studies* 34, no. 6 (2011): 825–852.

32. See, respectively, Evan Braden Montgomery, "Contested Primacy in the Western Pacific: China's Rise and the Future of U.S. Power Projection," *International Security* 38 no. 4 (2014): 115–149; Samir Puri, "The Strategic Hedging of Iran, Russia, and China: Juxtaposing Participation in the Global System with Regional Revisionism," *Journal of Global Security Studies* 2, no. 4 (2017): 307–323; and Gao Cheng, "Market Expansion and

Grand Strategy of Rising Powers," *The Chinese Journal of International Politics* 4 (2011): 405–446.

33. Julian Germann, "German 'Grand Strategy' and the Rise of Neoliberalism," *International Studies Quarterly* 58, no. 4 (2014): 706–716.

34. Christopher J. Fettweis, "Free Riding or Constraint? Examining European Grand Strategy," *Comparative Strategy* 30, no. 4 (2011): 316–332.

35. Jeffrey Legro, *Rethinking the World: Great Power Strategies and International Order* (Ithaca, NY: Cornell University Press, 2005).

36. David A. Welch, *Painful Choices: A Theory of Foreign Policy Change* (Princeton, NJ: Princeton University Press, 2005).

37. Kevin Narizny, *The Political Economy of Grand Strategy* (Ithaca, NY: Cornell University Press, 2007).

38. Colin Dueck, *Reluctant Crusaders: Power, Culture and Change in American Grand Strategy* (Princeton, NJ: Princeton University Press, 2006).

39. William R. Thompson, "The 1920–1945 Shift in US Foreign Policy Orientation: Theory, Grand Strategies, and System Leaders Ascents," *Foreign Policy Analysis* 12, no. 4 (2016): 512–532.

40. Popescu, *Emergent Strategy and Grand Strategy*, 5–9.

41. Hudson, *Foreign Policy Analysis*, 37-39

42. David G. Winter, et al, "The Personalities of Bush and Gorbachev Measured at a Distance: Procedures, Portraits, and Policy," *Political Psychology* 12, no. 2 (1991): 215–245.

43. Under this rubric, regional focus might be at one of three levels: (1) regional, (2) inter-regional, or (3) global. If not a global scope, a government might concentrate most of its security and diplomatic energy in its immediate neighborhood (1 - regional) or divide that energy between its immediate neighborhood and a few, select extra regional locations (2 inter-regional). In reality, *scope* is best understood as a sliding scale; however, segmented categories help the analyst identify and articulate differences within and between cases.

44. Stephen Walt, "Trump's Sound and Fury Has Signified Nothing," *Foreign Policy*, January 30, 2018, https://foreignpolicy.com/2018/01/30/trumps-sound-and-fury-has-signified-nothing/.

45. George Bennett and Alexander L. George, *Case Studies and Theory Development in the Social Sciences* (Cambridge, MA: MIT Press, 2005), 67–72.

CHAPTER 3

THE BEST PEOPLE

CANDIDACY AND EARLY 2017

Donald Trump's personal style immediately affected perceptions of US foreign policy. Still, his underlying strategy—if he held one—remained unclear. On the campaign trail, Trump boasted about hiring "the best people" and draining the Washington swamp, choked with elites and insiders. Yet by August 2017, key members of his original national security cohort had been driven out of the administration. Over those months, two basic camps grappled to define influence over the president and, in turn, shape US grand strategy.

The next four chapters will focus primarily on a narrative case history of the Trump administration's grand strategy. Empirically, they will provide the raw material to determine whether one can observe grand strategy as a *pattern of thought and policy*, as defined by the GSA approach in Chapter 2. In turn, that material will be used to address the book's core analytical questions: what was the administration's grand strategy and how, if at all, did Trump himself shape that grand strategy? Each narrative chapter will touch on these findings and revisit the book's frameworks. The conclusion draws those insights together in more detail. This first empirical chapter traces Trump's early national security impulses and strategic positions.

Campaigning, candidate Trump honed a message for his domestic support base. The United States, he told roaring crowds, was weaker than it should be, tolerated unfair trade deals, lived with unnecessary nuclear threats, and let in too many dangerous immigrants. In fact, he wanted a "total and complete shutdown" of Muslims entering the United States until officials "can figure out what the hell is going on." The phrases "America first" and "peace through strength" emerged as possible titles for this Trump approach. Critics called it rank nationalism, harkening back to the 1930s. Such an approach, they argued, ignored many US strengths and would in fact undermine global stability.

Temperamentally and professionally a delegator, Trump relied on advisors to lend credibility and substance to his strategic positions. Men like Steve Bannon and Michael Flynn, for instance, actively supported Trump's candidacy and had been critical of Washington's foreign policy elite. Now, the new president elevated them, though he also sought out more conventional options for senior positions. He appointed Marine Corps General Jim Mattis to be Secretary of Defense and, reaching for a political neophyte, Exxon CEO Rex Tillerson to be Secretary of State. Trump's vice president Mike Pence, meanwhile, played an intermediate role, a consummate Washington insider and politician sympathetic to Trump's strategic agenda.

Trump's team stumbled through the transition. This included several major gaffes and missteps, such as directly muddling the One-China policy by granting a phone conversation with Taiwan's president. Most notably, though, Trump removed Flynn as his National Security Advisor after less than a month of service. Driven by Flynn's own misbehavior along with external and internal pressure, the move also signaled an initial tilt away from the hard-core nationalists and toward a more mainstream strategy. For instance, H. R. McMaster, Trump's replacement for National Security Advisor, enjoyed bipartisan support. Over the next year, this lean would rebalance yet again to favor Trump's nationalist impulses and preference for hardline talk. In the meantime, however, Trump and his team responded to events and pushed their agendas with a mix of conventional Republican party line policies and the new president's unconventional "America first" nationalism.

The outlines of Trump's grand strategy emerged early and clearly. Recall the basic grand strategy dimensions adopted by this book: *scope, substance,* and *assertiveness.* Campaigning and through the transition, Trump's basic priorities remained—given the man's penchant for improvisation and even self-contradiction—remarkably consistent. He was worried about US interests around the world, but he also wanted to narrow the scope of US exposure to security and, perhaps even more, trade threats. "America first" in particular would prove durable. Both the nationalists and internationalists in the administration could agree on protecting US power and even reorganizing US interstate relations around shared respect for sovereignty. In practice, this meant the administration's more mainstream Republicans set out to reassure allies that the United States would respect its agreements, but it also meant that nationalists in the administration would aggressively push confrontation with allies and adversaries alike. Actual violence, however, remained a secondary tool for the administration. Trump appeared to prefer a high level of rhetorical, political, and trade assertiveness rather than resorting to force.

Trump's personal impact on US grand strategy, however, was muted during these early months. Over the next two years, the president would slowly winnow and restock his senior team, and, in turn, the administration's overall approach to the world increasingly tracked with Donald Trump's preferences. As this chapter finds, however, the new president only achieved a middling level of consistency between his own statements and the actual policies of the US government. Stated differently, Trump's positions and those of the government were only moderately correlated. Overall, White House rhetoric changed dramatically the day Obama walked out of the building for the last time as president, but

US policy changed far more slowly, and during these early months, Trump struggled to keep some of his senior officials in step with his nationalist approach.

"EVERY DREAM YOU'VE EVER DREAMED"

Forty-one days before the 2016 election, Donald Trump stood at a podium. Thousands of Americans had flocked to his rallies for over a year. Often, they showed up in their Trump gear. Shirts, flags, and especially the signature hats. "Make America Great Again" printed on a bold red, sometimes white, baseball cap. It was an unmistakable statement but often with an unclear message. Trump rallies had become electrified events. To observers, they represented the voice of the forgotten, Americans' worst instincts, classic election barnstorming, an angry cry, or a new political movement. Accepting the GOP's nomination that July in Cleveland, Ohio, Trump staked out a singular claim. "I am your voice," he said to a crowd of delegates chanting *build the wall!* "I alone can fix it."[1]

In Florida, a major swing state, the Trump team held 30 rallies. When the campaign rolled into our town, my students seemed bemused, excited, disdainful, uncomfortable, curious. No one, it seemed, was indifferent. Everyone had an opinion, though few expressly shared their views. "You should go," a few insisted in class, "If nothing else, it'll be great entertainment value!" Later that year at another rally, in Melbourne, Florida, the candidate reminisced about his great victory over bewildered GOP primary candidates. The crowd cheered. But the work was not done. "I'll tell you," his voice echoing, "Our country is being laughed at by the world. It's being laughed at. Remember that." Like a conductor, he moved his right hand to match the speech. Steadily up and down, often with his index finger up. In Trump style, he warned, "We have 41 days," in one of the most ambitious claims in American political history, "to make possible every dream you've ever dreamed for your country."[2]

Naming the Agenda

Trump liked to claim, as he did in the Melbourne speech, that he had forged his political career in just a few months. That was wrong. In fact, his publicly stated political views stretched back to the 1980s, and he had often toyed with and twice made short runs for president.[3] During the Obama years, Trump spent a lot of time in radio and television interviews honing his message. Most notoriously, he raised questions about Barack Obama's birth certificate, a "birther" conspiracy theory holding that the forty-fourth president had not, in fact, been born in the United States.[4] More often than not, though, Trump shared skepticism about "the swamp" in Washington. Nobody, he said, seemed to be fixing or protecting American jobs and industries. Republicans had drawn the United States into disastrous wars in Iraq and Afghanistan. Liberals like Hillary Clinton were corrupt and did not seem to care about American strength. Immigration was out of control.

By the time of the Melbourne speech, Trump had landed on a relatively consistent set of foreign policy views and statements. This was not quite a grand strategy; nevertheless, these campaign positions reflected a core set of priorities and approaches. On some issues, particularly trade, Trump had held a consistent position for decades. In more recent years, Trump had also road tested positions like building a border wall and found raucous support.[5] When he announced his presidential candidacy, he notoriously declared that Mexico "is not sending their best." In fact, "They're not sending you. They're sending people who have lots of problems ... They're bringing crime. They're rapists. And some, I assume, are good people."[6] Later, in the election cycle's final stretch, Trump appointed Steve Bannon to revive a stumbling campaign.[7] Bannon had become a kind of media activist who held that "traditional" Western civilization was collapsing under liberal elites and pro-immigration "globalists."[8] Trump never fully adopted Bannon's specific theories, but their visions converged.

Whatever the theme's source, Trump himself came to call it "America first." In a remarkable—in fact, transformative—March 2016 interview, reporter David Sanger of the *New York Times* tried to characterize Trump's foreign policy. He asked if it was defined by "a mistrust of many foreigners, both our adversaries and some of our allies, a sense that they've been freeloading off of us for many years."[9] Sanger called this "America first" in apparent reference to anti-Semitic and nationalist ideas of the 1930s. Most US foreign policy experts in 2016 would have read this question as almost an insult. After all, "America first" in the lead-up to World War II was typically held by fascist sympathizers and came to be seen by the public as catastrophically wrong-headed after the Pearl Harbor attack. Trump, however, liked the phrase. "I'm not isolationist," he answered, "but I am 'America First.' So I like the expression." Later, when advisers warned him about the term's negative associations, Trump said he believed voters would only care that it invoked optimistic change.[10] He explained in the Sanger interview that the United States was "the big stupid bully and we were systematically ripped off by everybody." Trump wanted to continue friendly relations "with everybody," but in his view, governments in East Asia and the Middle East, particularly, benefitted from the United States leasing land for military bases and helping those states make money hand-over-fist. NATO and the UN also received money from Washington, yet "we're a poor nation, we're a debtor nation."

Campaigning, Trump tended to play a range of popular hits, but "America first" broke into two basic categories: trade and security. In rallies, debates, and media appearances, the candidate hammered trade. Notably, many experts agreed with Trump on the problems.[11] China, for example, had manipulated its currency value and subsidized its own industries for years in order to keep its goods relatively cheap in international markets. Global trade in general had expanded the world's overall wealth, but wages in developed countries had grown stagnant and old middle-class jobs in manufacturing seemed to be vanishing. Trump's solution, however, defied the experts. Where they might suggest carefully targeted policy changes and trade deals, Trump railed in favor of trade war and protectionism. He also promised to pull the United States out of the Trans-Pacific Partnership, a multilateral trade deal among a wide range of Pacific Rim countries. If US allies were benefitting from US bases, they should pay for the privilege, he reasoned. If China was making money off Americans, the United States should raise tariffs on Chinese goods until Beijing's leaders accepted US demands. If globalization had hurt the coal and steel industries, they should be supported. In reality, manufacturing job losses occurred as much from automation as outsourcing. Trade and security commitments were far more complex than monetary gains and losses. Nevertheless, Trump had long stated that the United States was on the wrong end of zero-sum deals, and his nationalist supporters agreed.

One domestic episode symbolized Trump's emerging strategic approach. When, shortly after the 2016 election, heating and cooling manufacturer Carrier Corp. announced that it would lay off 1400 workers in Indianapolis and move those operations to Mexico, president-elect Trump pressured the company to keep the jobs in place and receive millions of dollars in state tax breaks.[12] The proposal catered to his base and offered effective photo opportunities. Trump could exploit political leverage held by his running mate Mike Pence, who was stepping down as Indiana's governor. The move also treated international economics as a zero-sum competition: under Trump's theory, Mexico would gain at the expense of the United States. Notions of classic economic dynamics like "creative destruction," comparative advantages, or market efficiency—normally guiding lights for Republican administrations—gave way to economic nationalism. Unfortunately for Trump, it was also not a sustainable approach. Would the new president personally intervene in other such cases? How would the administration decide which industries should be "saved"? Indeed, thirteen months later, Carrier announced that it would lay off hundreds of different employees at the same location. The jobs would be moved to Mexico.

Making America First

On security, Trump and his team framed a wide range of issues and actors as threats even as Trump himself insisted that Russia could be a useful partner rather than a growing adversary. Immigration in particular propelled the campaign. Rarely had human migration risen to the level of grand strategy in US politics. Parties had grappled with the issue as a domestic concern. Now, however, Trump insisted that he would build a massive wall on the US-Mexico border and force Mexico to pay for it.[13] Overlapping Islam with international terrorism, he called for a halt, even if temporary, to all Muslim immigration. Indeed, Trump argued that all immigration policy should be overhauled in favor of strict merit rather than, for example, family connections. For Trump and many of his senior advisors, a growing foreign-born population posed a basic—perhaps even existential—threat to US wealth and power as well as its international security. Looking overseas, he insisted that he would be far tougher on the Islamic State than the Obama administration, though he offered no specific details. He had long blamed Republicans for a needless war in Iraq and was skeptical of ongoing US military support in Afghanistan. In all three cases, Trump's impulse seemed to be hit hard, if necessary, and then get back out.[14] This also seemed to match a simmering mood on both the liberal and conservative ends of the political spectrum.

Pointedly, Trump rarely spoke about American values as a strategic goal or priority. Rather, he emphasized being tough and getting a fair deal. At one point, he even suggested torturing terrorists and targeting their families. He later insisted that he would never order the military to actually take such action, but as with all Trump rhetoric, observers struggled to discern his intention from his bluster. Supporters insisted that he should be taken "seriously but not literally," but, of course, that guidance still begged the question: when *was* Trump literal? On Iran's nuclear program, he agreed with hardliners that the United States should pull out of the multilateral agreement (the Joint Comprehensive Plan of Action, JCPOA) that Obama's team had spent years negotiating. Reneging on the other agreement signatories like France, Germany, and the United

Kingdom could hurt US credibility even with its long-standing allies, but Trump considered it "the worst deal ever negotiated" and insisted that it emboldened Iran and made the world more dangerous.[15] North Korea, similarly, was a nuclear menace that should be confronted.

Meanwhile, Trump consistently suggested that there should be no reason that the United States and Russia could not be fruitful partners and coordinate on, for example, ending war in Syria.[16] It was a notable position because in rare accord, the Republican-led House of Representatives and the Democratic president had agreed over previous years that Russia should be sanctioned for certain human rights abuses and, especially, its abuse of Ukrainian sovereignty. In theory, Trump's openness to Russia reflected his preference to treat all relationships as pragmatic opportunities for making deals. In reality, many observers found his position inexplicable given his tough rhetoric even toward Mexico and Canada. Even before the election, word started to trickle out that a Russian disinformation campaign attempted to tip the election against Hillary Clinton, and that the Trump Organization had been working on a Moscow real estate deal in early 2016. Trump found himself embroiled in accusations, questions, and investigations that would stalk his presidency.

RHETORIC MEETS REALITY

Modern presidents set an aggressive agenda for their "first 100 days." The tradition—and the term—emerged with Franklin D. Roosevelt, who wanted to prepare Americans for a flood of new laws and executive actions to address the Great Depression. One hundred days is an arbitrary timeframe, but it signals urgency and focus. Later administrations have believed, and political science has confirmed, that presidents' political capital declines over time. It is harder for them to set new precedents and push ambitious agendas as their popularity declines and they make enemies. Entering office with a clear agenda and a well vetted team are seen as essential for early success. The Trump team, unfortunately for the president's agenda, stumbled through the transition, never filled dozens of high level bureaucratic appointments, and only started to gain its footing as the first 100 days waned.

On-The-Job Training

One notorious account holds that Trump himself was convinced—and was hoping—he would lose the election.[17] That he sought not political power but to gain visibility and television contracts after running for president. That he and his team, along with his tearful wife, sat stunned and confused as election night results unfolded. Even if exaggerated, there is a reason this thesis feels plausible to many observers. Trump's transition team struggled to fill positions and work up a specific policy agenda. Typically, presidential campaigns are ready to spring into action by drawing upon existing lists of names and networks. By contrast, to take one example, many staffers at the National Security Council (NSC) later recounted Trump appointees belatedly sweeping into their positions "in a blur of chaos, disregarding legality and ethics and showing a deep hostility to the career professionals."[18] Many new Trump appointees declined to read the extensive policy guides worked up by the career staff, struggled to obtain security clearances, and disregarded the NSC's traditional policy process. Trump supporters argued that the Obama NSC had grown unwieldy and produced only bland technocratic policies; however, insiders suspected that "early on under Trump, there seemed to be no meaningful organization at all."

Still, as president-elect, Trump's basic grand strategy principles remained consistent. He threatened tariffs against Mexico and China as well as "retribution" against companies, like Carrier, contemplating international operations. He also vowed to massively overhaul or, failing that, terminate even long-standing trade agreements like NAFTA.[19] To lead his White House National Trade Council, Trump announced that China hardliner Peter Navarro would be joining the administration.

During a representative news cycle just before Christmas, the president-elect broadcast a bold statement on nuclear weapons then had to circle back to address cascading questions about its meaning and seriousness. Trump tweeted that the United States "must greatly strengthen and expand its nuclear capability until such time as the world comes to its senses regarding nukes." Earlier that day, Russian president Vladimir Putin had spoken to his military about strengthening the country's nuclear missile capabilities. Observers around the world suddenly wondered if Trump was pushing a new arms race. Sean Spicer, Trump's new spokesman, tried to redirect the narrative. Trump was not exactly proclaiming a new policy or strategy. He merely wanted to communicate that "he is going to do what it takes to protect this country and if another country or countries want to threaten our safety and sovereignty."[20] Another spokesman emphasized the president-elect's desire to "improve and modernize our deterrent capability as a vital way to pursue peace through strength." Trump, however, did not want to back down. Appearing on the cable show Morning Joe, he reiterated, "Let it be an arms race. We will outmatch them at every pass and outlast them all."[21] The president-elect never quite clarified his policy intention, but the issue was soon lost amidst other headlines and developments.

Similar uncertainty and reversals persisted throughout the transition. After Election Day, governments around the world scrambled to uncover personal links to the new president. Many were not even sure how to contact officials in the transition team. They were, however, determined to get in front of the next US president as soon as possible. Trump, accustomed to freewheeling communications and interpersonal relations, was happy to take congratulatory calls and hand out compliments. When he called the Pakistani Prime Minister Nawaz Sharif, he alienated Indian politicians by calling their archrival a "terrific guy."[22] When Trump accepted a call from Taiwan's President Tsai Ing-wen, he set off a firestorm of criticism. No US president had spoken directly with a Taiwanese leader since 1979. Generations of American administrations had carefully walked a fine line between supporting Taiwan as a partner and allowing Beijing to maintain its formal claims to sovereignty over the island. Prior administrations-elect had also carefully vetted contacts with foreign governments. Now, China issued an outraged denunciation of the call. Foreign policy experts were baffled. The national media was in an uproar. Congressional Republicans praised the president's boldness. Trump officials claimed that they had planned the call for months, had already spoken formally with Chinese President Xi Jinping, and wanted to send a signal of strength. No one, it seemed, even mentioned the Trump Organization's recent interest in Taiwanese real estate development.[23] In another pair of calls, eight days after the inauguration, Trump shared, by all accounts, a pleasant phone conversation with Russian president Vladimir Putin. Hours later, Trump bereted Australia's prime minister, Malcolm Turnbull, about an immigration policy and abruptly ended the call.[24] He attempted to mend relations with Turnbull in February, but the president-elect's early strategic approach, motivations, and agenda remained difficult to read.

These imbroglios faded from the public eye as Trump assumed the presidency, but they were not forgotten. Administration efforts to redirect grand strategy now faced preexisting skepticism and uncertainty. They also presaged Trump's bombastic approach to North Korea through 2017, and they underscored Trump's tendency to blur impulse and strategy. In analytical terms, Trump and his team had set clear expectations that their grand strategy approach would be global in scope. Substantively, it would emphasize zero-sum competition and transactionalism, and it would be skeptical of long-standing alliances. Whether it would be highly assertive was not well established. Critics feared that the new president would be a war monger, but Trump and his core advisers actually disdained the so-called neoconservatives of the G.W. Bush administration. Would Trump himself fundamentally alter US grand strategy? He certainly promised radical change, but in style and substance, his inconsistency and low level of knowledge about specific policies and relationships often undercut his dramatic pronouncements. As one of my graduate assistants observed, "There tends to be a discrepancy between what he tweets, what he says, and what he does." It was, she concluded, "difficult to discern if his Tweets should be considered his actual foreign policy goals."[25]

Help Wanted

Trump's personnel appointments added to this uncertainty. The transition team started with a personnel deficit. Dozens of experienced Republican foreign policy professionals had refused to endorse his candidacy and effectively refused to serve his administration. The feeling was mutual. Trump—along with many frustrated nationalists and libertarians—had long shared scorn for the overcommitments of the G.W. Bush years, whose officials had "very little to brag about except responsibility for a long history of failed policies and continued losses at war."[26] Trump was looking for "new people."

Conventional Choices

Still, his appointees tended to fall between two strategic poles: conventional Republicans and disruptive nationalists. At a victory rally in Cincinnati, for instance, Trump wound up the crowd for a big announcement. "Don't let it outside this room," he confided to cheers, "We are going to appoint 'Mad Dog' Mattis as our Secretary of Defense!"[27] James Mattis had risen through a career as a Marine officer to command the United States Joint Forces Command, NATO Allied Command Transformation, and United States Central Command. Along the way, he had developed a reputation for thoughtful analysis and tough but effective leadership. (He also, by most accounts, hated the nickname "Mad Dog.") Whether Trump realized it or not, Mattis also stood for continued and careful global leadership. A few months into his tenure, for instance, the former general praised initiatives like the Marshall Plan and arrangements like NATO that emphasized US power and leadership along with partnership and burden sharing.[28] Mattis was more than willing to use overwhelming force against adversaries, but he also displayed high regard for the type of committed international leadership that had been common among both Republican and Democratic foreign policy elites for decades.

Rex Tillerson, Trump's appointment for Secretary of State, ultimately appeared to support these basic priorities. Tillerson, however, arrived with no government service. He spent his career in the oil industry and had risen to become CEO of ExxonMobil, one of the largest corporations on Earth. Tillerson was an insider who had worked deals around the world. As a political actor, however, his views remained uncertain. He later intimated that he accepted the position out of a sense of duty. Critics charged that he symbolized the worst instincts of corporate influence in US strategy. Whatever his motivation, Tillerson shared Mattis' preference for a stable foreign policy and for protecting long-standing strategic priorities.

Other, more conventional appointments included Dan Coats, formerly a moderate US Senator from Indiana, as Director of National Intelligence and Nikki Haley, formerly a conservative but pragmatic governor of South Carolina, as US Ambassador to the United Nations. Vice President Mike Pence, Indiana's outgoing governor, carried, as Trump once commented in the Oval Office, a "central casting" demeanor for a politician: serious, but not menacing; white-haired but not elderly; grave but approachable. As Trump's man but also a dyed-in-the wool Republican, many wondered if he could span the Trump-GOP divide, or if he would be forced to fall into either fully supporting or leading opposition to Trump's nationalist instincts. In the White House, Reince Priebus, also a consummate party man and formerly chairman of the Republican National Committee, would become Chief of Staff.

Outside the White House, Trump appointed conservatives sympathetic to his hardline positions. Not quite fully "America first," their strategic agendas dovetailed with the president's. Perhaps most prominent proved to be Mike Pompeo. Initially Trump's CIA director, Pompeo would be elevated to Secretary of State in 2018. A West Point graduate, Pompeo left the Army after five years, obtained a Harvard law degree, and acquired a manufacturing business in Kansas. He later won a seat in the US House of Representatives, where he served on a number of prominent committees, including the CIA subcommittee and the House Select Committee on Benghazi, a years-long investigation into a deadly US consulate attack. The probe conveniently allowed Republicans also to scrutinize then

Secretary of State Hillary Clinton. In the House, Pompeo remained one among many nationally visible Republicans; however, his Benghazi work along with his hardline views on Russia, North Korea, and Iran, as well as his prominent support for Israel, lent him credibility to a new administration looking for "establishment" figures who would also follow Trump's lead. With these appointments, Trump may have been seeking to build bridges with elites in his party, or he was simply limited in his options. Either way, Trump's early foreign policy would be defined by tension among his principals and advisors. They largely agreed on the scope of US grand strategy. They would soon tussle, however, over the appropriate level of US assertiveness and, in particular, the nationalist substance that Trump and some of his favored appointees wanted to inject into US grand strategy.

Personal Preference

At the nationalist end of the spectrum, Trump's appointees received lower-profile appointments. Still, they remained influential with the president. Steve Bannon maintained his access and became a White House fixture. Trump appointed him to be Chief Strategist and even allotted him a seat with the regular principals in National Security Council meetings. The move immediately outraged traditionalists and critics, who believed Bannon landed a major position of influence without facing a Congressional hearing to vet his views. Bannon did little to help his standing among possible allies by constantly talking with the press and battling other Trump loyalists. Stephen Miller emerged as one of these core loyalists. Miller, still in his early 30's, was building a career as a conservative activist, with a particularly hard line on immigration. After working as a press official for members of Congress, he became a Trump speech writer, even helping pen Trump's inaugural address. Miller emerged as a senior advisor (and likely helped to oust Bannon later that year).

The president's son-in-law, Jared Kushner, also transitioned to an influential, semi-formal role. Married to Trump's daughter Ivanka,

Kushner himself was member of a wealthy New York real estate family. In reality, Jared and Ivanka held the relatively moderate political views shared by many of their urbane peers; however, the new president seemed to trust them implicitly and handed Kushner—despite lacking any government or national security background—a large foreign policy portfolio, including somehow achieving peace in the Middle East. In turn, during these early months, Jared and Ivanka would occasionally try to temper the new president's more excessive impulses even as they largely represented his agenda to the world.

By contrast, former Army general Michael Flynn arrived with extensive experience, was named Trump's National Security Advisor, but flamed out within weeks. During the US wars in Iraq and Afghanistan, Flynn proved adept at improving counterterror and insurgent strategy, and after retiring, he built a private intelligence company. Though a registered Democrat, he advised several Republican campaigns before lending his voice to the Trump team. When dozens of other national security professionals rejected candidate Trump, Flynn's prominence grew. He even started adopting more Trumpian rhetoric, famously calling for Hillary Clinton to be "locked up," admitting he was "reluctant to take options off the table" regarding torture, and roundly criticizing the Obama administration's extensive reliance on lethal drones. He also quietly maintained ties with the Turkish and Russian governments, connections that would collapse his appointment and end in a criminal conviction, one of a growing number of indictments associated with the Trump campaign.

On economic affairs, Trump also reached for sympathetic figures. For US Trade Representative (USTR), Trump called on Robert Lighthizer, a long time Washington lawyer and a Deputy USTR during the Reagan administration. Crucially, Lighthizer had previously defended the "venerable history of protectionism" and had long argued that the United States should more aggressively combat what he considered to be China's unfair trading practices.[29] Alongside Lighthizer, Trump appointed two investors individually worth hundreds of millions of dollars. Steven Mnuchin, appointed Secretary of the Treasury, emphasized domestic tax reform (namely, tax cuts and deregulation) and a strategy that switched the United States from multilateral trade deals to bilateral arrangements. Wilbur Ross, appointed Secretary of Commerce, was also pro-trade but skeptical about the ambitious, complex trade deals that the United States started signing in the 1990s.[30]

These high-level appointments masked a debilitating bureaucratic challenge: over the time covered by this book, the administration failed to fill dozens of lower level offices. Major partners like South Korea lacked permanent ambassadors for months and significant agencies like the State Department and National Security Council operated without the assistant secretaries and other administrators who typically head up regional or issue areas, interface with their counterparts around the world, and pass along strategy and policy analysis.

STARTS AND FALSE STARTS

Fulfilling Promises

Donald Trump and his White House team devoted their first weeks to undoing President Obama's agenda, talking with select world leaders, and rolling out signature campaign promises. Though rough, the outlines of candidate Trump's grand strategic scope, substance, assertiveness carried forward into President Trump's Oval Office. Trump's personal imprint on the tenor of US foreign policy also began to shape US foreign relations, but he and his team—like a cyclist suddenly mounting a hill—struggled to carry their momentum forward into profound strategic change. One of the most dramatic steps occurred when the new president signed a memorandum directing the US Trade Representative to withdraw the United States as a signatory to the Trans-Pacific Partnership (TPP).[31] It was both a symbolic and a strategic statement. Nine years earlier, the George W. Bush administration had initiated talks with a group of Pacific Rim governments who had formed a trade deal. After taking office, Obama green-lighted his Secretary of State, Hillary Clinton, to continue the talks.[32] When the United States signed the deal in 2016, it also included the Canada, Mexico, Peru, Chile, New Zealand, Australia, Singapore, Malaysia, Brunei, Vietnam, and Japan, or about 40 percent of world GDP. Its goals were manifold but simple. Under conventional economic theory, both wealthy and developing states hoped to see expanded markets for their goods and, in turn, economic and job growth. That in itself is a familiar strategic goal, but geopolitically, the TPP also put China in a bind. Officially, the deal was open to China and other governments willing to negotiate access. In practice, they faced economic and geostrategic marginalization in the region, but they would have to address the deal's standards on transparency, market access, intellectual property protection and so forth. For a single party state jealous of its power, those demands were a serious challenge. Indeed, TPP supporters argued that the deal cleverly knit together powerful and weak states in a coalition that would exert positive pressure on a rising China.

American voters, however, appeared to have soured on economic globalization. After the Great Recession of 2008-09, manufacturing outsourcing, suspicions about elites secretly negotiating away US sovereignty, and years of stagnant middle-class wages, the major presidential candidates—even Hillary Clinton—vowed to end or massively revise the deal. In its memo cutting ties with the TPP, the administration asserted that trade was of "paramount importance" but that the Trump team would "deal directly with individual countries on a one-on-one (or bilateral) basis in negotiating future trade deals." For Trump, China posed an ongoing economic threat. As such, it should be directly confronted rather than enmeshed in a complex web of strategic maneuvers. Alongside this move, Trump promised to renegotiate NAFTA, the North American Free Trade Agreement. Later, in March, the Trump team compelled the other ministers at the G20 (a semi-formal meeting of leaders from the world's largest economies) to drop a commitment to "resist all forms of protectionism."[33] This signaled a major shift for the United States, whose administrations since World War II had taken clearly pro-trade stances.

As *Washington Post* reporter Damian Paletta summarized, "The White House sent a clear signal that it would not accept existing trade norms and could pursue a more antagonistic approach with trading partners around the world."[34] In all these cases, Trump was carrying forward his promise to reorient not the importance of trade and international commerce, exactly, but the way that it was pursued. He was changing some aspects of the *substance* and *assertiveness* of trade strategy without redefining the basic US interest in global commerce and its global *scope*.

The administration's first major policy crisis also flowed from the president's desk. On January 27, Trump signed the executive order "Protecting the Nation From Foreign Terrorist Entry Into the United States."[35] This was the so-called "Muslim travel ban." By most accounts, it was largely pushed by Bannon and authored by Miller. It called for an overhaul of US immigration and visas, but in effect, it immediately halted anyone from a set of Muslim-majority countries from entering the United States.[36] The move sparked domestic protests as well as consternation and confusion in many foreign capitals. It appeared to confirm skeptics' greatest fears that the administration would dive toward ethnic nationalism as a policy and strategy direction. Trump officials—particularly those with nationalist outlooks—defended it as meeting a campaign promise and a necessary move to more effectively monitor or constrict travel from terrorist hotbeds. It also staked out one of the nationalists' strategic goals: reasserting cultural and practical sovereignty on American terms. The order was stayed by a judge and then collapsed under legal pressure, but it was later heavily revised. That later version was ruled constitutional by the Supreme Court. Strategically, the move seemed to send a message, but which message was unclear. Trump officials believed it broadcast strength after years of what they considered Obama's weakness. Indeed, a month later, they announced plans to create over 15,000 jobs to support immigration enforcement.[37] Critics believed that, instead, it broadcast incompetence as well as a general withdrawal from the United States' long-standing positions on global leadership and human rights.

National Security Counseling

In the National Security Council, Trump's early appointments proved calamitous. Rather than pushing out a clear strategic agenda, they refocused national and international attention on internal scandals. As early as January 26, acting Attorney General Sally Yates had warned White House personnel that Michael Flynn had been lying about his international contacts and they faced "a situation where the national security adviser essentially could be blackmailed by the Russians."[38] At one point, Vice President-elect Pence appeared on national television and repeated Flynn's assurances that he held no compromising ties. Meanwhile, permanent staffers later complained of an aggressive, unprofessional atmosphere created by Flynn and other Trump appointees. For instance, a proposal to support a longtime partner in the war against ISIS, the Kurdish fighters of Iraq, languished without action until May. Trump appointees countered that the career folks simply felt uncomfortable with a new administration challenging them to come up with less staid policy options.[39] Whatever his policy vision, Flynn was forced to resign on February 14.[40] He later pleaded guilty of lying to the FBI.

As this personnel drama played out, Steve Bannon attempted to imprint his vision on US national security strategy. The Trump administration had revised the NSC structure. It downgraded the Joint Chiefs of Staff chairman and the Director of National Intelligence and handed Bannon a permanent seat. This was a highly unusual move. Designed to offer the president candid and informed foreign policy advice, the NSC principals include some of the government's highest ranking officials. Elevating Bannon, a campaign advisor with little national security experience, no Congressional approval, and highly controversial views, set off alarm bells in the media and among former national security officials. Bannon supporters in the White House later claimed that Trump assigned him the position to monitor and channel Flynn.[41] Bannon himself stated, without clarification, that he was placed on the NSC to "de-operationalize" it after the Obama years. Trump's initial personnel arrangement seemed to favor nationalist prerogatives, yet by May, Bannon would also be removed from the NSC.

Still, Steve Bannon's nationalist theories seemed to lend shape to Trump's impulses. His theory of the world tended to exert a gravitational pull on Trump and some of his close advisers because he exuded a consistent agenda, had seemed to help turn the campaign toward victory, and actually did hold a unified theory of the world. At the height of his perceived influence, some of the media characterized him a "shadow president."[42] Indeed, Bannon heavily shaped the new president's inaugural address. It portrayed an unusually grim world of "American carnage."[43] By now, the themes were familiar: over recent decades, American prosperity had been siphoned out of the country. "Total allegiance" and "loyalty" would be crucial to revitalization. For grand strategy, the administration would respect other governments that "put their own interests first," and the United States would serve as an example rather than "impose our way of life on anyone." Bannon appears to have drawn his intellectual framework from an obscure account of American history that predicted a period of crisis in the early twenty-first century.[44] Western society would be in peril, a more traditional order would emerge, and old systems, like the "administrative state," should be torn down and renewed. Inside the White House, Bannon often dismissed Republicans, and even Jared Kushner, who held standard or pragmatic internationalist views on trade and security as "globalists" and "cucks." Tensions between the Kushner and Bannon camps grew. By April—perhaps in part *because* Bannon received such attention, including a cover on *Time* magazine—Trump had removed Bannon from the National Security Council and characterized him as simply "a guy who works for me." On key issues like China trade, Trump started siding against Bannon's policy preferences. Bannon's White House nemeses portrayed his aggressive version of nationalism as a public relations liability.[45]

SHIFTING GEARS

Bannon would occupy his perch in the White House through the summer, but he found himself increasingly marginalized when H.R. McMaster arrived on 20 February to assume the National Security Advisor position. Rising to Lieutenant General in the Army, McMaster brought a reputation as a serious thinker and theater commander. In many ways, he was an anti-Bannon: also tireless and ambitious but within existing strategic and professional frameworks. Where Bannon was an intellectual bomb thrower and entrepreneur, McMaster was studied and pragmatic. Along with advancing through a military career that included commands in the Iraq war as well as serving in the command for the International Security Assistance Force (ISAF) in Afghanistan, McMaster had earned an American history Ph.D. He was a member of the Council of Foreign Relations as well as a Consulting Senior Fellow at the International Institute for Strategic Studies (IISS). In Bannon's parlance, McMaster arrived as a globalist and a member of the administrative state. McMaster himself had published *Dereliction of Duty*, which critiques senior military officers during the Vietnam War who, he argued, failed to challenge the civilian leadership's failing strategies.[46] Observers now wondered whether McMaster would work within Trump's vision or build a creative tension with the president. Either way, Trump skeptics expressed relief that Trump had reached for an establishment figure—albeit another general—and that the nationalists seemed to have lost a key position of influence over US grand strategy.

IN SUM

When candidate Trump promised "every dream you've ever dreamed for your country," he seemed to mean something specific. It was a nationalist promise, an "America first" promise. The Republican nominee saw the world in transactional terms. The United States was losing while others were winning. Trump would get tough and bring Washington back to winning. Rather than convoluted trade deals and security agreements, this would mean trade wars and limited but serious violence. Rather than welcoming alliances and immigrants, the United States would build walls and demand compliance. Some of Trump's advisors and supporters may have worked to fashion Trump's positions into a coherent strategy; however, Trump himself emphasized a set of impulses, priorities, and practices, most of which fit broadly into either trade or security concerns. This was also not quite a commitment to all Americans. It was a set of campaign promises to his base. Research suggests that despite conventional wisdom, Trump voters' overarching concerns were not actually about economics and security but about partisanship and status anxiety.[47] If true, Trump's promises and nationalism proved to be politically potent as vague but bold campaign rhetoric. Whether they would transition into an effective grand strategy would unfold over the coming months.

The administration's transitionary grand strategy seemed clearly to fit a nationalist framework. Trump himself impacted the tenor but not always the content of US grand strategy. Like prior administrations, Trump and his team considered the *scope* of US grand strategy to be global; however, they made less effort to distinguish traditional allies from adversaries. Rather, Trump particularly emphasized that he was more concerned about transactional benefits than the value of long-standing partnerships. On *substance*, the new administration may have parted most dramatically from its predecessors. "America first" appeared to represent a real effort to reorient US priorities away from internationalism and toward a nationalist emphasis on sovereignty, bilateral relations, cultural protection, and self-reliance. On *assertiveness*, however, the administration's approach remained uncertain. Trump naturally used tough talk, and all sides of his administration agreed on building American power and directly challenging, for example, threats like ISIS and North Korea's nuclear program. Aggressive military force, however, was not an active option, and Trump himself campaigned on rolling back the perceived over-commitments of both Democratic and Republican administrations. Still, despite Trump roiling American politics, his team struggled to implement profound policy change. As a manager and public figure, the new president spun off a wide array of statements and commitments. His administration was understaffed and divided between change agents and party loyalists. For all these reasons, early efforts to shift US grand strategy were mostly abortive. Donald Trump surprised the world by carrying the 2016 presidential election, and that win immediately affected the tone of US grand strategy. Trump as a figure, however, had yet to fundamentally redirect America's ship of state.

Notes

1. Yoni Applebaum, "'I Alone Can Fix It,'" *The Atlantic,* July 21, 2016, https://www.theatlantic.com/politics/archive/2016/07/trump-rnc-speech-alone-fix-it/492557/.
2. Philip Bump, "Donald Trump pledges to make every dream possible, which seems ambitious," *The Washington Post,* September 28, 2016, https://www.washingtonpost.com/news/the-fix/wp/2016/09/28/donald-trump-pledges-to-make-every-dream-possible-which-seems-ambitious/?utm_term=.74b365737359.
3. Michael Kruse, "The True Story of Donald Trump's First Campaign Speech—in 1987," *Politico Magazine,* February 2016, https://www.politico.com/magazine/story/2016/02/donald-trump-first-campaign-speech-new-hampshire-1987-213595?o=1. Don Gonyea and Domenico Montanaro, "Donald Trump's Been Saying the Same Thing for 30 Years," National Public Radio, *Morning Edition,* January 20, 2017, https://www.npr.org/2017/01/20/510680463/donald-trumps-been-saying-the-same-thing-for-30-years.
4. Ryan Struyk, "67 Times Donald Trump Tweeted About the 'Birther' Movement" ABC News, September 16, 2016, https://abcnews.go.com/Politics/67-times-donald-trump-tweeted-birther-movement/story?id=42145590. Trump also carried extensive personal baggage, ranging from questionable business dealings to accusations of sexual harassment. On Trump's business career, see David Cay Johnston *The Making of Donald Trump* (Brooklyn, NY: Melville House, 2016). See also David Barstow, Susanne Craig, and Russ Buettner, "Trump Engaged in Suspect Tax Schemes as He Reaped Riches From His Father," *The New York Times,* October 2, 2018, https://www.nytimes.com/interactive/2018/10/02/us/politics/donald-trump-tax-schemes-fred-trump.html?action=click&module=Top%20Stories&pgtype=Homepage.
5. Joshua Green, *Devil's Bargain: Steve Bannon, Donald Trump, and the Storming of the Presidency* (New York: Penguin Press, 2017), 93–117.
6. Staff, "Here's Trump's Presidential Announcement Speech," *Time,* June 16, 2015, http://time.com/3923128/donald-trump-announcement-speech/.
7. Bannon ran Breitbart News, a provocative far right news and commentary website. He had long considered Trump a useful figure to advance his agenda.

8. Green, *Devil's Bargain*, 204–208.
9. Maggie Haberman and David Sanger, "Transcript: Donald Trump Expounds on His Foreign Policy Views." *The New York Times*, March 26, 2016, https://www.nytimes.com/2016/03/27/us/politics/donald-trump-transcript.html?_r=0.
10. Green, *Devil's Bargain*, 190–191.
11. Ben Casselman, et al, "The Consequences: How Trade Became a Major Issue in 2016," *FiveThirtyEight*, June 13, 2016, https://fivethirtyeight.com/features/the-consequences-how-trade-became-a-major-issue-in-2016/. See also Nick Corasaniti, Alexander Burns, and Binyamin Appelbaum, "Donald Trump Vows to Rip up Trade Deals and Confront China," *The New York Times*, June 28, 2016, https://www.nytimes.com/2016/06/29/us/politics/donald-trump-trade-speech.html.
12. Amanda Becker, "More layoffs at Indiana factory Trump made deal to keep open," *Reuters*, January 11, 2018, https://www.reuters.com/article/us-usa-trump-carrier/more-layoffs-at-indiana-factory-trump-made-deal-to-keep-open-idUSKBN1F02TL. Carrier did little to help public perceptions when the manager announcing the move assured employees that cutting their jobs was "the best way to stay competitive and protect the business for the long term." Cory Doctorow, "Watch: tone-deaf manager announces layoffs to 1400 Carrier Air Conditioner workers whose jobs are moving to Mexico," *BoingBoing*, February 12, 2016, https://boingboing.net/2016/02/12/watch-tone-deaf-manager-annou.html.
13. Donald Trump, "Full Text: Donald Trump immigration speech in Arizona," *Politico*, August 31, 2016, https://www.politico.com/story/2016/08/donald-trump-immigration-address-transcript-227614.
14. James Woolley, "The Foreign Policy Views of Donald Trump," Foreign Policy Research Institute, November 7, 2016, https://www.fpri.org/article/2016/11/foreign-policy-views-donald-trump/.
15. Yeganeh Tobari, "Trump election puts Iran nuclear deal on shaky ground," Reuters, November 9, 2016, https://www.reuters.com/article/us-usa-election-trump-iran/trump-election-puts-iran-nuclear-deal-on-shaky-ground-idUSKBN13427E.
16. Jeffrey Stacey, "The Trump Doctrine: The View From Russia an Syria," *Foreign Affairs*, November14, 2016, https://www.foreignaffairs.com/articles/middle-east/2016-11-14/trump-doctrine.
17. Wolff, *Fire and Fury: Inside the Trump White House*,18. In a testimony before the House Oversight Committee, Trump's former "fixer" Michael Cohen also stated that Trump did not believe he would win and was

hoping to use the campaign to gain greater notoriety as well as leverage for a Russian real estate deal. Trump, he said, called the campaign "the greatest infomercial in history." United States Cong. House. Committee on Oversight. Michael Cohen Testimony. Hearings, February 27, 2019, 115th Cong. 1st sess.

18. Nahal Toosi, "Inside the Chaotic Early Days of Trump's Foreign Policy." *Politico*, March 1, 2019, https://www.politico.com/magazine/story/2019 /03/01/trump-national-security-council-225442.

19. Ylan Q. Mui, "Trump warns of 'retribution' for companies that offshore jobs, threatening 35 percent tariff," *The Washington Post*, December 4, 2016, https://www.washingtonpost.com/news/wonk/wp/2016/12/04/trump-warns-of-retribution-for-companies-that-offshore-jobs-threatening-3 5-percent-tariff/?utm_term=.630f15dd918c. Staff, Reuters, "Trump's NAFTA revamp would require concessions, may borrow from TPP," CNBC, November 22, 2016, https://www.cnbc.com/2016/11/22/trumps-nafta-revamp-would-require-concessions-may-borrow-from-tpp.html.

20. Melissa Fares, "Trump 'arms race' comment sows more doubt on nuclear policy," Reuters, December 22, 2016, https://www.reuters.com/article/ us-usa-trump-nuclear-idUSKBN14B1ZZ.

21. Ed Pilkington and Martin Pengelly, "'Let it be an arms race': Donald Trump appears to double down on nuclear expansion," *The Guardian*, December 24, 2016, https://www.theguardian.com/us-news/2016/dec/2 3/donald-trump-nuclear-weapons-arms-race.

22. Charlie Campbell, "Donald Trump Angers China With Historic Phone Call to Taiwan's President." *Time*, December 5, 2016, http://time.com/4 589641/donald-trump-china-taiwan-call/.

23. Anne Gearan, Philip Rucker, and Simon Denyer, "Trump's Taiwan phone call was long planned, say people who were involved," *The Washington Post*, December 4, 2016, https://www.washingtonpost. com/politics/trumps-taiwan-phone-call-was-weeks-in-the-planning-say-people-who-were-involved/2016/12/04/f8be4b0c-ba4e-11e6-94ac-3d324 840106c_story.html?utm_term=.3d0cfbae8d09. Staff, "Trump wants to expand business empire to Taiwan, creating another potential conflict of interest," *Shanghaiist*, November 11, 2016, http://shanghaiist.com/20 16/11/18/trump_taiwan_expand/#disqus_thread.

24. Philip Rucker and Ashley Parker, "How Trump made up with Australia's prime minister after a 'most unpleasant call,'" *The Washington Post*, February 22, 2018, https://www.washingtonpost.com/ politics/how-trump-made-up-with-australias-prime-minister-after-a-

most-unpleasant-call/2018/02/22/e1c4a4c2-1737-11e8-b681-2d4d462a19
21_story.html?utm_term=.5306384925fb.

25. Kelly Dutton, "Trump and Nuclear Weapons," Background notes developed for the author, December 2017.

26. Doug Bandow, "Donald Trump Dismisses U.S. Foreign Policy Elite: Would He Save Americans From Unnecessary War?" *Forbes*, May 16, 2019, https://www.forbes.com/sites/dougbandow/2016/05/16/donald-trump-dismisses-u-s-foreign-policy-elite-would-he-save-americans-from-unnecessary-war/#15a13df14b80.

27. Donald Trump, "Trump announces he will appoint Gen. James Mattis to secretary of defense." Video Recording, CBS News, December 1, 2016, https://www.youtube.com/watch?v=xoTIJrkeKb8.

28. Teddy Fischer, "Full Transcript: Defense Secretary James Mattis' Interview with The Islander," *The Islander* (Mercer Island High School, WA), June 20, 2017, http://mihsislander.org/2017/06/full-transcript-james-mattis-interview/.

29. Robert E. Lighthizer, "The venerable history of protectionism." *The New York Times*, March 6, 2008, https://www.nytimes.com/2008/03/06/opinion/06iht-edlighthizer.1.10774536.html. Jennifer Jacobs, "Trump Taps China Critic Lighthizer for U.S. Trade Representative," *Bloomberg*, January 2, 2017.

30. Andrew Restuccia and Doug Palmer, "Billionaire investor Ross said to be Commerce pick," *Politico*, November 15, 2016, https://www.politico.com/story/2016/11/wilbur-ross-commerce-secretary-trump-231421.

31. The White House, *Presidential Memorandum Regarding Withdrawal of the United States from the Trans-Pacific Partnership Negotiations and Agreement: Memorandum for the United States Trade Representative, Donald Trump.* Washington, DC, January 23, 2017. See also Eric Braner, "Trump's TPP withdrawal: 5 things to know." CNN, January 23, 2017, https://www.cnn.com/2017/01/23/politics/trump-tpp-things-to-know/index.html.

32. James McBride and Andrew Chatzky, "What Is the Trans-Pacific Partnership (TPP)?" Backgrounder, Council on Foreign Relations, January 4, 2019, https://www.cfr.org/backgrounder/what-trans-pacific-partnership-tpp.

33. "G20 finance ministers drop anti-protectionist pledge." BBC News, March 18, 2017, https://www.bbc.com/news/business-39315098.

34. Damian Paletta, "New rifts emerge as Trump administration rejects free trade statement at G-20 meeting," *The Washington Post*, March 18, 2017, https://www.washingtonpost.com/business/economy/new-rifts-emerge-

as-trump-rejects-free-trade-statement-at-g20-meeting/2017/03/18/aa69
b1a2-0bf3-11e7-a15f-a58d4a988474_story.html?utm_term=.022adcb369
dd&wpisrc=al_alert-COMBO-world%252Bnation&wpmk=1.

35. The White House. *Protecting the Nation From Foreign Terrorist Entry Into
    the United States.* Executive Order 13769, FR Doc. 2017-02281, United
    States Federal Register. pp. 8997-8982. Washington, DC, January 27,
    2017, https://www.federalregister.gov/documents/2017/02/01/2017-022
    81/protecting-the-nation-from-foreign-terrorist-entry-into-the-united-
    states.

36. Opponents raised a massive outcry and thousands protested at
    international airports where some individuals would arrive having
    lost their ability to enter the United States. The executive order was
    overturned in the courts for religious discrimination. Administration
    officials later implemented a revised version that the Supreme Court, in
    summer 2018, accepted. Hilary Hurd and Yishai Schwartz, "The Supreme
    Court Travel Ban Ruling: A Summary," *Lawfare*, June 26, 2018, https://
    www.lawfareblog.com/supreme-court-travel-ban-ruling-summary.

37. Paul McGeough, "Donald Trump to form new deportation army but
    claims there will be no mass round-ups," *The Sydney Morning Herald*,
    February 23, 2017, https://www.smh.com.au/world/donald-trump-has-
    a-new-deportation-army-but-claims-there-will-be-no-mass-roundups-
    20170222-guib7g.html.

38. Riley Beggin and Veronica Stracqualursi, "A timeline of Sally Yates'
    warnings to the White House about Mike Flynn," ABC News, May
    8, 2017, http://abcnews.go.com/Politics/timeline-sally-yates-warnings-
    white-house-mike-flynn/story?id=47272979.

39. Toosi, "Inside the Chaotic Early Days of Trump's Foreign Policy."

40. Julian Borger, "Trump security adviser Flynn resigns after leaks
    suggest he tried to cover up Russia talks," *The Guardian*, February
    14, 2017, https://www.theguardian.com/us-news/2017/feb/13/michael-
    flynn-resigns-quits-trump-national-security-adviser-russia.

41. Peter Baker, Maggie Haberman, and Glenn Thrush, "Trump Removes
    Stephen Bannon From National Security Council Post," *The New York
    Times*, April 5, 2017, https://www.nytimes.com/2017/04/05/us/politics/
    national-security-council-stephen-bannon.html.

42. Philip Rucker, Ashley Parker, and Rober Costa, "Inside Bannon's struggle:
    From 'shadow president' to Trump's marked man," *The Washington
    Post*, April 12, 2017, https://www.washingtonpost.com/politics/inside-
    bannons-struggle-from-shadow-president-to-trumps-marked-man/201

7/04/12/1f5aabc0-1f99-11e7-ad74-3a742a6e93a7_story.html?utm_term=
.69cf8da90e38.

43. Donald Trump, "The Inaugural Address," The Capitol, Washington DC,
January 20, 2019, https://www.whitehouse.gov/briefings-statements/
the-inaugural-address/. Days later, several attendees recounted former
President George W. Bush's judgement of the speech: "That was some
weird shit." Ali, Yashar, "What George W. Bush Really Thought of Donald
Trump's Inauguration," *New York Magazine*, March 29, 2019, http://
nymag.com/intelligencer/2017/03/what-george-w-bush-really-thought-
of-trumps-inauguration.html.

44. Jeremy W. Peters, "Bannon's Worldview: Dissecting the Message of
'The Fourth Turning,'" *The New York Times*, April 8, 2017, https://www.
nytimes.com/2017/04/08/us/politics/bannon-fourth-turning.html?ref=
politics&_r=1.

45. Rosie Gray, "Kushner and Bannon Battle for the Soul of the Trump White
House," *The Atlantic*, April 6, 2017, https://www.theatlantic.com/politics/
archive/2017/04/kushner-and-bannon-battle-for-the-soul-of-the-trump-
white-house/522213/.

46. H. R. McMaster, *Dereliction of Duty: Lyndon Johnson, Robert McNamara,
The Joint Chiefs of Staff, and the Lies that Led to Vietnam* (New York:
Harper Perennial, 1997).

47. Diana C. Mutz, "Status threat, not economic hardship, explains the 2016
presidential vote," *Proceedings of the National Academy of Sciences of the
United States of America* 115, no. 19 (2018). Mark Setzler and Alixanra B.
Yanus, "Why Did Women Vote for Donald Trump?" *PS: Political Science
and Politics* 51, no. 3 (2018). See also John Sides, Michael Tesler, and Lynn
Vavrek, *Identity Crisis: The 2016 Presidential Campaign and the Battle for
Meaning of America* (Princeton, NJ: Princeton University Press, 2018).

CHAPTER 4

AMERICAN POWER 101

SPRING AND SUMMER 2017

Through the middle of 2017, Donald Trump's mark on US grand strategy slowly settled into a few unstable but recognizable patterns. According to the GSA approach, observing individuals, particularly the president and other leaders, is an effective way to evaluate grand strategy. Observers can evaluate the gaps and inconsistencies between individual statements and policies. As decision agents, leaders often reflect a state's strategic constraints and patterns. In this period, late spring and into summer, supporters insisted that Trump had become a "normal president," that he displayed "deeply familiar" and "prosaic" approaches to the Middle East, and that he "has hewed preternaturally closely to the policies of his Democratic predecessor and the Republican establishment."[1] Yet basic questions remained. The exact nature and trajectory of US grand strategy proved a pernicious problem. Assessing its relative success proved elusive. And the president himself left observers wondering about the degree to which calculation and intention versus images and impulses drove the US agenda. In an unusual intervention that summer, national security officials from across the administration set aside personal and policy differences to brief the president on the realities and benefits of the country's global commitments. One observer called it "American Power 101."

Events had been building to that moment for months. Almost immediately upon taking office, the new president had announced that he would withdraw the United States from the Trans-Pacific Partnership (TPP), a massive trade deal. Yet he and his senior officials conducted many meetings with Asian partners over the spring and summer to assure stability and determine new directions. The White House's budget plan, notably, proposed significant cuts to US diplomacy and aid but expanded defense spending. Trump publicly demanded a resolution to North Korea's nuclear program, and he shifted his rhetoric of confrontation with China to the more cooperative language of incentives and shared problems. When the Syrian government used chemical weapons in its civil war, Trump followed his national security advisor's recommendation and launched a large, one-off missile strike against a Syrian air base. It was a punishment and a warning. On Russia, mixed signals emerged. Secretary of State Rex Tillerson and UN Ambassador Nikki Haley criticized Putin for his policies in Syria, but Trump regularly indicated willingness to work with the government in Moscow, and he remained dogged by allegations that his campaign may have colluded with Russian agents during the 2016 election. Trump even reaffirmed the importance of NATO, which he had questioned, and reaffirmed US cooperation with India on issues like counterterrorism and nuclear power.

That August, events seemed to have settled into a new equilibrium. An observer could identify reliable elements of grand strategy *scope*, *substance*, and *assertiveness* that carried forward from the transition. Senior advisor Steve Bannon, a nationalist gadfly, was finally bumped out of the White House. He was pushed by retired General John Kelly, who had become Trump's chief of staff. National Security Advisor H. R. McMaster, meanwhile, drummed out some of the early appointees of his predecessor, Michael Flynn. The administration might well have landed on the early phases of a stable, albeit contested, grand strategy approach. Despite ousting some of his more strident nationalists, Trump held to his "America first" instincts, and hardliners like Kelly supported those basic principles. More conventional leaders like Mattis, Tillerson, and McMaster, meanwhile, continued to reassure US partners that American commitments and interests, as well as its use of force, remained within long-standing parameters. In reality, rather than creative tension, these differences represented substantive gaps between the president's positions and those of his government. Throughout this period, Trump's temperament and penchant for undisciplined public statements, his full support for Saudi Arabia in a diplomatic dispute with Qatar—seemingly an abrupt break in usual US positions—his lack of interest in human rights rhetoric, and his ongoing war of words with the North Koreans set him apart from many of his principals and their agencies.

ESCALATIONS AND CLARIFICATIONS

Familiar Force

Outside the United States, early policies related to military force revealed a gap between Trump's rhetoric and US policy. In late January, for example, an "intelligence gathering" raid in Yemen ended in nine civilian casualties and one American military death.[2] US forces had approached a local military leader's home. A massive firefight, including air support, erupted. The event revealed an administration willing to expand ground operations to a new theater. It also raised questions about internal decision processes and humanitarian standards. Within a week of his inauguration, the new president had greenlighted the strike after a relatively informal presentation over dinner with Defense Secretary Mattis and Chairman of the Joint Chiefs of Staff Gen. Joseph Dunford.[3] Michael Flynn sealed the decision by arguing that such a risky, bold step would set Trump apart from the process-oriented Obama. Afterwards, the president tried to distance himself by commenting about the fallen US serviceman, "They lost Ryan." Critics suspected that the administration had been hasty and given little regard for noncombatants. In Syria and Iraq, the US campaign against ISIS continued apace and even expanded as the administration, in March, deployed Marines and some Army Rangers into active combat zones.[4] Trump supporters and nationalists lauded the president's decisiveness and tough image but also wondered about his commitment to winding down American military commitments.

Campaign promises about a "secret" plan to win the war apparently shelved, Trump also tasked the Department of Defense (DOD) with identifying a strategy to defeat ISIS so that the United States could finally leave the region. At the same time, Secretary of Defense Mattis appeared to contravene Trump's impulses on Russia as well as the president's tendency to critique allies. In routine talks at NATO, he flatly stated—contrary to Trump's consistently optimistic line on Moscow—that the United States and Russia were "not in a position right now to collaborate on a military level" and that there was "very little doubt that they have either interfered or they have attempted to interfere in a number of elections in the democracies."[5] In general, over the next months, Mattis consistently emphasized long-standing US alliance commitments and strategic priorities. Behind closed doors, Mattis and his team were also pushing to reassign Trump's surrogate at Defense, Mira Ricardel, who had been vetting Mattis' "politically unacceptable" candidates for senior positions.[6]

Also seeking to calm fears that the United States would veer off its traditional strategic values, Vice President Mike Pence brought an "assurance" to the annual Munich Security Conference. "The United States of America," he declared in a speech to allied leaders, "Strongly supports NATO and will be unwavering in our commitment to this transatlantic alliance."[7] Still, reviewing postwar history and its optimistic institutions, he concluded that "peace only comes through strength." Namely, the United States would expand military spending, a claim backed up weeks later by a White House budget proposal that grew funds for the DOD, Department of Homeland Security (DHS), and Veterans

Affairs while cutting the foreign aid budget.[8] Pence also warned other NATO governments to meet their spending obligations, identified Iran and Russia as state challenges to global security, and renewed the familiar threats against ISIS and other non-state extremist groups. This *peace through strength* theme would be folded into "principled realism" (to be discussed later) and remain a common trope over the subsequent months among several senior administration officials. The term may have served as a compromise framing between the more traditional Republicans and Trump's inner circle. Over the next year, traditional Republicans in the administration tried to use these terms to draw together their outlook with that of Trump and his nationalist appointees. They were designed to bridge the gap between—on the one hand—the president's rhetoric and impulses and—on the other hand—his government's and his party's long-standing interests. As big tent concepts, they could encompass rather than exclude the United States' existing *scope*, *substance*, and *assertiveness* on grand strategy. As revealed in Chapter 5, the effort reached its peak in late 2017. Ultimately, the center could not hold and the nationalists and hardliner Trump loyalists slowly gained dominance.

Familiar Foes
As with prior administrations, Iran and North Korea would become ongoing strategic burrs. In his effort to contravene all things Obama and play the role of tough negotiator, Trump landed on diametrically opposing approaches for each government. Where he pushed to scrap Obama's nuclear deal with Iran, he simultaneously would push to meet directly with Kim Jong Un. Initially, though, policy toward each seemed to run parallel. When Iran tested ballistic missiles during Trump's fist weeks in office, White House officials asserted that the move contravened a United Nations Security Council resolution. They imposed a new round of sanctions on high-level individuals and a dozen companies.[9] Campaigning, Trump had condemned the Obama Administration's 2015 Joint Comprehensive Plan of Action (JCPOA). Typically referred to as "the Iran nuclear deal," the agreement outraged Obama critics and even

unsettled some of his supporters. At that time, negotiating with the United States, Russia and several European governments, Iran had promised to open up its nuclear facilities for regular inspections and not develop the capacity to create weapons-grade nuclear material for a decade or more. In exchange, the negotiating powers would end sanctions that had taken years to coordinate. Critics worried that Obama had lost all his leverage for a mere freeze on Iran's program. After all, Iranians could still have their program running in 12 to 18 months. Further, shortly after the deal, Iran launched missile tests and supported regional violence that, strictly speaking, fell outside the deal's parameters but antagonized the Americans and Europeans. For Trump, the arrangement epitomized the kind of weakness and "losing" that he had long ridiculed. As with the TPP, he wanted out of the JCPOA. Still, Congress had accepted the plan, and many of Trump's senior advisors, most notably Mattis, insisted that even if they personally agreed that it was a bad deal, reneging would undermine US credibility as well as violate the deal itself. It would, in short, hand Iran a free pass to restart whatever program it had halted.[10] Still, Trump wanted out. That the US president himself was required to certify Iranian compliance every 90 days further agitated the new executive. For the moment, Trump decided to follow the advice of "the generals," but as the year progressed, his determination to kill the deal only grew. Stated differently, consistency between the president, his advisors, and his government remained low, but over time, Trump would —at least nominally—prevail.

Relations with North Korea seemed to start off on even more confrontational footing. By summer 2018, though, Donald Trump was shaking hands with Kim Jong Un. For over 20 years, US officials had wrangled with the North Koreans over their nuclear weapons and missile programs. The Clinton administration had announced a deal with North Korea in which the country agreed to shut down its major nuclear facilities before it actually developed a weapon. In fact, North Korean leaders used negotiations as a kind of delay tactic and never stopped their development program. In 2003, they left the Nuclear Non-Proliferation

Treaty, and in 2006, they conducted a nuclear weapons test. Both the GW Bush and Obama administrations had attempted to lead multilateral negotiations to impose economic sanctions and come up with a deal to end North Korea's nuclear program and missile tests. Over these years, North Korea suffered international isolation, but it also appeared to leverage its nuclear program and the ongoing waves of negotiation to avoid foreign intervention.

Trump and his team seemed to feel confident that they could break this cycle. In a March trip to Asia, Rex Tillerson—who had proven relatively inaccessible and private for a Secretary of State—announced that the United States government was ready "to exchange views on a new approach."[11] North Korean officials in Beijing warned that any war would be the fault of the United States and reiterated their right to self defense with nuclear weapons. In Seoul, South Korea, Tillerson escalated the war of words by declaring that "the policy of strategic patience has ended" and that "all options are on the table."[12] Speaking on Fox News, UN Ambassador Nikki Haley warned that Obama's "soft approach" on China's support for North Korea would also be ending. Administration officials would start pushing regional governments for more sanctions, and they announced their own two weeks later.[13] In April, just ahead of Chinese president Xi Jinping's visit to the United States, North Korea launched medium range ballistic missiles into the Sea of Japan. What strategic end game could advance remained undefined, but relations over the next year would be characterized by spiraling threats.

At the end of February, Trump addressed Congress. Supporters insisted that this was the moment he transitioned from brash to presidential. Skeptics saw a man dully reading a teleprompter who, within 24 hours, would return to tweets and speeches with a stream-of-consciousness quality. Either way, the address itself distilled Trump's initial grand strategic *scope, substance*, and *assertiveness*. Americans confronted global threats from both traditional adversaries *and* allies. Threats and opportunities centered on sovereignty, trade and, to a lesser extent, terror; the

United States would lean less on military and more on economic and political coercion. Jobs and wealth, Trump explained, were flowing to foreign countries. American businesses were hobbled by high nominal taxes. "I believe strongly," he explained, "in free trade but it also has to be FAIR TRADE."[14] US borders stood "wide open" even as Americans defend others' sovereignty. A "beachhead of terrorism" might form in the United States, which could see attacks similar to those that Europe had recently experienced. The vast bulk of the speech was domestically oriented. Still, Trump was clear. His foreign policy called for "direct, robust, and meaningful engagement with the world," but US leadership would be based on "vital security interests that we share with our allies across the globe." Americans prefer to stay at home, but they also know that taking action abroad to ensure less rather than more conflict in the world is better for the United States. On democracy, "free nations are the best vehicle for expressing the will of the people," but the United States "respects the right of all nations to chart their own path." This deference to sovereignty snugly fit the nationalist vision of the world, and it seemed to break from the rhetoric of all presidents since at least Franklin Roosevelt. Revealingly, Trump bluntly declared, "My job is not to represent the world."

A Red Line in Syria

Despite this assertion, Trump felt pressure to respond to a foreign war crime. In early April, the Syrian government appeared to release chemical weapons that killed 60 to 100 civilians. Four years earlier, the Obama administration faced a similar situation. US and other analysts concluded that Syrian government forces, under Bashar al Assad, had used banned chemical weapons in a civilian area. By that point, the Syrian civil war had claimed nearly 80,000 dead, but these images of parents and children desperately gasping for breath captured world attention. Further, bans on any use of chemical weapons had been almost universally respected since the 1920s. President Obama himself had said chemical weapons in Syria would be a "red line." Yet, when Assad appeared to cross that line in 2013, Obama was reluctant to fall into a quagmire and leery about repeating mistakes from his 2011 Libya intervention. He agreed to a diplomatic solution proffered by Russia: Syria would agree to have its chemical weapons removed and destroyed, and the United States would withhold a military response. Now, Trump faced a parallel situation. In 2013, he publically stated that Obama should not expand American military force to yet another Middle Eastern country, but he had since criticized his predecessor for doing too little about Syrian chemical weapons.[15] The White House initially declared that the chemical attack was "reprehensible" and "cannot be ignored." Days later, US warships launched 59 Tomahawk missiles at a Syrian air base that the government asserted was associated with the chemical attack.[16] Damage appeared to be minimal. According to Secretary of State Tillerson, the administration's message was that, whereas defeating ISIS would remain the priority in Syria, "the violation of international norms, the continuing ignoring of U.N. resolutions, and the continuing violation of agreements that they, themselves, entered into will no longer be tolerated."[17]

Observers immediately wondered whether and to what degree this signaled an emerging strategy change that favored a higher level of assertiveness. Tillerson emphasized defeating ISIS and cooperating with Russia, an ally of the Syrian government, to wind down the war and allow Syrians to "lawfully be able to decide the fate of [Assad]."[18] At an emergency session of the UN Security Council, however, US ambassador Haley seemed unequivocal: "We are prepared to do more" and, later, "We don't see a peaceful Syria with Assad in there." She also used the crisis to highlight a hard line on Moscow that she would repeat throughout her tenure at the United Nations: "Russia should ask themselves, 'What are we doing here? Why are we supporting this murderous regime that is committing mass murder of its own population and using the most heinous weapons available?'"[19] Leading Republican Senator Lindsey Graham (R-SC) agreed, arguing that "regime change comes when we train up Syrians." As a bonus, crippling or removing Assad might undermine the Iran-Syria partnership that had vexed American strategists for years.

That month, Treasury Secretary Mnuchin announced new economic sanctions on employees of Syria's Scientific Studies and Research Center.[20] Trump's new National Security Advisor, H.R. McMaster, concurred that "there is no political solution that any of us can see with Assad at the lead," but he also insisted that the United States would not directly "effect that change." Weeks later, Trump approved an NSC plan that originally stalled under Flynn and his appointees: arming Kurds in Syria to help fight ISIS.[21] As an immediate objective, officials wanted to retake Raqqa from the insurgency. Turkish government officials denounced the decision. They considered Kurdish militants to be nearly as dangerous an insurgent threat as ISIS. Was Trump falling into the expansion of American war in the Middle East despite his promises?

The public debate among Trump's own top appointees highlighted ongoing uncertainty about "America first" as the actual substance of US grand strategy. Critics suspected—and supporters worried—that the air strike signaled betrayal of Trump's nationalist promises. More generally, the administration had lowered Obama-era standards for who can be targeted by airstrikes and how rigorously those "counterterrorism" raids were reviewed.[22] By the end of the year, for example, the Trump administration exceeded Obama's annual use of tactical airstrikes.[23] Journalist McKay Coppins speculated that a Trump militarization of US foreign policy was inevitable because "Trump's approach to matters of war and peace appears to be more attitudinal than philosophical—motivated by instinct, manifested in tough talk, and rooted in a worldview that holds up the cultivation of fear as the most effective way to win respect and obedience."[24] This approach was not quite borne out by subsequent decisions. The administration did not follow up with any campaign to pressure Assad and continued to expand resources devoted to ISIS. When the US government committed tactical resources and weapons to fight ISIS, the promises remained limited and narrowly targeted at ISIS rather than expanding into the wider civil war. Rather than an inflection point, the Syria air strike appeared to be a one-off event. Trump's impulse to talk tough appeared, despite fears of widening militarism, to be moderated by his disinterest in long-term military commitments. In this case, Trump's personal preferences were, again, subsumed by larger US strategic pathways, but over time, as in other areas, US policy would indeed move closer to the president's stated views.

RISING TEMPERATURES

Middle East

Trump boarded Air Force One on May 19 for his first international tour. Three weeks earlier, the administration and Americans took account of Trump's first one hundred days in office. A consummate self-promoter, Trump touted his relationships with foreign leaders, the executive actions he had signed, and the quality of his team. Insiders, however, portrayed "a White House on a collision course between Trump's fixed habits and his growing realization that this job is harder than he imagined."[25] All the snafus, policy reversals, and personnel fights of prior months remained. Trump's staff seemed plagued with "paranoia and insecurity, paralyzed by internal jockeying for power." They struggled to serve an executive who "can consult with 20 outside associates a day, change his mind in a minute and change his mood even quicker." Awkward stories about Trump officials' alleged ties to or communication with Russians continued to bubble into the media and seemed to culminate—and end, the president seemed to hope—in Trump firing FBI director James Comey, who he said was failing to pursue and end the unprecedented flood of leaks flowing out of the White House and agencies across Washington D.C.[26] The move immediately fueled speculation (sometimes hyperbolic speculation) that Trump had colluded with a foreign power and was obstructing investigations into Russia's attempt to sway the 2016 election. Trump did not help his case when he met Russia's foreign minister days after the firing in an Oval Office meeting closed to US press and claimed that firing "nut job" Comey would reduce the "great pressure" on him.[27] Still, the president forged ahead. In one head-spinning 24 hours, he reversed an earlier stance and insisted that NATO is "no longer obsolete" and then, separately, announced that he was no longer determined to officially categorize China as a currency manipulator.[28] Kushner and Bannon, meanwhile, had met at Mar-a-Lago, Trump's ostentatious resort in south Florida and his "winter White House," to smooth their working relationship. Trump himself had met China's premier, Xi Jinping, at Mar-a-Lago in a seemingly amiable visit. Trump and Xi released an agreement that would, among other friendly actions, ease trade restrictions on beef, chicken, and liquefied natural gas trade between the countries.[29] Now, Trump would travel to the Middle East and then to Europe for the forty-third G7 summit meeting of some of the United States' longest-standing economic and military partners.

In Saudi Arabia, Trump touted his deal making to American observers as he met with, and was feted by, regional leaders. After signing a $110 billion arms trade agreement with the Saudis, he heralded what it represented for "jobs, jobs, jobs" back home.[30] Tillerson emphasized the "very strong message to our common enemies" while also "lower[ing] the cost to the American people of providing security in this region." Specifically, US officials were clear: the deal should be read as the administration's commitment to confront "malign Iranian influence and Iranian related threats." Indeed, Iran had become the admiration's primary state adversary in the region. With ISIS an immediate threat to fight, Trump explained in his keynote speech to leaders from 50 Muslim-majority states, Iran still pushed "the fires of sectarian conflict and terror."[31] Candidate Trump once speculated aloud that "I think Islam hates us," and, of course, he was still fighting to implement some version of the "Muslim ban." Now, with Muslim leaders, he was more careful. Aligning with Saudi Arabia's hard line, Trump cast Iran specifically as a regional spoiler and global sponsor of terror. To temper the pressure, though, Tillerson stated that while he had no plans to contact his Iranian counterpart, he had "never shut off the phone to anyone that wants to talk or have a productive conversation."

In Israel, President Trump reiterated his Iran position. The conservative Prime Minister Benjamin Netanyahu—staunchly skeptical of Iranians and Obama's nuclear deal with them—welcomed the message as well as Trump's overall support for this long-standing US ally. Politically and strategically, Iran served as a useful common adversary. In fact, Netanyahu decided to gloss over allegations that Trump shared Israeli intelligence with Russia's foreign minister in that Oval Office meeting. For his part, Trump did little to pressure Israelis on complex issues surrounding the status and treatment of Palestinians.[32] Politically, Israel enjoyed deep support among many US conservatives and, in particular, one of Trump's most faithful supporters: Evangelical Christians. Casting Israel and Iran as a good versus evil duo served the president's domestic political base and, for the moment, fit his nationalist grand strategy.[33]

Europe

In Europe, Trump's visit inspired a rather different tone. His preference to shift the alliance and internationalist traditions of US grand strategy was clear. If successful, the effort would alter the face of US *scope* and *substance*. Trump the man, however, was constrained by those very traditions as well as his own inconsistency and top personnel. After meetings with the Pope as well as Italian, Belgian, French, and European Union leaders, the US president arrived at NATO headquarters to deliver a speech. It was unsparing. "I have been very, very direct with secretary Stoltenberg and members of the alliance in saying NATO members must finally contribute their fair share and meet their financial obligations," he explained.[34] Treaty members are obliged to spend at least two percent of their annual GDP on defense, yet 23 of the 28 had failed to do so for years. Trump portrayed the shortfall—misleadingly—as a kind of debt owed to American taxpayers. Trump's skepticism extended to European Union priorities, as well. Earlier that day, European Council president Donald Tusk told reporters that whereas he and the US president agreed on counterterrorism, they parted on trade, climate, and Russia policy. Tusk emphasized shared transatlantic values. Trump emphasized fair dealing.

Notably, though, Trump's economic advisor Gary Cohn emphasized that Russia sanctions would persist—and maybe get tougher—despite the US president's personal reluctance to stake out a hard line with Russia.[35] At the G7 meeting, Trump's final major event before heading home, leaders appeared to agree on the basics of terrorism and Syria policy, and Trump's team agreed, to the relief of Europeans following the president's rhetoric, "to fight all forms of protectionism."[36] Still, talks almost broke down over migration and climate.[37] Thousands of Arab and African migrants in recent years had been arriving on European—most often Italian—shores. Grappling with their own internal challenges, Italians had spent months working out a "human mobility" arrangement to share the burden. Trump's team balked. The final G-7 statement recognized migrants' human rights, but it broke with the usual internationalist language of such statements and instead emphasized "the sovereign rights of states to control their own borders and set clear limits on net migration levels as key elements of their national security." Only days later, Trump also announced that the United States would withdraw from the 2015 Paris climate agreement. Again, he explained that as it stood, the deal would cost the United States huge amounts of money and jobs and hurt industries like oil, gas, and coal.[38] And, again, characteristically, he said that he would be open to renegotiating the agreement on more favorable, though unspecified, terms.

The End of the Beginning

"On a sweltering Washington summer day," runs an account from the Associated Press, "President Donald Trump's motorcade pulled up to the Pentagon for a meeting largely billed as a briefing on the Afghanistan conflict and the fight against the Islamic State group."[39] The July meeting, Trump found, "was, in reality, about much more." Within weeks, Steve Bannon along with some of his key national security hires would be gone, as would the White House press secretary Sean Spicer and Chief of Staff Reince Priebus. Personnel turnover had been unusually high, and it had caught up figures from all sides of the internal grand strategy debate. By the end 2018, however, senior appointments would converge more closely with Trump's personal and ideological preferences. During this moment in mid-2017, though, an unsettled team agreed that the president needed to be schooled in "American Power 101."

The *scope, substance,* and *assertiveness* of Trump's strategic policies during his first foreign trip—to the Middle East and Europe—had proven relatively consistent. They represented the president himself and his team's preferences for nationalist and transactional solutions. Outside Trump's immediate influence, however, administration officials still groped for clear grand strategy positions. Such positions, they seemed to believe, needed to align the administration's competing schools of thought, but those positions also needed to remain flexible enough to incorporate the president's shifting rhetoric, personal impulses, and unpredictable statements. In short, the Trump administration needed a doctrine that allowed for the president's own mercurial statements.

When simmering relations between the Persian Gulf state of Qatar and its neighbors started to boil, for instance, Trump's administration faced a dilemma. On the one side, Qatar housed the region's largest US military installation, Al Udeid Air Base. On the other side, the president had just affirmed the personal, economic, and military value of Saudi Arabia and other regional partners. Qatar's neighbors accused it of supporting terrorism, and in early June they cut diplomatic ties and imposed sanctions. Tillerson and Mattis separately stated that the United States would play its typical role of mediator, encouraging the governments, respectively, to "sit down together" and assuring reporters that "it will be resolved."[40] Shortly afterwards, Trump claimed that during his trip he supported hardline policies against funding for terrorists, and now Arab governments had taken up his advice.[41] Alarmed, Qataris contacted Tillerson, who reiterated a conciliatory position. Trump himself told Qatar's emir that he could help resolve the dispute, but days later, in a press conference, Trump said, "I decided, along with Secretary of State Rex Tillerson, our great generals and military people, the time had come to call on Qatar to end its funding." No diplomatic movement occurred, and the standoff between the Arab governments persisted, though in August, Saudi Arabia did reopen its land borders with the peninsular nation. When confronted with this crisis, Trump faced two options. He could push conciliation and traditional strategic priorities, or he could side with his preferred regional partners. These partners toed a hard line, but they did not specify how to unwind the situation. He chose the latter: commit to his preferred partners but with no specific endgame.

Subsequent weeks saw the administration continue to grapple with how to define its strategic focus. At the G-20 meeting in Hamburg, Germany, Trump held a series of bilateral meetings with fellow executives. Raising his long-standing trade concerns, he pushed Xi Jinping of China to help the United States pressure North Korea over its nuclear program.[42] European leaders, after their initial introduction to Trump in May, accepted that the United States would remain isolated on climate commitments and determined to challenge it on trade. German Chancellor Angela Merkel personally emphasized her disappointment that the United States remained the only country that did not endorse the summit's final climate statement, and she bluntly stated that "markets need to be kept open."[43] Still, there appeared to be no specific policy fallout. At home, though, news broke that Trump spent "nearly an hour" speaking privately with Russia's Vladimir Putin after their scheduled, two-hour meeting earlier that day.[44] The president and his staff assured the public that this was simply a normal conversation at a dinner for all the G20 leaders. Unfortunately for them, that summer also saw ongoing reports and revelations about Trump 2016 campaign connections with Russians. Ten days prior, the president tweeted that he had "strongly pressed President Putin twice about Russian meddling in our election. He vehemently denied it."[45] The gap was growing between Trump's personal view of Russia and that of the US intelligence community, many Republicans in Congress, and large sections of the public. Undaunted, Trump pointed to possible agreements between Washington and Moscow in order to cooperate in the Syrian civil war. He also said the Washington and Moscow could resolve this cybersecurity irritant by creating "an impenetrable Cyber Security unit so that election hacking, [and] many other negative things, will be guarded." Such tone deaf assurances tossed gasoline on a growing media fire. Critical commentators ramped into overdrive speculating about the president's possible conflicts of interest and ignorance about cyber espionage. In the long term, Trump-Russia investigations would dog the administration and frustrate the president for years. In terms of grand strategy, they raised unresolved questions for observers and even fellow Republicans about Trump's exact agenda with a seemingly adversarial—if not quite enemy—power.

REMEDIAL WORLD POWER

Shortly after the president's return to US soil, his advisors organized that "American Power 101" briefing. Donald Trump, for as long as he had expressed public political views, had questioned open-ended military commitments and basing thousands of people abroad. Mattis and Tillerson, according to the reports, tailored the presentation for Trump by leaning on visuals and talking points to emphasize the importance of keeping the world safe for American business.[46] With the Chinese pushing for greater global economic access, they explained, the military helped ensure stability. Plus, diplomats helped maintain ties to avoid foreign corruption and the intelligence community provided information to keep the system on track.

Afterwards, the president branded the meeting "very good," but it is hard to know if it marked a moment of change or a null effort with no clear effect. Over the next weeks, Trump did stake out conventional but hardline positions on some key strategic issues. The specific agenda of that meeting, for example, was to begin final decision making about military engagement in Afghanistan and against ISIS. For at least two months, senior national security appointees, spearheaded by McMaster, had been floating a new Afghanistan strategy.[47] According to the plan, the Pentagon rather than the White House would set troop levels and would push up to 5,000 more into the conflict to compel final negotiations with the Taliban. By threatening to cut military aid, officials would also increase pressure on Pakistan, where Taliban and other militants enjoyed support networks and safe havens. This was the sort of cautious strategy that military and foreign policy planners had advanced for years and had led to long-term military commitments. Given Trump's personal preferences on the matter, his willingness to seriously entertain the plan showed real influence from his senior officials.[48] A month later, standing before assembled troops, he declared in a prime-time speech that the United States would "fight to win" in Afghanistan.[49] He offered no details, saying only, "I will not say when we are going to attack, but we will." That job fell to Mattis, who, in October, set out his strategy to the DOD. In a rare direct admission of deferring to others, Trump explained, "My original instinct was to pull out—and, historically, I like following my instincts. But all my life I've heard that decisions are much different when you sit behind the desk in the Oval Office." For the moment, the establishment was still giving direction to American wars. Over time, however, Trump would return to his own counsel. Indeed, by the end 2018, he felt comfortable accepting Mattis' resignation after the president abruptly declared that United States forces would, within months, leave the waning fight against ISIS in Syria.

IN SUM

On August 18, the White House announced that Chief Strategist Steve Bannon had departed the administration. Close observers suspected that the erstwhile Richelieu had finally overplayed his hand. In a candid media interview, he contradicted the president's ratcheting rhetoric. "There's no military solution [to North Korea's nuclear threats], forget it."[50] The real issue, he said, is that "we're at economic war with China." His administration enemies—the "globalists"—disagreed and hoped to work with Beijing on North Korea. They also worried about a spiraling trade conflict. "They're wetting themselves," Bannon crowed. Notably, later events would vindicate Bannon's China analysis. After he had packed his belongings out of the White House, Bannon was defiant, but not toward Trump. "If there's any confusion out there," he declared, "let me clear it up: I'm leaving the White House and going to war for Trump against his opponents—on Capitol Hill, in the media, and in corporate America."[51] For Bannon, Trump always represented a movement. He was an idea as much as a politician. In that sense, Bannon said, the presidency he fought to achieve "is over." For him, the nationalist revolution had already stalled inside the Washington beltway. Bannon vowed to continue the fight; however, scorned by mainstream figures, seen as a failure by his movement comrades, and unable even to land a footing among far rightists in Europe, Bannon's prominence faded.

Trump, however, remained engaged and active. As the next chapter shows, his rhetorical bombast, and his steady preference for "America first," persisted. Committed nationalists like Bannon could not score a dramatic revolution in the *scope, substance*, and *assertiveness* of US grand strategy, but Donald Trump's ongoing presence and preferences created steady policy pressure on more moderate members of his administration. Over summer of 2017, for instance, Trump and North Korea's Kim Jong Un had escalated a war of words, with Kim launching missile tests and Trump threatening utter destruction of the regime in Pyongyang. That spiral would reach an unexpected series of crescendos over the next year. What remained unclear, and what this book interrogates, is the degree to which Trump himself and his team shaped the core content of US grand strategy.

NOTES

1. Danielle Pletka, "On foreign policy, Trump has become—gasp—a normal president," *The Washington Post*, April 26, 2017, https://www. washingtonpost.com/opinions/on-foreign-policy-trump-has-become--gasp--a-normal-president/2017/04/26/197b0372-2542-11e7-b503-9d616 bd5a305_story.html?utm_term=.8f147c4e7841; Marc Lynch, "What kind of deal is Trump making with Saudi Arabia?" The Monkey Cage, *The Washington Post*, May 22, 2017, https://www.washingtonpost.com/news/ monkey-cage/wp/2017/05/22/what-kind-of-deal-is-trump-making-with-saudi-arabia/?utm_term=.d90d460b583c; Aaron David Miller and Richard Sokolsky, "Trump's Foreign Policy: 100 Days of Global Bafflement," *Politico*, April 24, 2017, https://www.politico.com/magazine/story/2017/ 04/24/trumps-foreign-policy-100-days-of-global-bafflement-215066.

2. Staff, "Yemen: US Should Investigate Civilian Deaths in Raid," Human Rights Watch, February 24, 2017, https://www.hrw.org/news/2017/02/2 4/yemen-us-should-investigate-civilian-deaths-raid.

3. Stephen Tankel, "Donald Trump's Shadow War," *Politico*, May 9, 2018, https://www.politico.com/magazine/story/2018/05/09/donald-trumps-shadow-war-218327.

4. Barbara Starr, "US Marines join local forces fighting in Raqqa," CNNpolitics, March 9, 2017, https://www.cnn.com/2017/03/08/politics/ marines-raqqa-assault-syria/.

5. Staff, "US Defence Secretary James Mattis rejects military collaboration with Russia," Australian Broadcasting Corporation, February 16, 2017, https://www.abc.net.au/news/2017-02-17/us-defence-secretary-rules-out-military-ties-with-russia/8278350.

6. Aaron Mehta and Joe Gould, "Sources: Mattis, Ricardel clashed over Pentagon appointees," *Defense News*, March 15, 2017, https://www. defensenews.com/pentagon/2017/03/15/sources-mattis-ricardel-clashed-over-pentagon-appointees/. In November 2018, Ricardel was later forced out as a deputy national security advisor when, issuing a rare personnel veto, Melania Trump demanded that she be dismissed. Nicole Gaouette, "Who is Mira Ricardel and why did Melania Trump want her fired?" CNN, November 14. 2018, https://www.cnn.com/2018/11/13/politics/who-is-mira-ricardel/index.html

7. Mike Pence, Remarks by the Vice President at the Munich Security Conference, Munich, Germany, February 18, 2017, https://www.whitehouse.gov/briefings-statements/remarks-vice-president-munich-security-conference/

8. Office of Management and Budget, *America First: A Budget Blueprint to Make America Great Again*, Government Publishing Office, March 16, 2017, p. 5.

9. Guy Taylor and Dave Boyer, "Trump slaps sanctions on Iran over missile test," *The Washington Times*, February 3, 2017, https://www.washingtontimes.com/news/2017/feb/3/donald-trump-slaps-sanctions-iran-missile-test/.

10. The United States adopted the JCPOA not as a treaty but as a Congressional-executive agreement, making it both easier to pass and easier to end.

11. Anna Fifield and Anne Gearan, "Tillerson says diplomacy with North Korea has 'failed'; Pyongyang warns of war," *The Washington Post*, March 16, 2017, https://www.washingtonpost.com/world/asia_pacific/tillerson-stresses-regional-cooperation-to-curb-north-koreas-weapons-programs/2017/03/16/4ec5e07c-09ab-11e7-bd19-fd3afa0f7e2a_story.html?utm_term=.972e3ca03ed4.

12. Anna Fifield and Anne Gearan, "Tillerson says 'all options are on the table' when it comes to North Korea," *The Washington Post*, March 19, 2017, https://www.washingtonpost.com/world/tillerson-says-all-options-are-on-the-table-when-it-comes-to-north-korea/2017/03/17/e6b3e64e-0a83-11e7-bd19-fd3afa0f7e2a_story.html?utm_term=.2cb6860e9259.

13. Press Release, "Treasury Sanctions Agents Linked to North Korea's Weapons of Mass Destruction Proliferation and Financial Networks," Washington, DC, Press Center, U.S. Department of the Treasury, March 31, 2017, https://www.treasury.gov/press-center/press-releases/Pages/sm0039.aspx.

14. Trump, Donald. "Remarks by President Trump in Joint Address to Congress." Remarks to Congress. The Capitol, Washington, D.C., 28 Feb 2018.

15. Anne Barnard and Michael R. Gordon, "Worst Chemical Attack in Years in Syria; U.S. Blames Assad," *The New York Times*, April 4, 2017, https://www.nytimes.com/2017/04/04/world/middleeast/syria-gas-attack.html.

16. Spencer Ackerman, Ed Pilkington, Ben Jacobs, and Julian Borger, "Syria missile strikes: US launches first direct military action against Assad,"

The Guardian, April 7, 2017, https://www.theguardian.com/world/2017/apr/06/trump-syria-missiles-assad-chemical-weapons,

17. John Dickerson, "Full Transcript: Rex Tillerson on 'Face the Nation,'" Television interview, *Face the Nation*, April 9, 2017, https://www.cbsnews.com/news/full-transcript-rex-tillerson-on-face-the-nation-april-9/.

18. Curt Mills, "Tillerson, Haley Appear to Differ on Assad," *U.S. News & World Report*, April 10, 2017, https://www.usnews.com/news/politics/articles/2017-04-10/nikki-haley-rex-tillerson-offer-different-statements-on-assad-and-syria. See also "U.N. ambassador Nikki Haley warns U.S. 'prepared to do more' after Syria strike," CBS News/AP, April 7, 2017, https://www.cbsnews.com/news/un-ambassador-nikki-haley-says-us-prepared-to-do-more-after-syria-strike/.

19. Maxwell Tani, "The Trump administration appears torn over whether to support removing Syria's Assad from power," *Business Insider*, April 9, 2017, https://www.businessinsider.com/trump-bashar-al-assad-nikki-haley-regime-change-rex-tillerson-mcmaster-2017-4.

20. Emily Tillett, "Treasury secretary Steven Mnuchin announces new Syrian sanctions," CBS News, April 24, 2017, https://www.cbsnews.com/news/treasury-secretary-steven-mnuchin-announces-new-syrian-sanctions/.

21. Michael R. Gordon, and Eric Schmitt, "Trump to Arm Syrian Kurds, Even as Turkey Strongly Objects," *The New York Times*, May 9, 2017, https://www.nytimes.com/2017/05/09/us/politics/trump-kurds-syria-army.html?_r=2.

22. Stephen Tankel, "Donald Trump's Shadow War," *Politico*, May 9, 2018, https://www.politico.com/magazine/story/2018/05/09/donald-trumps-shadow-war-218327.

23. Jennifer Wilson and Micah Zenko, "Donald Trump Is Dropping Bombs at Unprecedented Levels," *Foreign Policy*, August 9, 2017, https://foreignpolicy.com/2017/08/09/donald-trump-is-dropping-bombs-at-unprecedented-levels/.

24. McKay Coppins, "Donald Trump, Inevitable Hawk," *The Atlantic*, April 8, 2017, https://www.theatlantic.com/politics/archive/2017/04/donald-trump-inevitable-hawk/522390/.

25. Josh Dawsey, Shane Goldmacher, and Alex Isenstadt, "The education of Donald Trump," *Politico*, April 27, 2017, https://www.politico.com/story/2017/04/27/the-education-of-donald-trump-237669.

26. Philip Rucker, et al., "Inside Trump's anger and impatience—and his sudden decision to fire Comey," *The Washington Post*, May 10, 2017, https://www.washingtonpost.com/politics/how-trumps-anger-and-impatience-

prompted-him-to-fire-the-fbi-director/2017/05/10/d9642334-359c-11e7-b373-418f6849a004_story.html?utm_term=.6008d0fba3ad.

27. Matt Apuzzo, Maggie Haberman, and Matthew Rosenberg, "Trump Told Russians That Firing 'Nut Job' Comey Eased Pressure From Investigation," *The New York Times*, May 19, 2017, https://www.nytimes.com/2017/05/19/us/politics/trump-russia-comey.html.

28. Staff, "Trump reverses course in 24 hours from Nato to China to Fed," BBC News, April 13, 2017, https://www.bbc.com/news/world-us-canada-39591032.

29. "Initial Results of the 100-Day Action Plan of the U.S.-China Comprehensive Economic Dialogue," Joint Press Release, Washington, DC, U.S. Department of Commerce, Office of the Secretary, May 10, 2017, http://www.wsj.com/public/resources/documents/secretaryrossbriefing.pdf.

30. Jordyn Phelps and Ryan Struyk, "Trump signs $110 billion arms deal with Saudi Arabia on 'a tremendous day,'" *abcNews*, May 20, 2017, https://abcnews.go.com/Politics/trump-signs-110-billion-arms-deal-saudi-arabia/story?id=47531180.

31. Reuters staff, "Donald Trump hits out at Iran, says region 'held at bay by bloodshed and terror,'" *The Sydney Morning Herald*, May 22, 2017, https://www.smh.com.au/world/donald-trump-hits-out-at-iran-says-region-held-at-bay-by-bloodshed-and-terror-20170522-gw9whd.html.

32. Peter Baker and Ian Fisher, "Trump Comes to Israel Citing a Palestinian Deal as Crucial," *The New York Times*, May 22, 2017, https://www.nytimes.com/2017/05/22/world/middleeast/trump-israel-visit.html?hp&action=click&pgtype=Homepage&clickSource=image&module=b-lede-package-region&region=top-news&WT.nav=top-news.

33. Unfortunately for the White House, the image most Americans saw of the visit was vivid and awkward: Trump with the Saudi and Egyptian leaders placing hands on a glowing globe, their faces cast in stark shadows. Sophie Tatum, "6 Key moments from President Trump's first trip abroad." *CNNpolitics*, May 26, 2017, https://www.cnn.com/2017/05/26/politics/trump-trip-key-photos/.

34. Daniel Boffey and Jennifer Rankin, "Trump rebukes Nato leaders for not paying defence bills," *The Guardian*, May 25, 2017, https://www.theguardian.com/world/2017/may/25/trump-rebukes-nato-leaders-for-not-paying-defence-bills.

35. Alexaner Mallin and Jordyn Phelps, "President Trump attends G-7 meetings in Italy," *abcNews*, May 26, 2017, https://abcnews.go.com/Politics/president-trump-attend-g7-meetings-italy/story?id=47644029.

36. John Irish and Crispian Balmer, "G7 leaders divided on climate change, closer on trade issues," *Reuters*, May 25, 2017, https://www.reuters.com/article/us-g7-summit/g7-leaders-divided-on-climate-change-closer-on-trade-issues-idUSKBN18L2ZU.

37. Patrick Wintour, "Hopes for refugee crisis plan fall into chasm between G7 and Trump," *The Guardian*, May 26, 2017, https://www.theguardian.com/world/2017/may/26/trump-set-to-clash-with-other-g7-leaders-over-refugees-and-climate.

38. Valerie Volcovici, "U.S. submits formal notice of withdrawal from Paris climate pact," *Reuters*, August 4, 2017, https://www.reuters.com/article/us-un-climate-usa-paris/u-s-submits-formal-notice-of-withdrawal-from-paris-climate-pact-idUSKBN1AK2FM.

39. Matthew Lee and Jonathan Lemire, "How Trump's advisers schooled him on globalism," Associated Press, September 18, 2017, https://apnews.com/4cef63caf6b34cb796bc4c196d47c143.

40. Krishnadev Calamur, "What Exactly Is the U.S. Policy on Qatar?" *The Atlantic*, June 9, 2017, https://www.theatlantic.com/international/archive/2017/06/us-policy-qatar/529866/.

41. Krishnadev Calamur, "The Trump Tweet Tracker," *The Atlantic*, June 6, 2017, https://www.theatlantic.com/liveblogs/2017/06/donald-trump-twitter/511619/16596/.

42. Ali Vitali, "G-20 Summit: Top Five Takeaways from Trump's Trip," *NBC News*, July 8, 2017, https://www.nbcnews.com/politics/donald-trump/g-20-summit-top-five-takeaways-trump-s-trip-n780916.

43. Angela Dewan, "G20 closes with rebuke to Trump's climate change stance," *CNN World*, July 9, 2017, https://www.cnn.com/2017/07/08/europe/g20-merkel-trump-communique/index.html.

44. Eli Watkins and Jeremy Diamond, "Trump, Putin met for nearly an hour in second G20 meeting," *CNN Politics*, July 19, 2019, https://www.cnn.com/2017/07/18/politics/trump-putin-g20/index.html.

45. Yoni Applebaum, "The Trump Tweet Tracker," *The Atlantic*, July 9, 2017, https://www.theatlantic.com/liveblogs/2017/06/donald-trump-twitter/511619/16596/.

46. Lee and Lemire, "How Trump's advisers schooled him on globalism."

47. Isobel Thompson, "Not everyone in the White House is behind what some are calling 'McMaster's War,'" *Vanity Fair*, May 9, 2017, https://www.

vanityfair.com/news/2017/05/trump-afghanistan-troop-surge?verso=
true.

48. Jacqueline Klimas, "Trump on more U.S. troops in Afghanistan: 'We'll
    see,'" *Politico*, July 20, 2017, https://www.politico.com/story/2017/07/20
    /afghanistan-us-troop-levels-trump-240759.

49. Jeremy Diamond, "Trump declares US will 'win' in Afghanistan, but gives
    few details," CNN, August 22, 2017, https://www.cnn.com/2017/08/21/
    politics/trump-afghanistan-speech/index.html.

50. Robert Kuttner, "Steve Bannon, Unrepentant," *The American Prospect*,
    August 16, 2017, https://prospect.org/article/steve-bannon-unrepentant.

51. Harriet Alexander, David Millward, and Barney Henderson, "Steve
    Bannon declares 'Trump presidency is over' after being ousted as White
    House chief strategist," *The Telegraph*, August 19, 2019, https://www.
    telegraph.co.uk/news/2017/08/18/steve-bannon-donald-trumps-chief-
    white-house-strategist-mutual/.

Chapter 5

The Rise and Fall of "Principled Realism"

Fall 2017 to Spring 2018

Standing before the world's assembled leaders, the president of the United States declared that his government was willing to "totally destroy" North Korea. "Rocket man," Donald Trump's voice echoed across the audience, "is on a suicide mission for himself and his regime."[1] The president's first speech to the UN General Assembly was, given the forum, a remarkable statement. Underneath the bombast, it also set out a theory of international affairs based on "a coalition of strong and independent nations." *Principled realism*, Trump explained, reflected his administration's commitment to respecting other governments' sovereignty and challenging those that undermine basic stability in the state system. First and foremost, it also emphasized securing America's interests. This chapter will trace the administration's grand strategy and whether principled realism had, in fact, emerged from the fights of early 2017 to define the administration's grand strategy. The concept's rise and fall serves as a marker. Like a dye dropped into water, it reveals flows and influences. Analyzed through the lens of Grand Strategy Analysis (GSA), analysts can observe how Donald Trump's personal preferences slowly prevailed over official US policy.

The *scope*, *substance*, and *assertiveness* that he and his closest supporters displayed had been chastened or constrained, but through this period, they grew to be more consistent aspects of US grand strategy.

"Principled realism" represented the administration's maturing effort to settle on a single grand strategy framework. Months earlier, in his March address to a joint session of Congress, Trump was blunt: "My job is to represent the United States of America," not to worry about international commitments. As a political position, this mobilized voters and explained his moves on international trade deals and immigration. As a strategic agenda, it was thin. In May 2017, then-National Security Advisor H. R. McMaster and Gary Cohn, the National Economic Council director, published an effort to beef up the president's rhetoric. It proved to be one of most extensive—and ultimately abortive—efforts to unify the administration's nationalist and mainstream Republican camps. "America first," they said, "Doesn't mean America alone." According to this realist-tinted operating theory, the world is zero-sum. States compete with one another, and if one is winning, the others are losing. There is, they explained, no "'global community' but an arena where nations, nongovernmental actors and businesses engage and compete for advantage. ... Rather than deny this elemental nature of international affairs, we embrace it." Still, the United States could and would work with other governments "where our interests align." Rather than impose American values, the United States would, in Trump's words, "secure the blessings of liberty for ourselves and our posterity." That, in any case, was to be the grand strategic philosophy. In practice, this meant security for Americans, with a particular focus on terrorism. It also involved economic well-being, represented by new military trade agreements with Saudi Arabia but also confronting European allies on trade deficits. In turn, by demanding that NATO allies spend more on defense, "we have deepened our relationships." As a theory, principled realism was hazy, but in terms of this book's frameworks, it was designed to serve as an agreed set of positions on *scope*, *substance*, and *orientation*. That agreement would, officials like McMaster seemed to hope, reduce the gap between two schools of thought: on the one hand, traditional US strategic policy and, on the other hand, the president and his more hardline or nationalist appointees.

In practice, uniting competing visions was unsustainable. Principled realism served as a rhetorical tent that covered Trump's slow consolidation around his tough-talking nationalism. That August, Trump announced a plan for the war in Afghanistan. However, rather than tie US efforts there to a larger agenda, it called for a "win" and remained vague on substantive changes. As the year ended, officials released their National Security Strategy and, in January, the Nuclear Posture Review. These documents were clear, and Secretary of Defense Mattis reinforced their message during a January Congressional testimony. "We will continue to prosecute the campaign against terrorists," he explained, "but great-power competition—not terrorism—is now the primary focus of US national security."

On North Korea, Trump himself seemed to drive for confrontation, at least for a time. He threatened "fire and fury like the world has never seen" when the regime conducted its sixth nuclear test in September. He tweeted that Secretary of State Tillerson was "wasting his time" when reporting revealed that America's chief diplomat was pushing talks with Kim's regime. Nevertheless, just below this "maximum pressure" campaign, Joint Chiefs Chairman Dunford joined Tillerson in reassuring South Koreans that American commitments remained firm. Revealingly, by late winter and early spring 2018, boiling relations rapidly cooled. South Korean diplomats quietly dialogued with their American and North Korean counterparts. Symbolic diplomacy, like North Korean athletes at the Winter Olympics, signaled growing cooperation. Then, in March, Trump himself startled the world by agreeing to a one-on-one summit with Kim Jong Un. For White House officials, this represented a win for the Trump approach. It did not, however, guarantee actual negotiating success, and it did not clearly identify which version of the Trump approach was driving strategic policy.

Trump saw similar results in other categories. On Afghanistan, Mattis and Dunford fleshed out Trump's Afghanistan announcement. Americans would pursue a plausible but familiar plan for more troops, more liberal rules of engagement, and an open-ended commitment. On Iran, Trump again drove headlines by refusing to certify Obama's 2015 Iran nuclear deal, yet the action was a warning shot: Congress retained ultimate power over the agreement. When Trump visited Asia, he pushed his trade agenda, but he also reassured allies and partners around the region that the United States would remain reliable, despite dumping the Trans-Pacific Partnership trade deal. Playing to domestic audiences, particularly his Evangelical supporters, Trump announced that the United States would recognize Jerusalem as Israel's capital and move its embassy there. Back at home, in early 2017, Trump had initiated a renegotiation for the North American Free Trade Agreement (NAFTA), one of his favorite examples of a bad trade deal. By fall and winter, Canadian efforts to build some compromise solution were still being rejected by the Americans, yet the talks did persist. Overall, "principled realism" seemed to serve more as a bridge toward Trump's preferred grand strategy approach rather than a tent to house the administration's competing views.

"Fire and Fury"

Negotiating with North Korea

Trump's attack on Kim Jong Un from the UN rostrum culminated months of spiraling rhetoric. Whatever their respective motivations, both Trump and Kim found an opponent ready to clash. By April, Trump was assuring reporters that "North Korea is a problem. The problem will be taken care of."[2] Days later, North Korea tested yet another long-range missile. This prompted Secretary of State Tillerson personally to address the UN Security Council. He warned that it was "likely only a matter of time before North Korea develops the capability to strike the US mainland" and that "catastrophic consequences" would follow if the UN Security Council

(UNSC) refused to act. The North Koreans continued to test missiles and escalate their rhetoric. In response, trying to ratchet pressure on China and work his relationship with Xi Jinping, Trump tweeted, "North Korea disrespected the wishes of China & its highly respected President."[3]

That summer, leaders in both Washington and Pyongyang were warning that war was a real option. Tension reached new heights when the Defense Intelligence Agency (DIA) confirmed that the US government believed North Korea had developed the capacity to place miniaturized warheads atop intercontinental ballistic missiles (ICBMs). Stated simply, North Korea's nuclear missile program was improving. Tillerson had already promised a second round of sanctions. In early August, the UN Security Council, including Russia and China, unanimously adopted these punishments.[4] Speaking to the media, National Security Advisor McMaster said the threat of a nuclear North Korea was "intolerable" and that "I think it's impossible to overstate the danger associated with a rogue, brutal regime."[5] Days later, seated at a nondescript conference table at an event in New Jersey, Trump defiantly folded his arms and told the assembled media, "North Korea best not make any more threats to the United States." And if they do? "They will be met with the fire and fury and frankly power, the likes of which this world has never seen before."[6] In response, a North Korean People's Army spokesman stated that his government was "carefully examining" strike plans against Guam, a US territory. Secretary of Defense Mattis, ever careful about his public pronouncements, warned that if North Korea attacked the United States or its allies, it would face the "end of its regime and the destruction of its people."[7] For the moment, administration officials worked to present a single face on the issue. By this point, media headlines reflected a growing frenzy. Claiming to reassure the public, Trump goosed the hysteria. "If anything," he mused in front of cameras, "maybe that statement wasn't tough enough."[8]

A Theory of America First

As world leaders convened for the UN General Assembly, Trump's team seized the opportunity to fold the North Korea confrontation into their larger view of US grand strategy. Decades earlier, Trump explained in his speech, governments had agreed to form an international organization "based on the vision that diverse nations could cooperate to protect their sovereignty, preserve their security, and promote their prosperity."[9] He continued in a steadily nationalist strain, "We do not expect diverse countries to share the same cultures, traditions or even systems of government." Instead, "we do expect all nations to uphold these two core sovereign duties, to respect the interests of their own people and the rights of every other sovereign nation." Sovereignty and state interest, not cooperation or some notion of global good, fundamentally defined the administration's strategic agenda. Trump expected no less from his compatriots in the chamber who "will always and should always put your countries first." In this vision, the sovereign state had proven the most effective tool at creating human welfare. This was designated "principled realism." Cooperation is necessary, but, for its part, the United States would no longer accept "one-sided" arrangements.

Bridging to North Korea, the speech stated that threats to sovereignty in places like Ukraine or the South China Sea should be challenged. For Trump himself, though, those particular issues rarely figured in his list of threats. He consistently treated Russia as a possible partner, and he sought to confront China on trade rather than geopolitics. Iran, however, was always a more pressing concern than Russia for the new president, and he listed it as a "rogue state" exporting terrorism. With North Korea, Trump ticked off the usual list of humanitarian and security violations: murder, authoritarianism, regional instability, nuclear proliferation. Which ones actually drove his policy was unclear. Moving to other topics, Trump cited "uncontrolled migration" as Middle East concern alongside Syria's chemical weapons and ISIS. Unchecked migration is, he explained, "deeply unfair to both the sending and the receiving countries." Many of Trump's other greatest hits appeared, including disproportionate

US monetary support for the United Nations, unfair trade deals, and "socialism" in Venezuela.

This UN speech remains a useful cipher to understand "America first." Regarding grand strategy *substance*, it explicitly unfolded a theory of state interests and prerogatives, a theory that dovetailed with Trump's longstanding personal intuitions and preferences. It also designated specific issue areas for particular focus. By contrast, "principled realism" was reaching its apex. McMaster along with others tried to inject this concept into public discourse and into the administration's rhetoric. It helped define the National Security Strategy later that year, but the phrase gained little traction. Further, this book's GSA framework interrogates gaps between the president, his senior officials, and government policy. In this case, gaps grew between figures like McMaster and Trump. A big tent concept, "principled realism" was designed to enfold the administration's competing foreign policy camps. Trump himself, however, rarely incorporated it into his extemporaneous speaking and tweeting. Over the next year, it disappeared.

Theory in Action, Preference at the Wheel

White House officials further consolidated their strategic vision over the following months. Toward Latin America, policy seemed to tack with Trump's personal priorities. In August, after Mike Pence led talks in Buenos Aires, the White House announced a trade deal to resume pork exports to Argentina for the first time since 1992.[10] A clean win on trade. With Venezuela, however, Trump—alarming his advisors—had actively entertained a possible US invasion.[11] For years, first under Hugo Chávez and now under Nicolás Maduro, the Venezuelan government had loudly touted its socialist policies and anti-American rhetoric. By 2017, however, the Venezuelan economy was faltering and, through 2018, would stutter into almost complete collapse. Meanwhile, the new US president often recounted his esteem for Venezuelan expats visiting one of his Florida golf clubs: "I've gotten to know them well. They are great, great people. We are going to take care of those people."[12] When the wife of a jailed political dissident visited the White House in February, Trump was impressed. Upending calibrated diplomatic policies, he tweeted a picture of her with him and Senator Marco Rubio (R-FL), a prominent advocate for Latin American relations. That summer, advisors talked him out of military action, though the question would reemerge.

In the meantime, Treasury Secretary Steven Mnuchin announced economic sanctions. Dubious election results had formally created a National Constituent Assembly (ANC) and effectively allowed Maduro's party to overrule the National Assembly.[13] Administration officials condemned the erosion of democracy and imposed sanctions to fit long-standing US strategic priorities. For Trump, avowedly opposed to exporting "our values," a hardline against Venezuela brought domestic political benefits. He could rhetorically accuse Democrats of being Venezuela-style "socialists," and Hispanic swing voters in Florida might appreciate an anti-Maduro line. Whatever the motivation, Trump seemed to have set Maduro and his rule into the "enemy" category. "What I'm told," explained former Obama NSC staffer Mark Feierstein, "is he has three top foreign policy interests—North Korea, Iran and Venezuela."[14]

Afghanistan indeed appeared to lay outside the president's core strategic priorities. As the previous chapter describes, Trump had announced a plan to "win" against the Taliban, but the White House remained silent about details. Journalists speculated that Trump had rushed the announcement to shift attention away from a boiling domestic controversy. (Two weeks prior, a neo-Nazi accelerated his car into a crowd of counterprotesters and killed one woman. The president inflamed national outrage by saying that there had been "some very fine people on both sides.") Crucially, though, Trump did promise that he was trusting his military team. They would devise an endgame for the US intervention that the current president had long considered a drain on US resources. In October, Mattis and the Joint Chiefs of Staff Chairman, Gen. Joseph Dunford, carried their revised strategy to briefings before the Senate Armed Services Committee and a House panel. "We intend," Mattis explained, "To drive fence-sitters and those who will see that we're not quitting this fight, to reconcile with the Afghan national government."[15] It was a Clausewitzian strategy: apply force to drive political bargaining. Tactically, this would mean shifting from a mission defined by supporting the Afghan National Army to expanding Special Forces cooperation with Afghan units. The approach would also authorize a wider range of situations in which US troops could call air strikes for ground support. Mattis said the push would include a small surge of about 3000 more US troops. This was dubbed R4+S: regionalize, realign, reinforce, reconciliation, and sustain. Military officials declined to set any timeframe. They hoped to convince the Taliban that their "one more year" mentality of waiting out the US commitment would fold. Trump, however, said little about the change. As ever, the gap between Trump's stated prerogatives and energy commitments and those of his foreign policy principals persisted. Instead, his gaze returned to familiar themes: trade, immigration, Iran, and North Korea.

CONSERVATIVE PROGRESS

Pushing Multiple Agendas

In early October, the president posed with senior military leaders for a photograph. They were headed to dinner after discussing Iran and North Korea. "Maybe it's the calm before the storm," Trump mused over the clicking cameras.[16] Sensing a scoop, journalists asked which front clouded the horizon. "You'll find out," Trump replied with a smile. During the meeting, he had reiterated that toward North Korea, "our goal is denuclearization" and that "we will do what we must do to prevent that from happening." He added Iran to his list of security concerns. Its government, he said, refused to honor the spirit of Obama's nuclear agreement, an agreement Trump had always criticized. Perhaps impatient with having some of his plans slow-walked by a wary Department of Defense, he commanded security officials "to provide me with a broad

range of military options, when needed, at a much faster pace." Through
that fall and winter, pressure slowly escalated on Trump's priority
concerns. The president was apparently pushing more effectively to
close the gap between his positions and those of his senior officials and
the US government. In turn, this meant that Trump's grand strategic
scope, substance, and *assertiveness* were more likely to directly shape
US grand strategy.

A week later, Trump refused to certify the Iran deal. Under the
agreement's terms, the Joint Compressive Plan of Action (JCPOA) was
to be certified by the US president every 90 days. In other words, he
was to confirm that the Iranian government was abiding by the letter of
the deal. The deal itself included China, France, Germany, the European
Union, Russia, and the United Kingdom, along with the United States and
Iran. Formally, Congress would actually have to withdraw the United
States, but the president was taking the first step in that process. By
most accounts, including US government agencies, Iran was, in fact,
following the agreement's technical standards. Iran was also, by most
accounts, supporting Assad in Syria, distributing weapons to American
enemies, and contesting Saudi Arabia for regional dominance. Regularly
confronted with recertifying what he called "one of the worst and most
one-sided transactions the United States has ever entered into," Trump
argued that the JCPOA "threw Iran's dictatorship a political and economic
lifeline."[17] Even Trump skeptics like Sen. John McCain (R-AZ) agreed that
Iran had been "literally getting away with murder."[18] Pushing the United
States to leave the deal could undermine US credibility, and, legally, it
would leave fault with the US rather than the Iranian government. Still,
Trump saw this as an opportunity to initiate a "new strategy." The United
States would work with allies to counter Iran's terror proxies, would
apply new sanctions, confront Iran's conventional weapons proliferation
and "deny the regime all paths to a nuclear weapon." Despite all this,
Trump's administration never specified a clear end state for US-Iran
relations. In fact, Republicans in Congress declined to reinstate sanctions
and lent the JCPOA 90 more days of life.[19]

Trump's second trip to Asia followed that November. He used the publicity to argue that he was both reasonable and tough. In South Korea, the president and his counterpart, Moon Jae-in, restated their hope that North Korea would denuclearize. Over previous months, the administration had been pushing a State Department pressure campaign started under the Obama administration. By October, over 20 governments had agreed to tighten trade relations with Pyongyang.[20] Now, Trump said he wanted North Koreans to "come to the table" and "hoped to God" that military force would not be necessary.[21] (At one point, either bargaining or simply unable to pass up an insult, Trump wondered why Kim would call him old. After all, "I would NEVER call him 'short and fat?'"[22]) His basic agenda, however, had not changed. Near the end of his trip, speaking before the Asia-Economic Cooperation meeting in Da Nang, Vietnam, Trump reiterated two of his core demands: that the United States secure more favorable—but still global—trade arrangements, and that partner governments unify in opposition to North Korea's nuclear program.[23]

Consistent trade nationalism characterized Trump's visit to China. He called the relationship "very unfair" and "one-sided," but he also admitted, "I don't blame China. After all, who can blame a country for being able to take advantage of another country for the sake of its citizens?"[24] His comments framed a signing ceremony for trade deals worth an estimated $250 billion. Still, relations remained fundamentally fraught. Within the month, US federal prosecutors would unseal indictments against three Chinese nationals for hacking proprietary systems and stealing trade secrets from Moody's Analytics, Siemens AG, and Trimble Inc. (respectively, an economic analysis firm, a manufacturing conglomerate, and a Global Positioning System technology manufacturer).[25] No Chinese government officials were charged, but the case highlighted a long-standing grievance. Americans argued that the Chinese government facilitated theft of private intellectual property. Sometimes directly conducted by government agents and sometimes farmed out to "private" hackers, the espionage raised red flags for US leaders. They believed that officials in Beijing also distributed that information to Chinese businesses. They could use the information to catch or leapfrog American industry. For years, US officials considered this behavior a serious trade violation as much as a geopolitical threat. Whether intellectual property drove Trump's trade agenda or it was simply a convenient *casus belli* may be unknowable. What is known is that through December and January, the administration started to wind up a more direct confrontation with China. McMaster characterized Chinese policy as "economic aggression."[26] Treasury Secretary Mnuchin stated that the United States was "in economic competition with China." Risking tautology, he argued that "this isn't about trade wars. This is about reciprocal fair trade. And if we have to protect American workers and put on tariffs or other things, where they don't have fair trade with us, the president will do that." Speaking at Johns Hopkins University a month later, Mattis enlarged the scope of US-China competition. He made a case for more defense spending even as Congress faced a shutdown over budget debates. "Great-power competition—not terrorism," he explained, "Is now the primary focus of U.S. national security."[27]

National Security Strategy

In part, Mattis was referencing a pair of major strategy documents, the National Security Strategy (NSS) and the National Defense Strategy (NDS). The NDS remained classified (aside from a summary), but the White House released the NSS in mid-December. Required by Congress in the 1986 Goldwater-Nichols Act, the NSS is supposed to be a summation of how the Executive Branch interprets and addresses national security threats. Appearing about every four years, it is as close to an explicit statement on grand strategy as is possible for the US government. It is a multi-agency affair, so change from one document to the next is typically not dramatic; nevertheless, administrations use the NSS to signal general changes to priorities and approaches. Ideal snapshots of contemporary grand strategy *scope*, *substance*, and *assertiveness*, they also provide analysts a well-defined baseline to evaluate consistency between stated policy and statements from senior officials.

In this 2017 edition, administration officials used "principled realism" to frame the whole. Without the Cold War to concentrate planning, claimed the background narrative, US strategy had drifted.[28] All the administrations since the early 1990s leaned heavily on liberal internationalist assumptions. They built strategic policy on the assumption that economic globalization and political integration would slowly transform autocracies. In fact, the NSS authors argued, foreign governments had taken advantage of US-led international arrangements. They wanted to shift the US strategic footing from global terror threats back to great power competition. Most notably, Russia and China, along with Iran and North Korea, had been left to push their agendas. Meanwhile, the United States cut its military funding and assets. Now, the United States faced an impending security and economic crisis. It risked permanent compromise of its own sovereignty as well as international security. In response, the Trump administration would, above all, invest in its traditional military and economic strengths. "An America that successfully competes," it reasoned, "is the best way to prevent conflict."[29] In reality, the NSS shifted long-standing emphases, but it was not radical. Homeland security, prosperity, "peace through strength," and American influence were familiar agendas. Investments in leading technology, confronting terror threats, securing global trade, and other priorities remained fundamentally the same as ever. The crucial shift would be to rebalance from asymmetrical war and terrorism to traditional great power threats.

Three emphases, however, did underscore the administration's unique agenda. The border and migration were highlighted more than prior administrations allowed. Trade would be defined as "free, fair, and reciprocal," which emphasized a nationalist framing. And, perhaps most profoundly if pursued, the United States would return to "overmatch" as its basic military goal. In other words, where prior administrations tried to reduce and streamline funding and resources for the military and then compensate with technology investments, the Trump administration wanted to return the United States to Cold War-style preparedness. This meant remaining able to confront multiple adversaries in multiple theaters and in every domain. In fact, that basic goal had never been abandoned; nevertheless, the NSS captured a consensus among both Trump's White House team and the Department of Defense that the United States needed to return to deterring traditional great powers rather than fighting asymmetrical adversaries. The authors also pepper "American values" throughout the text. It appears as a justification and a guiding agenda alongside power, security, and trade. Trump himself, however, rarely used such language. Overall, the document used the compromise language of "principled realism," but when interpreted by the Trump White House, it reflected the administration's "America first" agenda: realist power politics; zero-sum competition; and American values used to frame the administration's normative agenda, which emphasized American free enterprise and American sovereignty.

Reactions, as ever, reflected Trump as a human Rorschach test. Researcher Ilan Goldenberg said the strategy was "dead on arrival."[30] With the president committed neither to personal consistency nor to the document's basic principles, "it is plain impossible to execute such a strategy." By contrast, at the conservative newsmagazine *National Review*, columnist Jerry Hendrix struggled to find sufficient praise for the document. "Remarkably coherent" for an NSS developed in less than a year, it was a "realistic distillation" of post-Cold War strategy and then took that approach a step further by pushing for technological readiness, and it bluntly stated that the United States needed to confront Russia and China as serious "great-power competition."[31] Evaluating strategy toward China, scholar Dingding Chen agreed that "this is a huge signal."[32] US officials were arguing that the "rules-based order" was now under siege from all sides. US foreign policy elites were grappling with how to maintain lead power status as well as confront rising challenges, particularly from China. "This shift," he concluded, "Means that the strategic repositioning of past U.S. administrations is being undone, and one can even say that the United States has also entered a new era." Richard Fontaine, president of the Washington think tank Center for A New American Security (CNAS), was studiously balanced. "The new strategy," he surmised, "Could mark a belated shift from a campaign-style approach to foreign policy to a more balanced and mature version."[33] Under most presidents, such a transition should be expected. Still, "it might simply be ignored, a valiant attempt to pull the administration in the direction of global leadership at a moment when presidential instincts and political winds are blowing the opposite way."

THE TRUMP AGENDA

Consolidating Control

New Year's Eve 2017 saw Donald Trump at Mar-A-Lago. The president spent time on his golf course, tweeted happy new year to "all of my friends, supporters, enemies, haters, and even the very dishonest Fake News Media," and hosted a red carpet gala where individual tickets for club members ran $750.[34] Outside the "Winter White House," Trump also notched a win against the United Nations, where the General Assembly agreed to cut the organization's budget by five percent.[35] How to interpret this Trumpian New Year likely depends on one's view of Trump. It was either classy or crass, practical-minded or short-sighted.

This ambiguity persisted as the president's grand strategy approach increasingly diverged from more mainstream Republican views. Still, many experts found the details and execution feckless. They also suspected that the administration's agendas would founder simply because, by this point, it was clear that the White House was suffering unprecedented personnel turnover and continued to elevate relative novices to positions of major influence.[36] On Middle East policy, for instance, Jared Kushner and a Trump Organization lawyer, Jason Greenblatt, were tasked along with the ambassador to Israel to work up a comprehensive peace plan. Neither Kushner nor Greenblatt brought any diplomatic experience.[37] Trump's core team waved away the critique. They argued that advancing US interests always leaves skeptics dissatisfied. The White House also publicized a bullet-pointed list of President Trump's foreign policy accomplishments.[38] These included setting tougher border and migration policies, military progress against ISIS, ratcheting pressure on North Korea, declining to certify the Iran deal, enforcing a hard line on chemical weapons, pushing for more military spending and capacity, advocating regional "quadrilateral cooperation" with Australia, India, and Japan, taking major foreign trips, and—less plausibly—"revitaliz[ing] the NATO alliance." Again, observers read this list as either demonstration of success for "America first" or a grab bag of semi-failures.

Favored Friends

Throughout that winter and early spring of 2018, new aspects of Trump's agenda emerged piecemeal. In a remarkable, but not surprising, move, the White House announced that the United States would recognize Jerusalem as Israel's capital. For decades, US administrations supported Israel but argued that Jerusalem's status should be part of a final deal with the Palestinians. Trump's White House officially announced that Congress' 1995 Jerusalem Embassy Act called for formal recognition. It would follow that standard.[39] One conservative commentator described this policy simply as "a victory for common sense." The move also perfectly squared with Trump's campaign promises to conservative Christians, and it supported his budding relationship with Israel's conservative prime minister, Benjamin Netanyahu.[40] As defined in Chapter 1, the pattern of thought and policy that characterized Trump's grand strategy could not be easily disentangled from his political and personal agendas.

Meanwhile, Russia remained the primary issue in which Trump consistently seemed to diverge even from some of his core Congressional supporters. The FBI's independent investigation under Special Counsel Robert Mueller quietly rolled forward. Mueller's team sought to uncover the scope and type of alleged Russian efforts, including possible conspiracy —often loosely referred to as "collusion"—with Trump campaign officials during the 2016 election. Late on a Friday in mid-February, the investigators made public an indictment against 13 Russian nationals. It detailed their specific plans and actions throughout 2016 to manipulate US voters through social media. No charges against Americans appeared, but, fueling frustration from the president, the investigation would persist for another year. Interpretations of the administration's motivations diverged. At the State Department, Rex Tillerson ended the office of Coordinator for Sanctions Policy and moved the function to the policy planning office. Earlier, the United States had missed an October 1 Congressional deadline to implement sanctions against Russia. Now, Democrats worried that the administration was using Tillerson's agency reorganization to, in fact, consolidate the president's nationalist agenda and, more specifically, soft peddle Congress's bipartisan hardline against Russia. When Treasury Secretary Mnuchin announced that the US government would impose new sanctions on 24 Russian organizations and individuals associated with the 2016 election, critics worried that the response had been slow and underdeveloped.[41]

That same month, March 2018, news broke that a former Russian spy and expatriate, Sergei V. Skripal and his daughter nearly were killed by a weapons-grade nerve agent. Unusual, certainly, the assassination attempt was stunning for many in the West because it occurred as the pair sat on a bench in a quiet English town. Prime Minister Theresa May called it a possible "unlawful use of force" and condemned "such a brazen act to murder innocent civilians on our soil."[42] Trump himself remained relatively quiet on the matter, but two weeks later, the US government joined over two dozen European governments expelling a large number of Russian diplomats from their countries' delegations.[43] Mattis, subtly breaking with Trump, was unequivocal. NATO had tried to work with Russia, but close cooperation, "regrettably, by Russia's choice, is now a thing of the past." Russia, he said, had clearly become a "strategic competitor" to the Western democracies, not just the United States.[44] When Syrian civilians suffered another chemical attack, Tillerson stated that "Russia ultimately bears responsibility."[45] Trump himself, however, continued to talk about Russia as a possible partner.

Relations with North Korea, meanwhile, saw a remarkable turn. On March 8, White House officials announced that Donald Trump had agreed to meet personally with Kim Jong Un. Leading up to this startling development, observers struggled to make sense of a relationship that seemed to tumble from a war spiral to open dialogue. In early January, South Korea and the United States had announced that they would not hold military exercises during the Winter Olympics, hosted by South Korea. At the same time, North and South Korea announced their own high-level talks.[46] In turn, North Korea agreed to send athletes to the games.[47] Such optimistic symbolism was tempered. Days before arriving in South Korea to visit the games, Vice President Mike Pence said that "the United States of America will soon unveil the toughest and most aggressive round of economic sanctions on North Korea ever."[48] For administration officials, tough sanctions and rhetoric had brought North Korea to the edge of cooperation. Ratcheting the pressure seemed sensible. Then, South Korea's US envoy Chung Eui-yong arrived the in Oval Office with news. South Korean officials had determined that Kim was "frank and sincere" about meeting with Trump about ending his nuclear program and the potential for a breakthrough summit.[49] As journalists Peter Baker and Choe Sang-Hung describe the meeting, "Mr. Trump accepted on the spot, stunning not only Mr. Chung and the other high-level South Koreans who were with him, but also the phalanx of American officials who were gathered in the Oval Office." Tillerson later suggested that Kim's position had suddenly changed "in a fairly dramatic way" and that "in all honesty that came as a little bit of a surprise to us."[50]

The meeting would be a first between a US and a North Korean leader. Indeed, a presidential one-on-one had been a diplomatic and public relations goal of North Korean negotiators for decades. Critics worried that Trump was giving away his leverage. Mattis and McMaster "both expressed caution," but "Mr. Trump brushed them off." Tillerson later insisted that Trump had considered this option "for quite some time," and a White House official reasoned that "it made sense to accept an invite to meet with the one person who can actually make decisions" rather than repeating the "long slog of the past." Conservative Trump skeptic and scholar Kori Schake argued that the administration deserved some credit for, to date, effectively managing this issue.[51] Administration officials had coordinated with, and given prominent visibility to, their South Korean partners. Their "maximum pressure" push had been consistent across the government and had opened a window for those negotiators. In Schake's view, the administration was seeking the wrong policy; nevertheless, she admitted, it had just notched an early success with its preferred policy. Trump himself later insisted that the United States would not ease its economic pressure until the North Koreans truly ended their nuclear program, but he also inflated expectations by publicly musing that "there's a great celebration to be had" in Korea's Demilitarized Zone (DMZ) if he scored a successful negotiation.[52]

Closer to home, administration nationalists pushed increasingly confrontational trade policies. In one notorious tweet in early March, Trump explained, "When a country (USA) is losing many billions of dollars on trade with virtually every country it does business with, trade wars are good, and easy to win."[53] Internationalists were aghast. Global economics, they argued, relied upon an open US economy that played within the rules and the organizations it had supported for decades.[54] A day prior, the president announced a 25 percent steel tariff and a ten percent aluminum tariff. In response, the Dow Jones industrial average dropped 420 points. For Trump and others, this was a necessary and natural culmination of American trade grievances. Already, the administration was aggressively renegotiating NAFTA. Other governments had been warned to play ball ever since Trump's inauguration. Nevertheless, though economists and business leaders had praised—or at least appreciated the need for—the GOP's 2017 tax reform bill, they carefully watched the president's call for retaliation against what he called the European Union's "very unfair" trade policies.[55]

Many Republicans were also nervous. House Speaker Paul Ryan (R-WI) and others privately warned the president that this tariff move could be politically unpopular and economically damaging; however, though trade fell within Congress' constitutional purview, Ryan and others did not publicly float any legislative alternative to Trump's trade war policy.[56] Inside the White House, some officials worried that Trump launched this policy in a fit of pique rather than after careful strategizing. Agitated by developments in the Mueller investigation and a White House personnel drama, he become "unglued" and, feeling confrontational, abruptly sided with Commerce Secretary Wilbur Ross and White House trade director Peter Navarro over the advice of Mnuchin and National Economic Council chair Gary Cohn.[57] The White House had prepared no official statement on the policy, no diplomatic strategy, and no legislative plan. Officials at the State, Treasury, and Defense Departments received no prior notice. Days later, Cohn—a "free-trade-oriented Democrat" per the *New York Times*—announced his resignation.[58] Whatever Cohn's motivation, which he did not spell out, the move left economic nationalists like Ross and Navarro clearly ascendant.

"PRINCIPLED REALISM" AND ITS DISCONTENTS

Over a stunning three weeks, two major figures joined Cohn: Secretary of State Tillerson and National Security Advisor McMaster. On March 13, Trump announced that Tillerson would be leaving, and that Mike Pompeo would transition from CIA Director to Secretary of State. For months, Tillerson and Trump—in both public and private—had diverged temperamentally and on policy.[59] In perhaps the most famous and telling episode, after a key meeting in summer 2017, Tillerson pointedly declined to deny leaks that had called his boss a "fucking moron." In a final break, Tillerson supported the UK government's condemnation of Russia—based on intelligence shared with the United States—for its apparent assassination attempt on Sergei Skripal. Trump, however, said he wanted to wait for more information rather than simply join the British government. The morning after his statement, Tillerson learned with the rest of the world via tweet that he would be replaced.[60] Expert observers tended to agree that Tillerson had fumbled the job. He was private in a job requiring high visibility, and he had cratered morale in his agency with a series of cuts and reorganizations. In one scathing assessment, economics Nobel laureate and liberal commentator Paul Krugman tweeted, "On one side, he was surely the worst Secretary of State since William Jennings Bryan. On the other, he was surely fired not for his failings but for his occasional lapses into principle."[61] On most major policy issues, Tillerson preferred caution and preserving America's existing system of alliances and agreements. In other words, he favored a conventional US grand strategy. The gaps between that preference and the president's nationalist positions only grew.

Just over a week later, Trump issued another personnel tweet. This time, McMaster was out. Rumors had swirled since February about the National Security Advisor's demise. He was never favored by Trump, who disliked the general's personal style and often dumped his advisor's carefully developed policy and strategic positions in favor of more nationalist or more confrontational approaches.[62] More startling for close observers is that Trump appointed John Bolton to serve as his next National Security Advisor. Bolton was a well-known, and often feared, national security professional. He had served as George W. Bush's ambassador to the UN and gained particular prominence for his neoconservative positions and his skepticism of international organizations. Trump regularly saw Bolton on Fox News and liked his tough talk and skeptical eye towards internationalism as well as toward Iran and North Korea; however, Bolton favored interventionism. Commentators shared a mix of fear that Bolton might make war more likely and bewilderment about how Bolton and Trump would synchronize their divergent views of military force and global leadership.[63]

In Sum

"Principled realism" had finally spun apart. Over Trump's first months in office, doctrinaire nationalists like Steve Bannon were pushed out of the administration. Now, at the other end of the Trump team, many of the so-called "adults in the room" (career professionals with relatively mainstream views), were departing. To replace them, Trump chose men with whom he thought he could work. The decision was personal as much as it was policy driven. Neither Pompeo nor Bolton would likely, on his own, be characterized as a nationalist; however, their conservative and hardline approaches, along with their personal temperaments, resonated with the president's preferences. Stated in this study's analytical terms, Trump was pushing for more consistency and fewer gaps between his positions and those of his government.

The president's preference to churn through rhetoric, policies, and personnel had spun off both unusually strident nationalists as well as many staid and careful mainstream practitioners. What was emerging seemed to reflect the president's tough-talking temperamental approach and nationalist policy preferences. Indeed, Trump's basic intuitions on *scope*, *substance*, and *assertiveness* remained relatively consistent. He wanted to engage the entire world but treat most governments as neither friends nor foes. He saw international politics and economics as thoroughly zero-sum, and he saw little need to tend to issues that did not directly affect the perceived interests of his base supporters. He wanted to expand military spending and to apply "maximum pressure" against trade and security threats, but he declined to expand US military commitments. Unfortunately for the administration, implementation remained messy and did not seem to enhance US credibility or influence. One observer sympathetic to Trump, Elliot Abrams, observed that military professionals and old hands around the president constantly battled to "constrain him, contain him, discipline him, box him in."[64] For Abrams, US security policy was not hitting a stride for this reason, and the solution would be a new set of personalities, like CIA director Mike Pompeo, who resonated with Trump's more intuitive, free-flowing (or perhaps undisciplined) style. Scholar and sometime Republican supporter Daniel W. Drezner, by contrast, recognized Trump's willingness to accept risk and take concrete strategic steps like reemphasizing "the Quad" cooperation between Australia, Japan, India, and the United States.[65] Unfortunately, explained Drezner, Trump's "I alone" mentality and "his mixture of erratic security pledges, mercantilist economic policy and transactional values is less appetizing to the rest of the world than he realizes." Every effort to implement his grand strategy would always "fail miserably" for this reason. Untested by an external crisis, administration officials wrestled with one another, with domestic political challenges, and with the sprawling commitments of the world's leading power.

NOTES

1. Donald Trump, "Full text: Trump's 2017 U.N. speech transcript," *Politico*, September 19, 2017, https://www.politico.com/story/2017/09/19/trump-un-speech-2017-full-text-transcript-242879.
2. Staff, "North Korea 'will be taken care of': Trump," *SBS News*, April 14, 2017, https://www.sbs.com.au/news/north-korea-will-be-taken-care-of-trump.
3. Staff, "North Korea crisis: Rex Tillerson urges international response," BBC News, April 28, 2017, https://www.bbc.com/news/world-asia-39749 670. Staff, "North Korea missile test: regime has 'disrespected China', says Donald Trump," *The Guardian*, April 29, 2017, https://www.theguardian.com/world/2017/apr/28/north-korea-test-fires-ballistic-missile.
4. Staff, "FACT SHEET: Resolution 2371 (2017) Strengthening Sanctions on North Korea," New York: United States Mission to the United Nations, August 5, 2017, https://usun.state.gov/remarks/7924.
5. Abby Hamblin, "Trump threatens 'fire and fury,' North Korea 'considering' strike on Guam," *The San Diego Tribune*, August 8, 2017, https://www.sandiegouniontribune.com/opinion/the-conversation/sd-north-korea-nuclear-weapons-20170808-htmlstory.html.
6. Joby Warrick, Ellen Nakashima, and Anna Fifield, "North Korea now making missile-ready nuclear weapons, U.S. analysts say," *The Washington Post*, August 8, 2017, https://www.washingtonpost.com/world/national-security/north-korea-now-making-missile-ready-nuclear-weapons-us-analysts-say/2017/08/08/e14b882a-7b6b-11e7-9d08-b79f191668ed_story.html?utm_term=.eb082180d43e.
7. Julian Borger, "US defense chief warns North Korea that it risks the 'destruction of its people,'" *The Guardian*, August 9, 2017, https://www.theguardian.com/world/2017/aug/09/north-korea-us-rex-tillerson-nuclear-war-threat.
8. Jacob Pramuk, "Trump: Maybe 'fire and fury' statement on North Korea wasn't tough enough," *CNBC*, August 10, 2017, https://www.cnbc.com/20 17/08/10/trump-maybe-fire-and-fury-statement-on-north-korea-wasnt-tough-enough.html.
9. Trump, "Trump's 2017 U.N. speech transcript."

10. Spencer Chase, "US pork cleared for export to Argentina," *AgriPulse*, August 17, 2017, https://www.agri-pulse.com/articles/9736-us-pork-cleared-for-export-to-argentina.

11. Joshua Goodman, "President Trump Pressed Aides About an Invasion of Venezuela, Says a U.S. Official," Associated Press, July 4, 2018, https://apnews.com/a3309c4990ac4581834d4a654f7746ef.

12. Jonathan Swan, "Inside Trump's Venezuela Pivot," *Axios*, February 24, 2019, https://www.axios.com/venezuela-donald-trump-foreign-policy-strategy-7f04c3da-fd30-4038-8fd1-e057b15c7f83.html.

13. Christine Wang, "Treasury sanctions Venezuelan President Nicolas Maduro," CNBC, July 31, 2017, https://www.cnbc.com/2017/07/31/treasury-sanctions-venezuelan-president-nicolas-maduro.html.

14. David Nakamura, "How an Oval Office meeting led to a Trump tweet that changed U.S. policy toward Venezuela," *The Washington Post*, October 6, 2017, https://www.washingtonpost.com/politics/how-an-oval-office-meeting-led-to-a-trump-tweet-that-changed-us-policy-toward-venezuela/2017/10/06/87e9b178-a52b-11e7-ade1-76d061d56efa_story.html?utm_term=.fe5c7fc4c0fb.

15. Jamie McIntyre and Travil J. Tritten, "Jim Mattis breaks down the new Afghanistan strategy: The goal, the plan, what's different and how it all ends," *The Washington Examiner*, October 4, 2017, https://www.washingtonexaminer.com/jim-mattis-breaks-down-the-new-afghanistan-strategy-the-goal-the-plan-whats-different-and-how-it-all-ends.

16. Jeff Mason, "In meeting with military, Trump talks of 'calm before the storm,'" *Reuters*, October 5, 2017, https://www.reuters.com/article/us-usa-trump-military/in-meeting-with-military-trump-talks-of-calm-before-the-storm-idUSKBN1CB03C.

17. Donald Trump, "Remarks by President Trump on Iran Strategy." Washington, DC: The White House, October 13, 2017, https://www.whitehouse.gov/briefings-statements/remarks-president-trump-iran-strategy/.

18. Ben Riley-Sith and Rob Crilly, "Donald Trump refuses to certify Iran nuclear deal," *The Telegraph*, October 13, 2017, https://www.telegraph.co.uk/news/2017/10/13/donald-trump-expected-promise-tough-action-iran-landmark-speech/.

19. Zeeshan Aleem, "Trump punted the Iran deal to Congress. Congress just punted it back," *Vox*, December 12, 2017, https://www.vox.com/policy-and-politics/2017/12/12/16767908/trump-sanctions-iran-deal-congress.

20. Paul Sonne and Felicia Schwartz, "U.S. Pressure on North Korea's Global Ties Bears Fruit," *The Wall Street Journal*, October 8, 2017, https://www.wsj.com/articles/state-department-pressure-on-north-koreas-global-ties-bears-fruit-1507492004.
21. Staff, "Trump urges N Korea to 'come to table' over nuclear issue," BBC News, November 7, 2017, https://www.bbc.com/news/world-asia-4189 6635.
22. Cited in Daniel W. Drezner, "Why Donald Trump's foreign policy ambitions will always collapse," *The Washington Post*, November 13, 2017, https://www.washingtonpost.com/news/posteverything/wp/2017/11/1 3/why-donald-trumps-foreign-policy-ambitions-will-always-collapse/?utm_term=.2f6d8031a528.
23. Donald Trump, Remarks by President Trump at APEC CEO Summit. Da Nang, Vietnam, November 10, 2017, https://www.whitehouse.gov/briefings-statements/remarks-president-trump-apec-ceo-summit-da-nang-vietnam/.
24. Staff, "Trump does not blame China for 'unfair' trade," BBC News, November 9, 2017, https://www.bbc.com/news/business-41924797.
25. United States of America v. Wu Yingzhuo, Dong Hao, and Xia Lei, No. 17-247, filed September 13, 2017, U.S. District Court, Western District of Pennsylvania, https://www.justice.gov/opa/press-release/file/10138 66/download.
26. Toluse Olorunnipa and Margaret Talev. "Trump 'America First' Plan Sees China, Russia as U.S. Frenemies," *Bloomberg*, December 18, 2017, https://www.bloomberg.com/news/articles/2017-12-18/trump-to-declare-china-strategic-competitor-in-security-speech.
27. Dan Lamothe, "Mattis unveils new strategy focused on Russia and China, takes Congress to task for budget impasse," *The Washington Post*, January 19, 2018, https://www.washingtonpost.com/news/checkpoint/wp/2018 /01/19/mattis-calls-for-urgent-change-to-counter-russia-and-china-in-new-pentagon-strategy/?utm_term=.0f9d11523de8.
28. White House, *National Security Strategy of the United States of America*, Washington, DC, December 20, 2017, https://www.whitehouse.gov/wp-content/uploads/2017/12/NSS-Final-12-18-2017-0905.pdf. p2.
29. Ibid., 3
30. Ilan Goldenberg, "Trump's National Security Plan is Pure Fantasy," *Newsweek*, December 18, 2017.
31. Jerry Hendrix, "Trump's New National-Security Strategy Projects Confidence," *National Review*, December 18, 2017, https://www.

nationalreview.com/2017/12/donald-trump-foreign-policy-increases-defense-capability/.

32. Dingding Chen, "The Trump Administration's National Security and National Defense Strategies Reveal a Change in Mindset Toward China," *The Diplomat*, January 26, 2018, https://thediplomat.com/2018/01/the-trump-administrations-national-security-and-national-defense-strategies-reveal-a-change-in-mindset-toward-china/.

33. Richard Fotaine, "Trump Should Min the Gaps in His National Security Strategy," *War on the Rocks*, December 21, 2017, https://warontherocks.com/2017/12/trump-mind-gaps-national-security-strategy/.

34. Emily Cochrane and Michael S. Schmidt, "For Trump, a Glittering Gala Ends a Winter Vacation Rooted in Routine," *The New York Times*, December 31, 2017, https://www.nytimes.com/2017/12/31/us/politics/trump-new-years-eve-mar-a-lago.html. Alexandra Clough, "EXCLUSIVE: Sources tell Post prices upped for Trump's New Year's Eve party," *The Palm Beach Post*, November 28, 2018, https://www.palmbeachpost.com/news/20181128/exclusive-sources-tell-post-prices-upped-for-trumps-new-years-eve-party.

35. Editorial Board, "Trump Gets the U.N. to Cut Spending," *The Wall Street Journal*, January 1, 2018, https://www.wsj.com/articles/trump-gets-the-u-n-to-cut-spending-1514839180?mod=searchresults&page=55&pos=1.

36. Jeff Shesol, "A Year Into The Trump Era, White House Staff Turnover Is 'Off The Charts,'" *The New Yorker*, December 15, 2017, https://www.newyorker.com/news/news-desk/a-year-into-the-trump-era-white-house-staff-turnover-is-off-the-charts.

37. Michael Warren, "The Man with Trump's Peace Plan," *The Weekly Standard* 23, no. 3 (2017): 17–19.

38. White House, "President Donald J. Trump's First Year of Foreign Policy Accomplishments. Fact Sheets," Washington, DC, December 19, 2017, https://www.whitehouse.gov/briefings-statements/president-donald-j-trumps-first-year-of-foreign-policy-accomplishments/.

39. White House, *Presidential Proclamation Recognizing Jerusalem as the Capital of the State of Israel and Relocating the United States Embassy to Israel to Jerusalem*, Proclamation, Foreign Policy, Donald Trump, Washington, DC. December 6, 2017, https://www.whitehouse.gov/presidential-actions/presidential-.proclamation-recognizing-jerusalem-capital-state-israel-relocating-united-states-embassy-israel-jerusalem/.

40. Elliott Abrams, "A Capital Idea," *The Weekly Standard* 23, no. 15 (2017): 16–17.

41. Elana Schor, Andrew Restuccia, and Cory Bennett, "U.S. imposes new sanctions on Russian entities over 2016 election meddling," *Politico*, March 15, 2018, https://www.politico.com/story/2018/03/15/us-russia-sanctions-election-meddling-465475.
42. Ellen Barry and Richard Pérez-Peña, "Britain Blames Moscow for Poisoning of Former Russian Spy," *The New York Times*, March 12, 2019, https://www.nytimes.com/2018/03/12/world/europe/uk-russia-spy-poisoning.html.
43. Angela Dewan, Milena Veselinovic, and Carol Jordan, "These are all the countries that are expelling Russian diplomats," CNN, March 28, 2018, https://www.cnn.com/2018/03/26/europe/full-list-of-russian-diplomats-expelled-over-s-intl/index.html.
44. Dave Majumdar, "Mattis: Russia Has Chosen To Be a 'Strategic Competitor,'" *National Interest*, March 27, 2018, https://nationalinterest.org/blog/the-buzz/mattis-russia-has-chosen-be-strategic-competitor-25105.
45. Cristiano Lima, "Tillerson: Russia 'bears responsibility' for suspected chemical attack in Syria," *Politico*, January 23, 2018, https://www.politico.com/story/2018/01/23/rex-tillerson-russia-syria-359092.
46. Min Sun Lee, "North and South Korea Agree to High-Level Talks Next Week," *The Wall Street Journal*, January 4, 2018, https://www.wsj.com/articles/north-and-south-korea-agree-to-hold-high-level-talks-next-week-1515122447?mod=searchresults&page=53&pos=14.
47. Choe Sang-Hun, "North Korea to Send Olympians to South Korea, in Breakthrough," *The New York Times*, January 8, 2018, https://www.nytimes.com/2018/01/08/world/asia/north-korea-south-olympics-border-talks.html.
48. Louis Nelson, "Ahead of Olympics, Pence says U.S. will impose new sanctions on North Korea," *Politico*, February 7, 2018, https://www.politico.com/story/2018/02/07/sanctions-north-korea-mike-pence-395965.
49. Peter Baker and Choe Sang-Hun, "With Snap 'Yes' in Oval Office, Trump Gambles on North Korea," *The New York Times*, March 10, 2018, https://www.nytimes.com/2018/03/10/world/asia/trump-north-korea.html.
50. Ali Vitali, "President Trump agrees to meet with North Korea's Kim Jong Un," *NBC News*, March 8, 2019, https://www.nbcnews.com/politics/white-house/south-koreans-deliver-letter-trump-kim-jong-un-n855051.

51. Kori Schake, "Give Trump Credit for the North Korea Opening," *The Atlantic*, March 12, 2018, https://www.theatlantic.com/international/archive/2018/03/trump-north-korea/555341/.

52. On economic pressure, see Michael R. Gordon, Jonathan Cheng, and Michael C. Bender. "Trump Will Tell Kim Jong Un That Dismantling Nuclear Arsenal Must Precede Economic Benefits," *The Wall Street Journal*, April 22, 2018, https://www.wsj.com/articles/trump-will-tell-kim-jong-un-that-dismantling-nukes-must-precede-economic-benefits-1524433979?mod=searchresults&page=1&pos=20. On Trump's optimism, see Mark Landler, "Trump, Hoping for 'Great Celebration,' Wants to Hold North Korea Talks in DMZ," *The New York Times*, April 30, 2018.

53. Thomas Franck, "Trump doubles down: 'Trade wars are good, and easy to win,'" CNBC, March 2, 2018, https://www.cnbc.com/2018/03/02/trump-trade-wars-are-good-and-easy-to-win.html.

54. Chad P. Bown, "Trump has announced massive aluminum and steel tariffs. Here are 5 things you need to know," *The Washington Post*, March 1, 2018, https://www.washingtonpost.com/news/monkey-cage/wp/2018/03/01/trump-has-announced-massive-aluminum-and-steel-tariffs-here-are-5-things-you-need-to-know/?utm_term=.ff59fb53d20d.

55. Wiktor Szary and Emre Peker, "President Trump Hints at Retaliation Against EU for Unfair Trade Policies," *The Wall Street Journal*, January 28, 2018, https://www.wsj.com/articles/president-trump-hints-at-retaliation-against-eu-for-unfair-trade-policies-1517157101?mod=searchresults&page=4&pos=20.

56. Rachael Bade, Burgess Everett, and Doug Palmer. "Republicans blitz Trump to head off tariffs," *Politico*, March 3, 2018, https://www.politico.com/story/2018/03/05/trump-tariffs-republican-response-436382.

57. Stephanie Ruhle, "Trump was angry and 'unglued' when he started a trade war, officials say," NBC, March 2, 2018, https://www.nbcnews.com/politics/white-house/trump-was-angry-unglued-when-he-started-trade-war-officials-n852641.

58. Kate Kelly and Maggie Haberman, "Gary Cohn Says He Will Resign as Trump's Top Economic Adviser," *The New York Times*, March 6, 2018, https://www.nytimes.com/2018/03/06/us/politics/gary-cohn-resigns.html.

59. Peter Baker, Gardiner Harris, and Mark Landler, "Trump Fires Rex Tillerson and Will Replace Him With C.I.A. Chief Pompeo," *The New York Times*, March 13, 2018, https://www.nytimes.com/2018/03/13/us/politics/trump-tillerson-pompeo.html?smid=tw-share. That December, Tillerson

observed that Trump *tries* not to act on impulse, is "pretty undisciplined ... doesn't read briefing reports" and often, wittingly or otherwise, attempted to take illegal actions. Aaron Blake, "Rex Tillerson on Trump: 'Undisciplined, doesn't like to read' and tries to do illegal things," *The Washington Post*, December 7, 2018, https://www.washingtonpost.com/ politics/2018/12/07/rex-tillerson-trump-undisciplined-doesnt-like-read-tries-do-illegal-things/?utm_term=.f96a46d815ec.

60. David Frum, "Why Did Trump Fire Tillerson Now?" *The Atlantic*, March 13, 2018, https://www.theatlantic.com/politics/archive/2018/03/exodus-rex/555473/.

61. Paul Krugman (@paulkrugman), Twitter, March 13, 2018, 6:02 a.m., https://twitter.com/paulkrugman/status/973544891811794944?lang=en.

62. Alex Ward, "Trump's national security adviser, H. R. McMaster, is out. It was a long time coming," *Vox*, March 22, 2018, https://www.vox.com/ 2018/3/22/16065042/hr-mcmaster-trump-john-bolton-fired.

63. Colin Kahl and Jon Wolfsthal, "John Bolton is a National Security Threat," *Foreign Policy*, March 23, 2018, https://foreignpolicy.com/2018/03/23/ john-bolton-is-a-national-security-threat/; David Frum, "What Trump's Choice of Bolton Reveals," *The Atlantic*, March 23, 2018, https://www. theatlantic.com/politics/archive/2018/03/what-trumps-choice-of-bolton-reveals/556352/; Peter Feaver, "Give John Bolton a Chance," *Foreign Policy*, March 23, 2019, https://foreignpolicy.com/2018/03/23/give-john-bolton-a-chance/.

64. Abrams, "A Capital Idea."

65. Daniel W. Drezner, "Why Donald Trump's foreign policy ambitions will always collapse," *The Washington Post*, November 13, 2017, https://www. washingtonpost.com/news/posteverything/wp/2017/11/13/why-donald-trumps-foreign-policy-ambitions-will-always-collapse/?utm_term=.68 d54354e06f.

CHAPTER 6

DONALD TRUMP
IS A NATIONALIST

SUMMER AND FALL 2018

Midterm election season turned into a desperate fight for President Trump and the Republicans. Democrats were highly energized. Both Trump and the GOP's legislative record had proven consistently unpopular. For Trump, losing a majority in either the House or Senate would threaten his agenda and possibly hobble his grand strategy ambitions. It might also lead to Congressional investigations. Some Democrats talked about impeachment. Thus, when Republican incumbent senator Ted Cruz of Texas faced an unexpectedly tight race, Trump flew to Houston to rally his supporters. Nearly two years into his administration, the president's pitch revealed grand strategy *scope*, *substance*, and *assertiveness* now firmly consolidated around Trump's own "America first" preferences.

During their first months in office, White House officials tried to bridge the divide between the administration's nationalists and its more conventional Republican internationalists. In one interview, Trump himself insisted that "I'm both" a nationalist and a globalist.[1] As Chapter 5 shows, however, by spring 2018, Trump had fully reorganized his personnel and firmly established his strategic priorities. As one observer noted, he finally had "the White House he always wanted."[2] When he was a private citizen in Trump Tower, "There was no business plan, no development strategy, no layers of authority; instead, Trump would come up with an idea, work it up in his head, and tell one of his hand-picked diamonds in the rough to get moving on it." Now in the White House, Trump allowed his team members to fight amongst themselves— and, less directly, with him—until he found people whose temperaments synced with his and who were willing to flesh out and implement his national security preferences.

Rallying his base in Houston, the president was clear about which agenda now reigned. "A globalist," he explained, "is a person that wants the globe to do well, frankly not caring about our country so much. And you know what? We can't have that."[3] He admitted that, instead, he preferred an old-fashioned word to describe himself: "I'm a nationalist, OK—I'm a nationalist. Use that word."

Whether Trump's nationalism fundamentally altered US grand strategy was less clear. As the GSA approach suggests, individual leaders matter to grand strategy, both as agents and as indicators of *other* types of influences. These influences could include variables ranging from strategic culture to relative power to geography. In these first two years, despite his efforts, Trump could not escape domestic institutional and international systemic constraints on US grand strategy. In one incident that July, the president tweeted a threat against Iran: "NEVER, EVER THREATEN THE UNITED STATES AGAIN OR YOU WILL SUFFER CONSEQUENCES THE LIKES OF WHICH FEW THROUGHOUT HISTORY HAVE EVER SUFFERED BEFORE."[4] Concerned headlines flew around the world. Trump's senior foreign policy principals were besieged with questions. The National Security Advisor, John Bolton, confirmed that be believed the president was serious.[5] Iran's Foreign Minister Mohammad Javad Zarif replied, also via tweet, "COLOR US UNIMPRESSED."[6] Indeed, within days, the incident had largely disappeared from the president's agenda. Administration officials returned to an Iran policy that Trump and his team had started unfurling over the previous year. Most media, Americans, and foreign governments seemed to assume that Trump was not particularly serious about this extravagant threat, and many speculated that he was really blowing off steam after feeling frustrated about—or deliberately trying to distract from—his recent, now-notorious, press conference with Russian President Vladimir Putin (described elsewhere).[7] When news broke in October that the president insisted on using his personal phone despite its known vulnerability to hacking, staffers stunned journalists by insisting that the problem was not as dire as it might seem. Trump, they admitted, typically knew too few operational details on any given topic to cause real harm.[8] Alternatively, maybe the president was indeed playing a long game with Iran and wanted to bid up tensions only to negotiate later. Not unlike Richard Nixon's "madman theory," his standard approach for decades had been to inflate his position, which he combined with a willingness to cause havoc in order to pressure his target. Whatever Trump's motivation, most observers now seemed to assume that the president's comments on any given day could not or should not be treated as directly shaping US policy positions. US grand strategy had become a mix of unpredictable, often short-lived, eruptions coupled with steady, relatively conventional policy work.

This chapter covers spring 2018 through the November midterm election. It will complement Chapters 3, 4, and 5 as a history of Trump's first two years of grand strategy. And as with those chapters, it seeks to set out the content and decisions that shaped the administration's most prominent strategic efforts. The final chapter, in turn, uses this material to define Trump's grand strategy and evaluate his impact upon American grand strategy more generally. In early 2018, for instance, scholar Hal Brands was skeptical that the year would unfold well for Trump's grand strategy. "Fundamentally," he concluded, the president "remains as erratic, volatile, and destructive as ever." At home, winter saw Trump's White House grappling with, among other challenges, an immigration reform deal collapsing in the Senate, a series of near-misses on prolonged government shutdowns, the growing Russia investigation, relentless media scrutiny, outrage over two mass shootings, a salacious best seller about White House dysfunction, rumors swirling that Chief of Staff Kelly and National Security Advisor McMaster might be ousted, and the president's abrupt announcement of major steel and aluminum tariffs, with the latter justified by a tweet that "trade wars are good and easy to win." Trump's leadership style did little to alleviate this pressure.

Still, with his preferred personnel in place, and a year of experience in hand, Trump and his team could face the coming months with optimism. Under the GSA framework, the president's personal preferences and stances were increasingly—though still not highly—correlated with those of his principals and his government's official positions. Trump began settling into a core set of national security and foreign policy principals. American economic growth and power remained steady. US representatives below the president had spent months reassuring allies that despite shifting priorities, America's basic commitment to stability and partnership remained solid. Indeed, rather than tackle new strategic issues, Trump and his team largely sought "wins" on a host of existing concerns: North Korea, immigration, trade, and Iran along with, to a lesser extent, NATO relations, Russia, Syria, and Department of Defense priorities. What White House officials could not control were developments overseas, the President's behavior, and, just as ominously for their agenda, a midterm election season in which a projected Democratic wave could end the GOP's hold on Congress.

Maximal Pressure, Minimal Commitment

The Middle East

For Trump nationalists, the Middle East was simultaneously a morality tale of wasted resources and a theater for resolve. In early April, with ISIS "close to 100 percent" defeated, Trump told military leaders to plan withdrawal as soon as possible and to hand off responsibility to Arab partners.[9] Many military officials, including Secretary of Defense James Mattis, worried that despite territorial defeat, ISIS could reconsolidate. Trump had listened to conventional wisdom from his generals and agreed to push back withdrawal every six months since assuming office, but now he was ready leave. Days after this announcement, however, images of suffocating adults and children emerged after an apparent chemical weapons attack near the Syrian capital. US officials faced a problem they hoped had been solved with their massive missile strike one year prior. They vowed that all possible responses were under consideration.[10] Breaking with his usual deference, Trump specifically blamed Putin for supporting "Animal Assad," though critics also pointed out that Syria's President Bashar al Assad may have felt emboldened by Trump's public readiness to leave the region.[11] As the world waited to discover the American response, Mattis privately pushed the White House team to secure Congressional support before launching another round of air strikes. The effort died. According to one journalist, Mattis' approach was "overruled by Mr. Trump, who wanted a rapid and dramatic response."[12] On April 13, Britain, France, and the United States launched missile strikes against suspected Syrian chemical weapons facilities. Though larger than the 2017 missile strike, the damage was again relatively limited. Mattis confirmed that no further strikes were planned.[13] Reactions were mixed. Former foreign policy official and commentator Eliot Cohen complained that "this attack was unserious but intended to relieve emotional pressure, a kind of martial onanism masquerading as strategy."[14] Whatever Trump's motivation, Syria's president Bashar al Assad seemed to believe Western threats and for the next six months no alleged chemical attacks occurred.

The president's early Iran agenda, meanwhile, culminated when he announced that the United States would withdraw from the nuclear deal. President Obama's team had negotiated and enjoined the Joint Comprehensive Plan of Action (JCPOA) along with Russia and several European governments. Trump had insisted since it was announced that it was one of the worst deals ever signed.[15] He refused to certify it in fall 2017. Now, he was bolstered by his new Secretary of State, Mike

Pompeo, and National Security Advisor, John Bolton, who himself had long treated Iran as a bête noire. In his first international trip as chief diplomat, Pompeo asserted that the JCPOA was too weak to achieve the administration's chief goal: "to make sure [Iran] never possesses a nuclear weapon."[16] Trump's personal lawyer even announced at the Iran Freedom Convention for Human Rights and Democracy that Trump was "as committed to regime change as we are." It was, he explained, "the only way to peace in the Middle East."[17] Certainly officials throughout the government believed that Iran had supported, and continued to foster, instability, and sometimes violence (including against Americans) in Iraq in order to gain influence after the 2003 US invasion.[18] Crucially, Israel's hardline prime minister, Benjamin Netanyahu, actively supported these positions. Trump had personally bonded with Netanyahu, who shared similar nationalist impulses. For decades, all American presidents strove to support Israel and satisfy domestic interest groups, but that interest had grown far more pronounced for Republicans thanks to Evangelical beliefs that Israel deserved special support, a theological view Pompeo himself personally shared.[19] Israel was also a crucial intelligence, political, and military partner. As the JCPOA's next certification period arrived in May 2018, Netanyahu seized the opportunity. Standing before a screen that read "IRAN LIED," he announced in front of cameras that his government was releasing documents from early in the previous decade. They showed, he said, Tehran's interest in developing a nuclear weapons program.[20] Most experts agreed that the information had been well known for some time; however, they also speculated that the blunt display was specifically designed to capture Donald Trump's attention. A week later, Israel continued a related, low-level conflict by launching a series of strikes against Iranian military assets and partners in Syria.[21]

Few observers were surprised when Donald Trump stood in the White House and announced that "the United States no longer makes empty threats." It would withdraw from the JCPOA and apply maximum pressure through aggressive economic sanctions. The Obama deal "didn't bring calm, it didn't bring peace, and it never will."[22] Trump's specific strategy, however, was unclear. A State Department official later asserted that the administration hoped to gain European support with the renewed sanctions. Hopefully, ran the reasoning, sanctions would coerce Iranian leaders *back* to the negotiating table. Many observers and allied governments, however, expressed concern and confusion. After all, whatever its faults, the Obama deal already capped years of coordinated sanctions and negotiations. Now, the United States had effectively broken the deal, allowed Iran to legitimately return to its old program, and wanted to restart the entire process. In the immediate term, however, both the European signatories and the Iranians stated that they would continue to abide by the deal even though, technically, the United States had ended it.

Pompeo later explained in a speech to the Heritage Foundation, a conservative think tank, that former President Obama's administration had taken a bet. Obama officials hoped that Iran would not cheat on the deal, and they hoped that time would allow space to improve the regional and security situation.[23] By contrast, the Trump administration planned to impose "unprecedented financial pressure," use a more assertive military posture to deter "Iranian aggression," and "advocate tirelessly for the Iranian people." His theory of the case seemed to be that, like the USSR imploding under its own political and economic contradictions, "the Iranian regime will come to its senses and support—not suppress —the aspirations of its own citizens." His long list of demands included nuclear facilities inspections, ending support for terror organizations, and ending interference in the affairs of regional governments. For Trump's team, the strategic challenge of Iran was not its nuclear program but the *regime itself.*

North Korea

This process of ratcheting "maximum leverage," or "maximum pressure," also continued to be applied to North Korea. Trump and Kim Jong Un had committed to meeting in June, yet both continued to jockey for position. In April, White House officials signaled to the press that the president would only reduce existing sanctions if North Korea clearly moved to dismantle its nuclear weapons capability.[24] Trump praised Kim when his government released several American detainees, but in mid-May, bluster between the leaders peaked when Trump released a letter announcing his withdrawal from the meeting.[25] Speaking on Fox News two weeks earlier, John Bolton explained that "we have very much in mind the Libya model from 2003, 2004."[26] At that time, Libya's dictator, Muammar Gaddafi, watched the United States invade Iraq based on a belief that Saddam Hussein was hiding a nuclear weapons program. Gaddafi quickly dismantled his own program, and he allowed inspectors to confirm the move. Now, Bolton explained, the Trump administration's "maximum pressure campaign" had brought Kim to the same conclusions as Gadaffi. North Koreans, however, balked. They threatened to call off the summit if the US administration continued to demand "unilateral nuclear abandonment."[27] Concerned that Kim would preempt him, Trump listened to two rounds of discussion on the topic among his top foreign policy and national security principals.[28] Within 24 hours, he was announcing that the summit would be cancelled. Reports suggested that the debate broke between Pompeo, favoring diplomacy, and Bolton, favoring confrontation. Mattis, notably, remained off site and peripheral. Whiplash continued, however, when, just a day after this announcement, Trump responded to reporters that US officials were still talking with the North Koreans and the meeting "could even be the twelfth."[29] White House Press Secretary Sarah Huckabee Sanders confirmed that "the White House pre-advance team for Singapore will leave as scheduled in order to prepare should the summit take place." Throughout this entire imbroglio, Pompeo had been shepherding plans with his counterparts.[30] His goal remained denuclearizing North Korea, and the United States continued to exert full economic pressure through sanctions and North Korea's international financial networks. After years of null outcomes and heightened tensions the previous year, the simple fact of a Trump-Kim meeting assumed the appearance—if not the actual substance—of a strategic win.[31]

Two weeks later in Singapore, Trump and Kim strode toward one another between a row of their nation's flags and a massive bank of cameras. When the men emerged from a closed-door meeting, each claimed success. Their signed agreement included further normalizing relations; a reaffirmation of the recent Panmunjom Declaration between the two Koreas (in which the North committed to full denuclearization of the peninsula); and a commitment to recover US service members' remains from the 1950–1953 Korean War.[32] Trump also suspended routine military exercises with South Korea.[33] The first-ever meeting between a US and North Korean leader appeared remarkable, and the administration pitched it as a major success. Reading between the lines, however, close observers noted that North Korea maintained its view that "denuclearization" meant *all* nuclear powers should give up their weapons. For them, unilateral disarmament was not an option. The Trump administration, of course, understood "denuclearization" to apply *only* to North Korea. Further, North Korea had not committed to an immediate or even a clearly specified timeline for its weapons program. Such seemingly minor details would later bedevil negotiators. Indeed, Trump himself walked out of talks with Kim less than a year later. He realized immediate denuclearization was not actually on offer and that he would be attacked at home for returning with a weak agreement after years of ambitious promises.

TRADING REALITIES

Throughout 2017 and early 2018, Trump waved the flag of trade war. He had long warned that he wanted to correct "terrible" trade arrangements in which, he said, the United States was losing money. Still, playing the roles of both bad cop and good cop, he also expressed willingness to work out deals before imposing maximum pressure. He said he was ready to deal if the terms met his conditions. In early March (see Chapter 5), the administration announced significant tariffs across several major goods, particularly steel (25%) and aluminum (10%). Implementation was less than smooth. Evaluated through the GSA framework, the move demonstrates how Trump and his core team were working to align US grand strategy with the president's preferred, nationalist stances on *scope*, *substance*, and *assertiveness*.

Friends and Neighbors

Within weeks, Commerce Secretary Wilbur Ross and his team faced a growing "tsunami" of over 1,200 requests for tariff exemptions.[34] Already, the administration had granted short term exemptions for about 63 percent of imports from entire countries, such as Canada, Mexico, South Korea, Argentina, Australia, Brazil, and several European Union partners. The situation was so complex, and Republican officeholders across the country were so concerned about hurting business, that, at one point, Trump told US Trade Representative Robert E. Lighthizer and National Economic Council Director Larry Kudlow to investigate a possible return to the Trans-Pacific Partnership.[35] That deal, after all, had been designed to coordinate closely with partners on more equal trade and, as a side benefit, pressure China also to meet those standards. Perhaps realizing the optics of walking back one of his signature policies, Trump later tweeted —without details—that he would only rejoin the TPP if he got a better deal than Obama had. Indeed, by the end of May, temporary exemptions for even close US allies lapsed when Ross announced that trade talks had made insufficient progress.[36] The Trump administration appeared to be launching a trade war against its friends. Ongoing negotiations with Mexico and Canada, already fraught, were imperiled.[37] European Commissioner Jean-Claude Juncker stated that the EU would be forced to respond in kind and initiate a dispute settlement at the World Trade Organization (WTO).[38] Other leaders, like French president Emmanuel Macron, agreed that the move was an illegal protectionist measure. Economist Douglas Irwin observed, "It's more than highly unusual. It's unprecedented to have gone after so many U.S. allies and trading partners, alienating them and forcing them to retaliate."[39] According to White House staffers, Trump was unmoved. One advisor recounted the president's private response: "'We're already getting screwed. What are we supposed to do, sit here and beg for them to leave us alone?'" In practical terms, administration officials also pointed out that the United States enjoyed higher domestic economic growth and lower percentages of foreign trade than other wealthy states.[40]

Allied relations seemed to reach a nadir at the June G7 meeting. Delegations believed that they had worked out a mutual statement, but tensions between Trump and the other leaders came to a head when the US president flew out early to attend his summit with Kim Jong Un. From the plane, he tweeted a series of insults against Canada's Prime Minister, Justin Trudeau. The G-7's joint statement had carefully avoided the tariff question, but after the conference, Trudeau said Canada would still retaliate in response to US tariffs. Trump called his counterpart "weak and dishonest."[41] Reporting then revealed that Trump had alienated his counterparts. He pressed them to readmit Russia to the group (reinstating it as the G-8) and called out each government for its unfair treatment of the United States. In a photo released by the German delegation, Trump sits at a table, arms crossed. The other leaders, standing and leaning forward, surround him in a semi-circle. German Chancellor Angela Merkel leans forward, as if lecturing the president. As other signature Trump moments, the image serves as a perception test. Either Trump is standing firm against the world like a strong leader, or he is shutting down all information like a petulant toddler.

China
Trade tensions with China actually grew more slowly, but they would prove less tractable over the long term. Within weeks, Steve Mnuchin arrived in Beijing to lead talks alongside US Trade Representative Robert E. Lighthizer, Commerce Secretary Wilbur Ross, trade advisor Peter Navarro, and National Economic Council head Larry Kudlow. Few concrete agreements emerged that first week of May, but the US delegation set out its terms while the Chinese reconsidered their own personnel, who brought only general knowledge of trade.[42] Administration officials

focused particularly on the two countries' trade deficit, and at a second round of talks in Washington D.C., Chinese representatives agreed, in principle, to buying more US goods.[43] Along the way, to show good faith, Trump and Mnuchin offered olive branches. The president said he would consider easing restrictions on ZTE, a Chinese telecommunications firm accused of violating US trade sanctions on Iran and North Korea. Mnuchin, meanwhile, cited progress and commented on *Fox News Sunday*, "We're putting the trade war on hold."[44] Critics worried that the administration had whipped up global economic anxiety only to settle for relatively minor concessions and soft-peddle consequences for ZTE, but when pressed, neither Mnuchin nor his Chinese interlocutors offered details and Trump himself conceded "we have a long way to go."[45] A month later, Mnuchin scored an internal win over the most serious China hardliners, Navarro and Lighthizer. The White House announced that, rather than invoking emergency powers to protect US intellectual and technical property, it would channel Chinese investment through the existing Committee on Foreign Investment in the United States.[46] For the moment, Mnuchin seemed to be emphasizing lucrative deals, whereas hardliners saw immediate punitive measures as part-and-parcel of a nationalist strategy. The division would not last.

Despite these signs of budding comity, trade war was still, in fact, an ongoing concern. In early July, the administration announced that 34 billion more dollars of Chinese goods would receive tariffs, and, again, Beijing reciprocated.[47] US farmers in particular started to see prices fall, and critics worried that a trade war could easily spiral. In response, the administration arranged $12 billion of subsidies for the agricultural sector.[48] Officials argued that with a growing economy and low unemployment there was no better time to confront China's trade practices, an issue that most observers agreed needed to be addressed in some form. The problem, worried former US trade negotiator Wendy Cutler, was that Trump was "very quick to pull the trigger. I don't know that he knows how to get off the cliff." His strategy remained unclear beyond increasing pressure and working trade talks. Concerned but reluctant to contradict Trump, Senate Republicans joined Democrats to pass a nonbinding motion stating that Congress would retain some influence over a subset of tariffs: those imposed under a national security justification.[49] Given Congress' constitutional supremacy on commerce and spending, it was a modest gesture. Largely discounting concerns from Republican and business leaders—and, later, even Trump's own Federal Research chairman—Mnuchin told delegates at the G-20 that US tariffs on *all* Chinese imports remained a real possibility.[50] Indeed, over the next two months, the Office of the US Trade Representative (USTR) announced two more rounds of tariffs, one for $16 billion and the next for $200 billion.[51] In response, China canceled a round of trade talks in September.[52]

Dealing With Reality

Back in North America, Trump claimed a victory. On October 1, he announced that after more than a year of high-profile presidential threats, near failures in talks, new tariffs, and bureaucratic negotiations, Mexico, Canada and the United States had agreed to a new free trade deal. It would be called, ponderously, the United States-Mexico-Canada Agreement (USMCA). Back in the 1990s, Bill Clinton's administration pushed and achieved the North American Free Trade Agreement (NAFTA). Officials and many economists argued that it would increase commerce, global competitiveness, and economic growth for all three members. And on balance, it did. At the time and ever since, however, critics complained that US workers could not compete with Mexican wages and lower labor standards, and that all three governments unfairly subsidized their own preferred industries at the expense of the others. Indeed, like Carrier in Indianapolis after Trump's election, thousands of US businesses relocated operations to Mexico. Now, standing on the White House lawn, he crowed about his success. Threatening and imposing tariffs worked, he said, saying the situation could have become truly "nasty" but mocking "those babies out there who keep talking about tariffs."[53] Trump now turned his sights on Congress, which would have to adopt the agreement.

Free-trade Republicans felt uncomfortable with Trump aggressively threatening such close partners. Others worried that the deal would not help industries in their own states. Democrats, meanwhile, remained reflexively skeptical of all things Trump, but they argued that the USMCA was especially weak on labor standards, environmental protections, and agricultural fairness.

Indeed, despite its new name, the USMCA was, in effect, an updated NAFTA. It made changes to tariffs on automobile parts, sorted out a long-standing dispute over Canada's milk subsidies, updated some labor and environmental rules, modernized intellectual property protections, opened Canada's market to more access from US drug companies, and stipulated that the deal would have to be reviewed after six years.[54] It did not, however, overhaul the original free trade arrangement. In real estate terms, Trump had rebranded and renovated an existing and proven property. Rather than a revolution, it was a measured update. White House officials treated the USMCA as a clear vindication of Trump's approach to his strategic agenda: escalating rhetoric and pressure—specifically tariffs—then using that leverage to negotiate and obtain deals. This was "maximal pressure." Still, such a win could be overstated. After all, Canada and Mexico had little leverage over the United States, and they were already amenable to talks. Rather than uniquely tough negotiating, Trump's real contribution may have been his willingness, as the president, to prioritize trade issues.

Whatever the lesson, here, China remained the real prize, but the contest was shaping up to be an extended battle royal. Over the fall, trade relations were fraught. Trump continued to cultivate personal relations with Xi Jinping, but he and his trade team also demanded real concessions. Domestically, this strategy was pulled in two directions. Most US experts agreed that China needed to be confronted. For instance, federal prosecutors revealed changes against a Chinese technology firm accused of intellectual property violations.[55] Still, many Americans worried that "trade war" would become an economic mill stone. Stock markets—one of Trump's favored bellwethers—regularly slumped and spiked in tandem with US-China trade updates.[56] Further, the Chinese leadership, and Xi in particular, seemed to be just as committed as Trumpian nationalists to pushing their sovereign rights, and they knew that they held significant leverage over key US industries. For two years, the Trump administration's approach had been about ratcheting trade pressure. Such "maximum pressure" seemed to have worked with allies. With the Chinese, however, maximum pressure could not easily be limited to trade or economic matters. It always risked spilling over into larger geopolitical issues.

UNCERTAIN DEFENSE

The Border
Throughout 2018, the president also pushed his vision of tough nationalism across several other grand strategy concerns. On immigration, Trump had actually ordered National Guard troops to the US-Mexico border. Stationed in Texas and Arizona, military leaders kept the troops "as far away from the border as possible" and directed them to provide surveillance and logistical support for the US Border Patrol.[57] That spring, Trump had been frustrated that his requests for border wall funding had been largely sidelined by the Republicans' latest spending bill. Then, around Easter, he tweeted outrage after seeing reports on Fox News about a caravan of Central American migrants working their way through Mexico to the US border.[58]

For Trump and other nationalists in the White House, like Stephen Miller, the imagery of foreigners pushing toward the United States confirmed their greatest fears about national security and cultural identity being swamped by outsiders. Politically, it also signaled that despite campaign promises, Trump's administration—after an initial dip—had only seen *increases* in people crossing the border legally and illegally.[59] Under the US Constitution and international law, many of these migrants could, and did, apply for asylum.[60] Frustrated, the administration quietly approved a "zero tolerance" policy to deter would-be migrants. Adults were prosecuted and children separated from their parents and placed in shelters or foster care.[61] When news of the policy broke, critics were outraged at the apparent and deliberate abuse of human rights. In response, senior officials characterized illegal migrants as criminals and said the policy was standard in that context, but they also ended the policy and worked to reunite families. Trump, however, was undeterred. He insisted that many of the people crossing the border were "animals" and members of the violent gang MS-13, pushed Mexico to absorb more of the asylum seekers, and threatened to reject Congress' next spending bill and shut down the government if legislators did not commit far more resources to "Border Security, which includes the Wall!"[62] At one point, he even threatened to sign an executive order ending birthright citizenship.[63] Then, just days before the midterm election, Trump ordered 3,500 active duty troops—under the encouragement of John Bolton, according to insiders—to areas of the border where officials believed the latest migrant caravans might arrive.[64] In short, constricting immigration had become a strategic objective for which the administration was willing to sacrifice an extraordinary amount of political capital. It was also a strategic objective that allowed the president to energize his electoral base.

Pentagon Relations

At the Department of Defense, Secretary Mattis supported the administration, but he also stood as something of a holdout. Since assuming his office, Mattis had played the role of military diplomat. He vocally supported existing allies and partners at home and, abroad, worked to assure them that the United States remained as reliable as ever. When reporters pressed him about North Korea in spring 2018, he emphasized diplomacy and "confidence-building measures."[65] In Afghanistan, Mattis pushed to revive peace talks with the Taliban as a complement to the DOD's 2017 strategy for the country, and that autumn, he joined Secretary of State Pompeo to call for a cease-fire in Yemen.[66] Consistent with the administration's emphasis on traditional great power politics, he regularly warned that China was a long-term geopolitical challenge that was using "intimidation and coercion" in the South China Sea.[67] He also made a visible effort to visit Beijing that summer and "have a conversation." During a flare-up in autumn, when US and Chinese vessels penetrated each other's normal operating space, Vice President Pence warned, "We will not back down."[68] Mattis, by contrast, said, "We'll sort this out." Overall, he explained, he did not foresee worsening relations.[69]

Mattis also supported, or at least raised no public objections to, the White House's defense politics. Despite this, the personal and policy gaps between the core White House team and Mattis grew insurmountable. In June, the president announced that he wanted to create a "Space Force" alongside the major service branches. Most public reaction ranged from baffled to bemused. Close observers explained that updating and reconsolidating US military capabilities in or related to Earth orbit could be sensible. Department of Defense officials saluted and started drawing up a plan despite Mattis' stated opposition, just one year earlier, to "the creation of a new military service and additional organizational layers at a time when we are focused on reducing overhead and integrating joint warfighting functions."[70] Pence defended this government expansion and possible militarization of space in sloganeering terms: "What we want to do is continue to advance the principle that peace comes through strength."[71]

Whatever Trump's motivation for creating a Space Force, it was assimilated into the administration's larger push to grow military spending and capabilities. For instance, the administration continued to expand US airstrikes in places like Yemen and, with Congressional approval, more direct Special Forces support with partners throughout Africa.[72] Over its first two years, the White House had also been able to secure hundreds of billions of dollars in new defense spending, leading to bumper profits for US defense contractors.[73] Though he kept a steady public face, Mattis nevertheless found himself subject of a whisper campaign, allegedly stoked by National Security Advisor Bolton and his deputy Mira Ricardel, that the Defense Secretary "is done for."[74] As described in the next chapter, at this same time, Trump confided to a television interviewer that he thought Mattis, as a "globalist," may no longer be a good fit for the administration. Weeks later, the secretary of defense resigned.

Another Chapter in *L'Affaire Russe*

Russia also epitomized Trump's tension between personal prerogatives and national strategy. US officials and members of Congress argued that Moscow must be held to account for a record of confrontational behavior. From absorbing Crimea to supporting Syria's Bashar al Assad to political assassinations to 2016 election interference, Vladimir Putin's government seemed to be challenging traditional US leadership. The president, however, continued to insist that Russia could and should be a useful partner. In April, when UN Ambassador Nikki Haley announced new economic sanctions for Russia, the White House almost immediately walked back the statement.[75] Still, policy leaders around the government remained wary. Over the next months, the State Department pushed the Russian government to release political and religious prisoners, senators advanced a rare bipartisan sanctions bill, and senior intelligence and law enforcement officials warned about another Russian disinformation campaign for the 2018 midterm election.[76]

Amidst all this, Trump stunned even his White House team. After a closed-door meeting with Putin, during a July visit to Helsinki, Finland, a reporter asked if Trump believed US intelligence agencies or if he believed Russia's president about 2016 election interference. Standing at a podium next to the man himself, Trump said, "President Putin says it's not Russia. I don't see any reason why it would be."[77] On US-Russia relations in general, and perhaps true to his personal notions of nationalism and deal making, Trump reflected that "both sides have made mistakes." The reaction was extensive. Former Obama-era ambassador to Russia Michael McFaul called it "the most appalling public display of capitulation by a US president to a Kremlin leader ever," and the widely respected GOP senator John McCain (R-AZ) said Trump now boasted "one of the most disgraceful performances by an American president in memory."[78] Most Republicans, however, avoided directly challenging their party's leader, but even senior Congressional leaders like House Speaker Paul Ryan (R-WI) and Senate Majority Leader Mitch McConnell (R-KY) released statements defending the US intelligence community. Trump himself appeared to leave the summit energized, believing that he had effectively parleyed with a second adversarial leader in as many months. However, back in Washington, Pence, Bolton and Chief of Staff Kelly, in a rare intervention, joined messages from Mattis and Pompeo. They tried to convince the president that he had taken a major misstep.[79] A day later, Trump waved away the firestorm by telling the press, "The sentence should have been: I don't see any reason why I wouldn't—or why it wouldn't be Russia." Unfortunately for the White House, over the next month, he also wondered publicly why the United States would commit to protecting small states in NATO, continued to attack the Mueller investigation as a "witch hunt," and faced polling that most Americans disapproved of his handling of both Russia and the Mueller investigation.[80]

Still, over the following months, Trump's personal views of Putin and Russia did not appear to change, but his administration added more Russians to the sanctions list for the 2016 election. That October, Trump also agreed to withdraw from the Intermediate-Range Nuclear Forces (INR) Treaty, which US President Ronald Reagan and Soviet Premier Mikhail Gorbachev signed in 1987. For years, Americans claimed that Moscow was violating the agreement, so in February 2017 when it deployed what analysts believed to be a fully-operational, land-based cruise missile (dubbed the SSC-X-8 by US intelligence), hardliners argued that that Russia had broken its commitments.[81] Bolton himself had pushed for US withdrawal. The treaty had put the United States in an "excessively weak position," not just with Russia, but "more importantly China." Beijing was never a party to the treaty and was developing its own missile systems.[82] Whatever the administration's core motivation for ending the treaty, Trump offered the press a basic nationalist logic, saying, "We're not going to let them violate a nuclear agreement and go out and do weapons and we're not allowed to." Still, no clear endgame emerged. Pressure and leverage along with a tough stance in themselves may have been the goal.

LOSING GRIP

The Morning After

That year's midterm election results immediately changed the climate in Washington. Election night showed a surge of support for Democrats as they gained a solid majority in the House of Representatives and saw gains in states across the country. Relatively moderate Republicans in swing districts were swept out. Within days, stories emerged detailing dozens of possible House investigations into the administration's behavior. Incoming leaders like Adam Schiff (D-CA) particularly wanted to hold officials to account on major international issues like immigration, trade, the war in Yemen, and Russia relations. "Credible allegations," Schiff said, existed "that the Russians may have laundered money through the Trump Organization."[83] More generally, Schiff continued, "We have a president who makes common cause with autocrats and has made the United States unrecognizable to a lot of our allies." In reality, the House would not be able to fundamentally change the direction of US grand strategy. Instead, Democrats like Joaquin Castro of the House Foreign Affairs Committee committed to a broad "reevaluation of America's engagement with the world."[84] Many of these efforts would sputter. Still, voters had largely pushed back against Trump's own effort to push the limits of American politics.

In response, reported the *Los Angeles Times*, Trump "retreated into a cocoon of bitterness and resentment."[85] *The Washington Post* characterized the week after Election Day as "five days of fury."[86] White House staff worried about approaching the president. A day after the election, Trump requested Attorney General Jeff Sessions' resignation and installed a skeptic of the Russia investigation, Matthew Whitaker, to serve as interim AG. This mood also poisoned a largely ceremonial trip to France. The president had accepted an invitation to join European leaders in commemorating the centennial of the World War I armistice. Along the way, however, Trump "berated" UK prime minister Theresa May during a phone call, declined to visit the Aisne-Marne American Cemetery and Memorial due to the weather, exchanged a conspicuously friendly wave with Vladimir Putin, showed up too late—as did Putin—to participate in a parade of leaders, and later issued tweets criticizing French president Emanuel Macron.[87] Macron, by contrast, took the stage to directly criticize both Trump and Putin. "Patriotism is the exact opposite of nationalism. Nationalism is a betrayal of patriotism," Macron declared, and then continued, "In saying, 'Our interests first, whatever happens to the others,' you erase the most precious thing a nation can have, that which makes it live, that which causes it to be great and that which is most important: its moral values."[88] For Trump, though, liberal solidarity and morals had always been irrelevant next to sovereign prerogatives.

Less than a week after the election, *The New York Times* ran another damning story. "North Korea," it led, "Is moving ahead with its ballistic missile program."[89] Commercial satellite images aimed at the North's rolling mountains showed ongoing activity and infrastructure improvements at 16 bases. Only five months prior, Trump had met North Korea's Kim Jong Un. Trump insisted for months that he could read Kim and get a deal that would end North Korea's pursuit of nuclear weapons as well as the means to deliver them. Most experts criticized the president for giving away American leverage in exchange for a vague agreement. For Trump, the fact of meeting and the handshake *were* the breakthrough. Talks could follow. Further, several American prisoners in North Korea had been returned. Despite all that, sanctions coordinated amongst major players like Russia and China began to fall away, and North Korea— aside from halting actual missile tests—continued its programs effectively unabated. Promised follow-up talks with Secretary Pompeo remained fraught to the point that North Koreans demanded Pompeo be replaced with another interlocutor. Trump's diplomatic coup had been consummated but bore no clear fruit.

Temperamental Nationalism

Midterm elections rarely bring direct change to US grand strategy. They do, however, often lead presidential administrations to evaluate and defend their foreign policy records. After all, midterms are also seen by many voters as well as observers as a referendum on the person sitting in the Oval Office. Through the latter half of 2018, critics saw a lot of froth but not much substance. Even worse, they charged, the president's mercurial rhetoric and rolling personnel changes made coherent grand strategy, or any kind of foreign policy, impossible. Rather than strength, Trump projected unreliability. Trump and his team, however, made the case that, among other agendas, they had secured unprecedented talks with North Korea, effectively managed a complex relationship with Russia, secured a new North American trade agreement, pushed tough immigration policies, and worked up "maximum pressure" on allies and adversaries alike.

Applying the GSA framework, this study draws some specific observations about the shape of Trump's grand strategy in the latter half of 2018. On balance, the president's preferences on *scope*, *substance*, and *assertiveness* remained relatively stable. Toward trade, nonproliferation, alliances and a host of other issues, "America first" meant nationalism. It meant embracing military power without making major commitments. It meant treating longtime partners and competitors as equally worthy of confrontation and cooperation. It meant "maximum pressure" and trade war without, in most cases, a resort to violence. It meant talking about sovereign fairness rather than international goods or American values. Candidate Donald Trump did not run as a self-conscious nationalist. Instead, his personal impulses and the political positions he had evolved in front of television cameras and his rallies, he seemed to realize, were nationalist. By October, the president was unequivocal: "I'm a nationalist."

Over this period, the president also saw his preferences and those of his foreign policy principals—as well as the official policies of the United States—pushed into closer alignment. Under the GSA approach, this book interrogates the president's personal influence by examining his own stated positions and actions with those of his senior officials as well as official US government actions and policies. For nearly two years, factions in the administration tried to bridge the gap between competing schools of thought. Perhaps inevitably, this "principled realism" collapsed. Mattis would be the last of the "adults in the room" to leave.[90] Pompeo, Bolton, Pence, Miller and others in some form or another comported with the president and his positions. By the end of 2018, US grand strategy more closely followed the president's own positions than at any other time over the previous two years. Trump himself—both his temperament and his views—would remain the key pivot point for the administration's approach to grand strategy. Still, Trump's effect remained moderate. Congress still pushed back on contentious adversaries like Russia, the United States still worked within its long-standing network of alliances, and the military still maintained its many global assignments. The next, and final, chapter unpacks these findings and arguments in greater detail.

NOTES

1. Jennifer Jacobs and Alyza Sebenius, "Trump Says 'I'm a Nationalist' in Appeal to Texas Republicans." *Bloomberg*, October 22, 2018, https://www.bloomberg.com/news/articles/2018-10-23/trump-says-i-m-a-nationalist-in-appeal-to-texas-republicans.
2. Gwenda Blair, "Trump Has the White House He Always Wanted," *Politico*, April 5, 2018, https://www.politico.com/magazine/story/2018/04/05/trump-tower-white-house-217778.
3. Jacobs and Sebenius, "Trump Says 'I'm a Nationalist.'"
4. Joshua Berlinger, "Trump tweets explosive threat to Iran," CNN, July 23, 2018, https://www.cnn.com/2018/07/23/politics/trump-iran-intl/index.html.
5. Andrew Buncombe, "John Bolton doubles down on Trump's Iran threat to inflict 'a price few countries have ever paid,'" *The Indepenent*, July 23, 2018, https://www.independent.co.uk/news/world/americas/us-politics/trump-iran-john-bolton-rouhani-mike-pompeo-tweet-threat-us-a8460736.html.
6. Joshua Berlinger, "Iran shoots back at Trump: 'Color us unimpressed,'" CNN, July 24, 2018, https://www.cnn.com/2018/07/24/politics/iran-trump-intl/index.html.
7. See, for example, Alex Ward, "Here's why Trump is blasting Iran on Twitter," *Vox*, 23 July 2018, https://www.vox.com/world/2018/7/23/17602978/trump-iran-twitter-threat-us; Tim Fernholz, "Donald Trump already told us why he's shouting at Iran," *Quartz* 23 July 2018, https://qz.com/1334536/donald-trump-already-told-us-why-hes-shouting-at-iran/.
8. Matthew Rosenberg and Maggie Haberman, "When Trump Phones Friends, the Chinese and the Russians Listen and Learn," *The New York Times*, October 24, 2018, https://www.nytimes.com/2018/10/24/us/politics/trump-phone-security.html.
9. Karen DeYoung and Shane Harris, "Trump instructs military to begin planning for withdrawal from Syria," *The Washington Post*, April 4, 2018, https://www.washingtonpost.com/world/national-security/trump-instructs-military-to-begin-planning-for-withdrawal-from-syria/2018/04/04/1039f420-3811-11e8-8fd2-49fe3c675a89_story.html?utm_term=.beb852ec3d71.

10. Eli Okun, "All options on table after Syria chemical attack, White House says," *Politico*, April 8, 2018, https://www.politico.com/story/2018/04/0 8/syria-chemical-attack-trump-508167.

11. Matthew Nussbaum, "Trump blames Putting for backing 'Animal Assad,'" *Politico*, April 8, 2018, https://www.politico.com/story/2018/04/08/trump-putin-syria-attack-508223.

12. Helene Cooper, "Mattis Wanted Congressional Approval Before Striking Syria. He Was Overruled," *The New York Times*, April 17, 2018.

13. Nancy A. Youssef and Michael C. Bender, "U.S., U.K. an France Launch Strikes Against Syria," *The Wall Street Journal*, April 14, 2018, https://www.wsj.com/articles/u-s-u-k-launch-strikes-against-syria-1523668212?mod=searchresults&page=1&pos=8

14. Eliot A. Cohen, "Neither Precise Nor Proportionate," *The Atlantic*, April 15, 2018, https://www.theatlantic.com/politics/archive/2018/04/neither-precise-nor-proportionate/558068/.

15. Presumably alongside other historically bad deals, such as lending the Trump Organization money in the 1980s and 1990s. Russ Buettner and Susanne Craig, "Decade in the Red: Trump Tax Figures Show Over $1 Billion in Business Losses," *The New York Times*, May 7, 2019, https://www.nytimes.com/interactive/2019/05/07/us/politics/donald-trump-taxes.html.

16. Sheena McKenzie, "Pompeo uses meeting with Saudis as an opportunity to slam the Iran nuclear deal," CNN, April 29, 2018, https://www.cnn.com/2018/04/29/politics/pompeo-iran-nuclear-deal-intl/index.html.

17. Brent D. Griffiths, "Giuliani: Trump is 'committed to' regime change in Iran," *Politico*, May 5, 2018, https://www.politico.com/story/2018/05/05/giuliani-trump-iran-regime-change-570744.

18. Isabel Coles and Ghassan Adnan, "Low Turnout Reported in Iraqi Election as U.S. and Iran Vie for Influence," *The Wall Street Journal*, May 12, 2018, https://www.wsj.com/articles/iraqis-vote-as-u-s-and-iran-vie-for-influence-1526103590?mod=searchresults&page=1&pos=2.

19. Later, Pompeo mused that Trump himself may have been ordained by God to help protect Israel. Daoud Kuttab and Luke Moon, "Perspectives on Pompeo, Evangelicals, and Their Love of Israel," *Providence*, March 29, 2019, https://providencemag.com/2019/03/providence-perspectives-pompeo-evangelicals-love-israel/.

20. Tom DiChristopher, "Netanyahu says files show Iran lied 'big time' about developing nuclear weapons," CNBC, April 30, 2018, https://www.cnbc.

com/2018/04/30/netanyahu-claims-to-show-irans-secret-nuclear-files-obtained-by-israel.html.

21. For years, groups like Hezbollah had attacked Israel using Iranian weapons. Krishnadev Calamur, "The Battle Between Israel and Iran Is Spreading," *The Atlantic*, May 10, 2018, https://www.theatlantic.com/international/archive/2018/05/israel-strikes-iran/560111/; Dan Williams and Angus McDowall, "Israel strikes Iranian targets in Syria after rocket fire," Reuters, May 9, 2018, https://www.reuters.com/article/us-mideast-crisis-syria-israel/israel-strikes-iranian-targets-in-syria-after-rocket-fire-idUSKBN1IA3GF.

22. Kevin Liptak and Nicole Gaouette, "Trump withdraws from Iran nuclear deal, isolating him further from world." CNN, May 9, 2018, https://www.cnn.com/2018/05/08/politics/donald-trump-iran-deal-announcement-decision/index.html; Nahal Toosi, Louis Nelson, and Cristiano Lima, "Trump says U.S. pulling out of 'rotten' nuclear deal," *Politico*, May 8, 2018, https://www.politico.com/story/2018/05/08/iran-responds-trump-nuclear-deal-573252.

23. United States Department of State, "After the Deal: A New Iran Strategy," Remarks by the Secretary of State, Mike Pompeo, The Heritage Foundation, Washington, DC, May 21, 2018, https://www.state.gov/secretary/remarks/2018/05/282301.htm#.

24. Michael R. Gordon, Jonathan Cheng, and Michael C. Bender, "Trump Will Tell Kim Jong Un That Dismantling Nuclear Arsenal Must Precede Economic Benefits," *The Wall Street Journal*, April 22, 2018, https://www.wsj.com/articles/trump-will-tell-kim-jong-un-that-dismantling-nukes-must-precede-economic-benefits-1524433979?mod=searchresults&page=1&pos=20.

25. Louis Nelson and Zoya Sheftalovich, "Trump thanks Kim Jong Un as he welcomes home detainees from North Korea," *Politico*, May 10, 2018, https://www.politico.com/story/2018/05/10/trump-north-korea-detainees-579899. David Nakamura, Anna Fifield, and John Wagner, "Trump's cancellation of summit with Kim raises fears of renewed tensions, destabilization," *The Washington Post*, May 24, 2018, https://www.washingtonpost.com/politics/trump-cancels-nuclear-summit-with-north-korean-leader-kim-jong-un/2018/05/24/e502d910-5f58-11e8-a4a4-c070ef53f315_story.html?utm_term=.393e74c61056.

26. Transcript, "John Bolton on push to rid North Korea of nuclear weapons," *Fox News Sunday*, Chris Wallace, host, April 29, 2018, https://www.

foxnews.com/transcript/john-bolton-on-push-to-rid-north-korea-of-nuclear-weapons.

27. Choe Sang-Hun and Mark Landler, "North Korea Threatens to Call Off Summit Meeting With Trump," *The New York Times*, May 15, 2018, https://www.nytimes.com/2018/05/15/world/asia/north-korea-postpones-talks.html?module=inline.

28. Courtney Kube, et al., "Trump wanted to cancel North Korea summit before Kim Jong Un could," NBC News, May 24, 2018, https://www.nbcnews.com/politics/national-security/inside-summit-collapse-trump-wanted-cancel-n-korean-leader-could-n877291?cid=sm_npd_nn_tw_ma.

29. Cristiano Lima, "Trump teases that summit with Kim may be back on," *Politico*, May 25, 2018, https://www.politico.com/story/2018/05/25/trump-north-korea-statement-reaction-608628.

30. Julian Borger, "US presses North Korea for 'historic' plan to disarm as Pompeo meets Kim aide," *The Guardian*, May 31, 2018, https://www.theguardian.com/world/2018/may/31/us-presses-north-korea-for-historic-plan-to-disarm-as-pompeo-meets-kim-aide.

31. Ian Talley, "U.S. Sanctions Target North Korea's Vast International Finance Network," *The Wall Street Journal*, May 28, 2018, https://www.wsj.com/articles/u-s-sanctions-target-north-korea-s-vast-international-finance-network-1527548907?mod=searchresults&page=1&pos=4.

32. Staff, "Full Text: The Statement signed by Trump and Kim," *Politico*, June 12, 2018, https://www.politico.com/story/2018/06/12/full-text-trump-kim-korea-summit-637541.

33. Julian Borger, "US to suspend military exercises with South Korea, Trump says," *The Guardian*, June 12, 2018, https://www.theguardian.com/us-news/2018/jun/12/us-to-suspend-war-games-with-south-korea-donald-trump-kim-jong-un-north-summit.

34. Heather Long, "There's a 'tsunami' of companies applying for relief from Trump's steel and aluminum tariffs," *The Washington Post*, April 16, 2018, https://www.washingtonpost.com/news/wonk/wp/2018/04/16/theres-a-tsunami-of-companies-applying-for-relief-from-trumps-steel-and-aluminum-tariffs/?utm_term=.a740e4a1cfc5.

35. Erica Werner, Damian Paletta, and Seun Min Kim, "Trump weighs rejoining Trans-Pacific Partnership amid trade dispute with China," *The Washington Post*, April 12, 2018, https://www.washingtonpost.com/business/economy/trump-weighs-rejoining-trans-pacific-partnership/2018/04/12/37d59500-3e71-11e8-8d53-eba0ed2371cc_story.html?utm_term=.a83576f9edd9.

36. Larry Elliott, Richard Partington, and Edward Helmore, "US on brink of trade war with EU, Canada and Mexico as tit-for-tat tariffs begin," *The Guardian*, May 31, 2018, https://www.theguardian.com/business/2018/may/31/us-fires-opening-salvo-in-trade-war-with-eu-canada-and-mexico.

37. Paul Vieira and Kim Mackrael, "U.S. Tariff Moves Jolt Nafta Talks," *The Wall Street Journal*, May 31, 2018, https://www.wsj.com/articles/u-s-tariff-moves-jolt-nafta-talks-1527809622?mod=searchresults&page=1&pos=1.

38. European Commission, "European Commission reacts to the US restrictions on steel and aluminium affecting the EU," press release, Brussels, Belgium, May 31, 2018, http://europa.eu/rapid/press-release_IP-18-4006_en.htm.

39. David J. Lynch, Josh Dawsey, and Damian Paletta, "Trump imposes steel and aluminum tariffs on the E.U., Canada and Mexico," *The Washington Post*, May 31, 2018, https://www.washingtonpost.com/business/economy/trump-imposes-steel-and-aluminum-tariffs-on-the-european-union-canada-and-mexico/2018/05/31/891bb452-64d3-11e8-a69c-b944de66d9e7_story.html?utm_term=.02be7eaa88a9.

40. Peter Eavis, "Trump's Trade War Faces Its First Big Test: DealBook Briefing," *The New York Times*, June 8, 2018, https://www.nytimes.com/2018/06/08/business/dealbook/justice-department-fox-disney-comcast.html.

41. Peter Baker and Michael D. Shear, "Trump's Blasts Upend G-7, Alienating Oldest Allies," *The New York Times*, June 9, 2018, https://www.nytimes.com/2018/06/09/world/g7-trump-russia.html?hp&action=click&pgtype=Homepage&clickSource=story-heading&module=b-lede-package-region&region=top-news&WT.nav=top-news; Staff. "G7 summit ends in disarray as Trump abandons joint statement," BBC News, June 10, 2018, https://www.bbc.com/news/world-us-canada-44427660.

42. Keith Bradsher, "As U.S. and Chinese Teams Meet on Trade, One Side Has an Edge in Expertise," *The New York Times*, May 3, 2018, https://www.nytimes.com/2018/05/03/business/china-trade-negotiations.html; Louis Nelson, "'Relatively big' issues remain on U.S.-China-trade, Chinese state media says," *Politico*, May 4, 2018, https://www.politico.com/story/2018/05/04/china-us-trade-568595.

43. Ana Swanson, "U.S. and China Tout Trade Talks as Success, but Leave the Details for Later," *The New York Times*, May 19, 2018, https://www.nytimes.com/2018/05/19/us/politics/china-trade-deal.html.

44. Ana Swanson, Mark Landler, and Keith Bradsher, "Trump Shifts From Trade War Threats to Concessions in Rebuff to Hard-Liners," *The New York Times*, May 14, 2018, https://www.nytimes.com/2018/05/14/business/china-trump-zte.html; Ana Swanson and Alan Rappeport, "U.S. Suspends Tariffs on China, Stoking Fears of a Loss of Leverage," *The New York Times*, May 20, 2018, https://www.nytimes.com/2018/05/20/us/politics/mnuchin-kudlow-china-trade.html.

45. Lindsay Dunsmuir and Howard Scheider, "U.S., China putting trade war on hold, Treasury's Mnuchin says," Reuters, May 20, 2018, https://www.reuters.com/article/us-usa-trade-mnuchin/u-s-china-putting-trade-war-on-hold-treasurys-mnuchin-says-idUSKCN1IL0JG; Doug Palmer and Louis Nelson, "Trump says China trade talks progressing 'nicely' but hints at trouble," *Politico*, May 23, 2018, https://www.politico.com/story/2018/05/23/trump-china-trade-603436.

46. Doug Palmer and Lorraine Woellert, "White House softens plans to block Chinese investment," *Politico*, June 27, 2018, https://www.politico.com/story/2018/06/27/white-house-china-investment-restrictions-654337.

47. David J. Lynch, Danielle Paquette, and Emily Rauhala, "U.S. levies tariffs on $34 billion worth of Chinese imports," *The Washington Post*, July 6, 2018.

48. Damian Paletta and Caitlin Dewey, "White House readies plan for $12 billion in emergency aid to farmers caught in Trump's escalating trade war," *The Washington Post*, July 25, 2018, https://www.washingtonpost.com/business/economy/white-house-readies-plan-for-12-billion-in-emergency-aid-to-farmers-caught-in-trumps-escalating-trade-war/2018/07/24/7bec9af4-8f4d-11e8-b769-e3fff17f0689_story.html?utm_term=.9bf753bb9789. Less than a year later, they sought another round of farm subsidies.

49. Al Weaver, "Senate sends Trump a warning shot on tariffs," *Washington Examiner*, July 11, 2018, https://www.washingtonexaminer.com/news/congress/senate-sends-trump-a-warning-shot-on-tariffs.

50. Jeffrey T. Lewis, "Mnuchin Says He 'Wouldn't Minimize' Chance of Tariffs on All Chinese Imports," *The Wall Street Journal*, July 21, 2018, https://www.wsj.com/articles/treasury-secretary-mnuchin-says-resolving-trade-issues-with-canada-mexico-is-a-big-priority-1532174708?mod=searchresults&page=1&pos=1; Tory Newmyer, "The Finance 202: Trump and his Fed chair present conflicting views on trade," *The Washington Post*, September 27, 2018, https://www.washingtonpost.com/news/powerpost/paloma/the-finance-202/2018/09/27/the-finance-202-

trump-and-his-fed-chair-present-conflicting-views-on-trade/5babbb5c1
b326b7c8a8d16a9/?noredirect=on&utm_term=.5bbc7189cae3.

51. United States Trade Representative, "USTR Finalizes Second Tranche
of Tariffs on Chinese Products in Response to China's Unfair Trade
Practices," press release, Policy Offices, Press Office. Washington, DC,
August 7, 2018; United States Trade Representative, "USTR Finalizes Tar-
iffs on $200 Billion of Chinese Imports in Response to China's Unfair
Trade Practices," press release, Policy Offices, Press Office. Washington,
DC, September 18, 2018.

52. Lingling Wei, "China Cancels Trade Talks With U.S. Amid Escalation in
Tariff Threats," *The Wall Street Journal*, September 22, 2018, https://www.
wsj.com/articles/china-cancels-trade-talks-with-u-s-amid-escalation-of-
tariff-threats-1537581226?mod=searchresults&page=1&pos=4.

53. Doug Palmer and Rebecca Morin, "Trump begins push to win approval of
new Canada, Mexico trade deal." *Politico*, October 1, 2018, https://www.
politico.com/story/2018/10/01/trump-trade-deal-mexico-canada-nafta-8
54310; Damian Paletta and Erica Werner, "Trump says USMCA trade
deal with Mexico and Canada proves tough talk and tariffs work," *The
Washington Post*, October 1, 2018, https://www.washingtonpost.com/
business/economy/2018/10/01/cae5b7fa-c588-11e8-b1ed-1d2d65b86d0c_
story.html?noredirect=on&utm_term=.c14c1e4719a2.

54. Heather Long, "U.S., Canada and Mexico just reached a sweeping new
NAFTA deal. Here's what's in it," *The Washington Post*, October 1,
2018, https://www.washingtonpost.com/business/2018/10/01/us-canada-
mexico-just-reached-sweeping-new-nafta-deal-heres-whats-it/?utm_
term=.5fcd25faace0.

55. Vivian Salama, Aruna Viswanatha, and Kate O'Keffe, "Trump and
Xi Talk as U.S.-China Tech Fight Brews," *The Wall Street Journal*,
November 1, 2018, https://www.wsj.com/articles/trump-signals-progress-
on-trade-after-phone-call-with-chinese-president-xi-1541083811?mod=
searchresults&page=1&pos=2.

56. Saumya Vaishampayan, "Fading Hopes for U.S.-China Trade Truce Hit
Markets," *The Wall Street Journal*, November 4, 2018, https://www.wsj.
com/articles/fading-hopes-for-u-s-china-trade-truce-hit-markets-15413
93410?mod=searchresults&page=1&pos=1.

57. Bryan Bender, "Trump Ordered Troops to the Border, But They're Doing
Busywork," *Politico*, June 14, 2018, https://www.politico.com/magazine/
story/2018/06/14/trump-ordered-troops-to-the-border-but-theyre-doing-
busywork-218821.

58. Louis Nelson, "Trump credits Mexico for reportedly breaking up migrant caravan," *Politico*, April 5, 2018, https://www.politico.com/story/2018/04 /05/trump-mexico-migrant-caravan-503665. Alicia A. Caldwell, "Trump Sees 2,000 to 4,000 National Guard Troops at the Border," *The Wall Street Journal*, April 5, 2018, https://www.wsj.com/articles/trump-sees-2-000-to-4-000-national-guard-troops-at-the-border-1522968839?mod=searchresults&page=1&pos=13.

59. Miriam Jordan, "More Migrants Are Crossing the Border This Year. What's Changed?" *The New York Times*, March 5, 2019, https://www.nytimes. com/2019/03/05/us/crossing-the-border-statistics.html?module=inline.

60. Kirk Semple, "U.S. Lets a Few Members of a Migrant Caravan Apply for Asylum," *The New York Times*, April 30, 2018, https://www.nytimes.com/ 2018/04/30/world/americas/mexico-migrants-caravan-asylum-seekers. html.

61. Miriam Jordan, "Family Separation May Have Hit Thousands More Migrant Children Than Reported," *The New York Times*, January 17, 2019, https://www.nytimes.com/2019/01/17/us/family-separation-trump-administration-migrants.html.

62. Julie Hirschfeld Davis and Niraj Chokshi, "Trump Defends 'Animals' Remark, Saying It Referred to MS-13 Gang Members," *The New York Times*, May 17, 2018, https://www.nytimes.com/2018/05/17/us/trump-animals-ms-13-gangs.html; Kirk Semple, "U.S. Pushes Plan to Make Mexico Handle Asylum Seekers," *The New York Times*, May 17, 2018, https://www.nytimes.com/2018/05/17/world/americas/mexico-migrants-caravan-asylum.html; Sherly Gay Stolberg, "G.O.P. Faces Another Midterm Threat as Trump Plays the Shutdown Card," *The New York Times*, July 29, 2018, https://www.nytimes.com/2018/07/29/us/politics/ trump-shutdown-republicans-midterms.html?module=inline.

63. By all accounts, it was an empty threat: the president on his own lacked authority to overthrow established legislation. Alex Leary and Jess Bravin, "Trump Wants to Curb Birthright Citizenship, Escalating Immigration Debate," *The Wall Street Journal*, October 30, 2018, https://www.wsj.com/ articles/trump-plans-executive-order-to-end-birthright-citizenship-in-u-s-1540901506?mod=searchresults&page=1&pos=7.

64. According to one White House leaker, Bolton rejected a Department of Homeland Security (DHS) proposal to work with the UN Refugee Agency, which could set up camps in Mexico. He then bypassed Chief of Staff John Kelly and DHS Secretary Kirstjen Nielsen to push the troop deployment by "yelling fire in the crowded movie theater that is Trump's

mind." Kimberly Dozier, Spencer Ackerman, and Asawin Suebsaeng, "Bolton Kept DHS in the Dark in His Push to Seal the Border Against the Migrant Caravan," *The Daily Beast*, October 26, 2018, https://www.thedailybeast.com/bolton-kept-dhs-in-the-dark-in-his-push-to-seal-the-border-against-the-migrant-caravan. On the troop deployment, see Nancy A. Youssef and Alicia A. Caldwell, "Troops Deploy to Parts of Border Where Migrant Caravans Are Deemed Most Likely to Go," *The Wall Street Journal*, November 2, 2018, https://www.wsj.com/articles/troops-deploy-to-parts-of-border-where-migrant-caravans-are-deemed-most-likely-to-go-1541160003?mod=searchresults&page=1&pos=1.

65. United States Department of Defense, *Secretary Mattis Hosts an Honor Cordon Welcoming Poland Defense Minister Mariusz Blaszczak to the Pentagon*, James Mattis and Mariusz Blaszczak, transcript, Washington, DC, Legacy Homepage: News, April 27, 2018, https://dod.defense.gov/News/Transcripts/Transcript-View/Article/1505983/secretary-mattis-hosts-an-honor-cordom-welcoming-poland-defense-minister-marius/.

66. Rod Nordland and Fahim Abed, "Jim Mattis Visits Afghanistan Amid Push for Peace Talks." *The New York Times*, September 7, 2018, https://www.nytimes.com/2018/09/07/world/asia/mattis-afghanistan-ghani-taliban-talks.html; Warren P. Strobel and Dion Nissenbaum, "U.S. Steps Up Bid to Halt War in Yemen," *The Wall Street Journal*, October 31, 2018, https://www.wsj.com/articles/u-s-steps-up-bid-to-halt-war-in-yemen-1541026803?mod=searchresults&page=1&pos=4.

67. Thomas Gibbons-Neff, "Amid Tensions, Mattis Arrives in China to 'Have a Conversation,'" *The Washington Post*, June 26, 2018, https://www.nytimes.com/2018/06/26/world/asia/jim-mattis-china.html. See also Nancy A. Youssef, "Jim Mattis Warns of Consequences If Beijing Keeps Militarizing the South China Sea," *The Wall Street Journal*, June 2, 2018, https://www.wsj.com/articles/mattis-says-u-s-remains-committed-to-allies-in-asia-1527906395?mod=searchresults&page=1&pos=1.

68. Gregory Hellman, "Pence to warn China after naval dustup," *Politico*, October 4, 2018, https://www.politico.com/newsletters/morning-defense/2018/10/04/pence-to-warn-china-after-naval-dustup-362505.

69. Lolita C. Balor and Robert Burns, "Mattis: US relations with China not worsening despite bumps," Associated Press, October 1, 2018, https://apnews.com/cc708022a70f479a9dc59d90fd135ea6.

70. Sarah Kaplan and Dan Lamothe, "Trump says he's directing Pentagon to create a new 'Space Force.'" *The Washington Post*, June 18, 2018, https://www.washingtonpost.com/news/speaking-of-science/wp/2018/

06/18/trump-says-hes-directing-pentagon-to-create-a-new-space-force/
?utm_term=.0204f8c557dc.

71. Robert Costa, "Pence leaves open the possibility of nuclear weapons in space: 'Peace comes through strength,'" *The Washington Post*, October 23, 2018, https://www.washingtonpost.com/politics/pence-leaves-open-the-possibility-of-nuclear-weapons-in-space-peace-comes-through-strength/2018/10/23/801a732a-d6d9-11e8-83a2-d1c3da28d6b6_story.html?utm_term=.28751af6982d.

72. Wesley Morgan, "Behind the secret U.S. war in Africa," *Politico*, July 2, 2018, https://www.politico.com/story/2018/07/02/secret-war-africa-pentagon-664005; Christina Goldbaum, "A Trumpian War on Terror That Just Keeps Getting Bigger," *The Atlantic*, September 11, 2018, https://www.theatlantic.com/international/archive/2018/09/drone-somalia-al-shabaab-al-qaeda-terrorist-africa-trump/569680/.

73. Scott R. Anderson, Sarah Tate Chambers, and Molly E. Reynolds, "What's in the New NDAA," *Lawfare*, August 14, 2018, https://www.lawfareblog.com/whats-new-ndaa; Aaron Gregg, "U.S. defense contractors report that business is booming—thanks to new spending, lower taxes," *The Washington Post*, October 26, 2018.

74. Lara Seligman, "Bolton's Whisper Campaign to Oust Mattis," *Foreign Policy*, October 25, 2018, https://foreignpolicy.com/2018/10/25/boltons-whisper-campaign-to-oust-mattis/

75. Philip Rucker, et al., "Trump puts the brakes on new Russian sanctions, reversing Haley's announcement," *The Washington Post*, April 16, 2018, https://www.washingtonpost.com/politics/trump-puts-the-brake-on-new-russian-sanctions-reversing-haleys-announcement/2018/04/16/ac3ad4f8-417f-11e8-8569-26fda6b404c7_story.html?utm_term=.feef60636ac2.

76. Michael R. Gordon, "U.S. Urges Russia to Release More Than 150 Political and Religious Prisoners," *The Wall Street Journal*, June18, 2018, https://www.wsj.com/articles/u-s-urges-russia-to-release-more-than-150-political-and-religious-prisoners-1529364745?mod=searchresults&page=1&pos=4; Elana Schor, "Russia sanctions bill gains bipartisan traction in Senate," *Politico*, July 20, 2018, https://www.politico.com/story/2018/07/20/senate-russia-sanctions-bill-rubio-van-hollen-734904; Michael R. Gordon, "Officials' Stark Warnings on Russia Diverge From White House View," *The Wall Street Journal*, July 22, 2018, https://www.wsj.com/articles/officials-stark-warnings-on-russia-diverge-from-white-house-view-1532317165?mod=searchresults&page=1&pos=1.

77. Staff, "Trump sides with Russia against FBI at Helsinki summit," BBC News, July 16, 2018, https://www.bbc.com/news/world-europe-44852812.
78. Michael McFaul, "The Trump-Putin summit in Helsinki was a historic event—in the worst possible way," *The Washington Post*, July 17, 2018, https://www.washingtonpost.com/news/global-opinions/wp/2018/07/17/the-trump-putin-summit-in-helsinki-was-a-historic-event-in-the-worst-possible-way/?utm_term=.d0bf36dfcf73; Felicia Sonmez and Mike DeBonis, "Trump's defense of Russia prompts outrage from some Republicans," *The Washington Post*, July 16, 2018, https://www.washingtonpost.com/politics/trumps-defense-of-russia-prompts-outrage-from-some-republicans/2018/07/16/adc9c52c-8914-11e8-a345-a1bf7847b375_story.html?utm_term=.dbff42a223a3.
79. Associated Press, "Pence, Bolton, Kelly confronted Trump in Oval Office about Russia comments," *Los Angeles Times*, July 21, 2018, https://www.latimes.com/nation/la-na-trump-russia-comments-20180721-story.html?utm_source=feedburner&utm_medium=feed&utm_campaign=Feed%3A+latimes%2Fsports%2Fcollege%2Fusc+%28L.A.+Times+-+USC+Trojans%29.
80. Krishnadev Calamur, "Trump Goes After Montenegro, a 'Tiny Country' With 'Aggressive People,'" *The Atlantic*, July 18, 2018, https://www.theatlantic.com/international/archive/2018/07/trump-montenegro/565475/; Mark Landler, Michael D. Shear, and Maggie Haberman, "A One-Two Punch Puts Trump Back on His Heels," *The New York Times*, August 21, 2018, https://www.nytimes.com/2018/08/21/us/politics/trump-manafort-cohen-mueller.html; Gary Langer, "Little public support for Trump in doubting Russian interference (POLL)," ABC News, July 22, 2018, https://abcnews.go.com/Politics/public-support-trump-doubting-russian-interference-poll/story?id=56734301.
81. Michael Gordon, "Russia Deploys Missile, Violating Treaty and Challenging Trump," *The New York Times*, February 14, 2017, https://www.nytimes.com/2017/02/14/world/europe/russia-cruise-missile-arms-control-treaty.html
82. Gregory Hellman, "Bolton in Russia after Trump announces INF withdrawal," *Politico*, October 22, 2018, https://www.politico.com/newsletters/morning-defense/2018/10/22/bolton-in-russia-after-trump-announces-inf-withdrawal-382068.
83. Uri Friedman, "House Democrats Want to Investigate Trump's Foreign Policy," *The Atlantic*, November 9, 2018, https://www.theatlantic.

com/international/archive/2018/11/house-democrats-investigate-trump-foreign-policy/575401/.

84. Alex Ward, "Democrats won the House—and Trump's foreign policy may be in trouble," *Vox*, November 7, 2018, https://www.vox.com/policy-and-politics/2018/11/1/18044158/midterm-elections-democrats-house-foreign-policy-trump-military-russia-intel.

85. Eli Stokols, "Trump, stung by midterms and nervous about Mueller retreats from traditional presidential duties," *Los Angeles Times*, November 13, 2018, http://www.latimes.com/politics/la-na-pol-trump-absent-201 81113-story.html.

86. Josh Dawsey and Philp Rucker, "Five days of fury: Inside Trump's Paris temper, election woes and staff upheaval," *The Washington Post*, November 13, 2018, https://www.washingtonpost.com/politics/five-days-of-fury-inside-trumps-paris-temper-election-woes-and-staff-upheaval/2018/11/13/e90b7cba-e69e-11e8-a939-9469f1166f9d_story.html?utm_term=.f434 dc446b23.

87. Dawsey and Rucker, "Five days of fury." Jen Kirby, "The controversies of Trump's Paris trip," *Vox*, November 12, 2018, https://www.vox.com/2 018/11/12/18087478/trump-paris-trip-macron-wwi-memorial.

88. Jane Dalton, "Emmanuel Macron warns of 'dangers' of nationalism in Armistice speech aimed at Trump and Putin," *Independent*, November 11, 2018, https://www.independent.co.uk/news/world/europe/remembrance-day-emmanuel-macron-speech-nationalism-patriotism-trump-putin-war-arc-de-triomphe-a8628856.html.

89. David E. Sanger and William J. Broad, "In North Korea, Missile Bases Suggest a Great Deception," *The New York Times*, November 12, 2018, https://www.nytimes.com/2018/11/12/us/politics/north-korea-missile-bases.html.

90. Nikki Haley, another more conventional foreign policy voice announced before the election that she would step down as UN Ambassador.

CHAPTER 7

ANALYZING TRUMP'S GRAND STRATEGY

FINDINGS AND CONCLUSIONS

NATIONALISM AS GRAND STRATEGY

Every September, presidents and prime ministers follow one of the globe's great annual migrations as they and their delegations fly to New York to open the United Nations General Assembly. Politicians deliver predictable speeches and shake hands before dispersing. To the 2017 session, though, the United States had sent, it seemed, a new type of American president.

This book has proposed two major research agendas. First, it argues that the most effective way to study grand strategy is via Grand Strategy Analysis (GSA). This approach is flexible and based upon the well-established foreign policy analysis research agenda among political scientists, but GSA is fundamentally interdisciplinary. Second, the book analyzes the sources, formation, and typology of the Trump administration's grand strategy. Applying the GSA framework allows us to systematically observe many variables related to grand strategy, and the book's simple *scope*, *substance*, and *assertiveness* rubric allows us to categorize the grand strategy in simple terms without committing to any one school of thought. To these agendas, this final chapter also provides an early evaluation of effectiveness. The following pages draw upon the book's core chapters—four case studies that create an early history of the Trump administration's grand strategy—to define and evaluate Trump's grand strategy based upon those frameworks.

Back at the UN, the president's team knew that the world was looking to understand what type of world Trump would work to create. Framed by the General Assembly's gold and marble dais, Trump stepped to the podium and presented his international agenda. His speech was divided between traditional Republican and insurgent nationalist agendas, but the nationalist vision largely carried the day. Trump declared to the world's leaders that he would elevate national sovereignty rather than American values as a guiding principle. He would work with flexible partners. He would be prepared to destroy "rocket man"—Kim Jong Un of North Korea—and confront the dictator's "suicide mission" to develop nuclear weapons. He would stop "radical Islamic terrorism," and he would start with Iran and his own country's nuclear agreement with that government. He would support refugees in their regions rather than bringing them to other countries. He would demand a better deal from the billions of dollars the United States had passed to the UN. He would push Venezuela to dump its socialist regime. And to make the world a better place, he rejected internationalism and called for "a great reawakening of nations, for the revival of their spirits, their pride, their people, and their patriotism."

A year later, Trump's team, now more closely tied to the president's personal preferences, worked up a reaffirmation of its worldview. Foreign delegations returned and leaders took their seats in the General Assembly chamber. "In less than two years," Trump boasted, "my administration has accomplished more than almost any administration in the history of our country." Laughter trickled across the room as the audience received its translations. The president of the United States paused and said, "I didn't expect that reaction, but that's OK." After the clapping and laughter subsided, President Trump proceeded to describe his administration's successes and priorities. He defended his trade war with China, US withdrawal from the UN Human Rights Council, and American preferences to keep refugees in their home regions. Trump touted America's energy sector along with his tough stand on Iran and his work with North Korea. His central strategic logic, however, remained unchanged: nationalism. Carefully guarded sovereignty and state prerogatives can combine with love and loyalty to homeland to "unleash ... incredible potential." By contrast, "globalism," with its institutions and integration, was dead to the administration's grand strategy.

Trump's presidential predecessors created the United Nations. They built it, in part, upon the promise of internationalism. Now, before that institution, Trump embraced nationalism. As a strategic and ideological framework, nationalism had defined Japanese, German, and even US strategic priorities in the 1930s. That approach ended in catastrophe and created the ground for the very organization Trump now challenged. Many of the world's leaders may have been alarmed by this nationalist turn. However, after nearly two years in office, they also knew Trump's record, and from where many of those leaders sat, that record was ambiguous.

Individuals and Grand Strategy
That same day, on another American coast, I rolled up my sleeves in the Florida humidity and walked to class. The topic that day was nuclear weapons and strategic policy. I chalked some key words onto a classroom blackboard and got to work with my students. Was the administration right to scuttle the JCPOA with Iran? Should Trump have met with Kim Jong Un, and was Kim's promise on nuclear weapons really what Trump sought? We wrestled with how to determine strategic priorities and long-term investments. As the discussion wound down, a student wondered about reputation. Can a unique president like Trump permanently change American strategy and reputation? Would a new, more conventional president return American security policy to an old standard?

It seemed to me that there are two basic ways to think about American strategic policy. GSA helps us disentangle and evaluate them. One is that grand strategy is ever changing as leadership changes. The second is that it rolls in long waves and remains relatively stable no matter who pulls the levers of American foreign policy. In the first, specific approaches and psychologies matter most. In the latter, a host of variables affect grand strategy and stabilize it. No doubt, there is a spectrum of other options between those poles. Wherever one stands on this analysis, individual and group decision makers remain the crucial unit of analysis. These are the agents articulating and interacting with strategies. It is amidst their words and decisions that one can identify and evaluate grand strategies. This is the insight of GSA. If observers want to know whether Donald Trump could fundamentally change US grand strategy or the American reputation in the world, they would need to observe the people at the heart of that strategy.

Man versus System

A month later, in the waning weeks of the 2018 midterm election season, Donald Trump confided something to interviewer Leslie Stahl, of the television newsmagazine *60 Minutes*. His no-nonsense Secretary of Defense and former Marine general James Mattis was "something of a Democrat."[1] Trump admitted that "he may leave." A two-year stint as Secretary of Defense would be short but not terribly unusual, particularly if the president and the incumbent diverge personally. However, Mattis' challenge was not that he and Trump had developed interpersonal problems; rather, Mattis' more internationalist view of national security and grand strategy was out of sync with Trump's. For Trump, Mattis being "something of a Democrat" meant that the man was one of *them*. An enemy of Trump's approach, nationalism, and possibly Trump himself.

Still, even if this is a fair portrait of Trump's personal approach to grand strategy—making it personal and individual rather than national and integrated—did his personal approach actually shape US grand strategy?

IDENTIFYING GRAND STRATEGY

Recall that this book applies a simple three-part rubric to identify a grand strategy: *scope, substance,* and *assertiveness.* It uses these three dimensions to "measure" the Trump administration's grand strategy.

Scope

Like administrations since the 1940s, the Trump team held that no part of the Earth—or even cislunar orbit—was irrelevant to US national interests. Its scope was *global* throughout this period. In his 2018 address to Congress, for instance, the president emphasized that the United States held "vital security interests" found "across the globe." This does not mean that administration officials saw interests evenly distributed. Trump and his team treated certain regions and issues with more attention. As a candidate and new president, Trump focused particularly on Mexico, China, the Middle East, and US allies. Many of these actors, he complained, had been poaching US wealth for decades. On the Middle East, Trump characterized his campaign adversaries as incompetent or foolish next to the task of dealing with terror threats, Islamic extremism (and possibly Islam itself), Iran, and ISIS. Mexico, meanwhile, served as a symbol of both trade injustice and migration threats.

Overall, Trump tended to drop traditional US distinctions between "allies" and "adversaries." Instead, just about every government could be an adversary if it declined to work with the United States on, for example, improving trade relations. Trump himself held some personal preferences for leaders in Saudi Arabia as well as Vladimir Putin in Russia. He also prided himself on working personally with Xi Jinping of China and even Kim Jong Un of North Korea. In those cases, though, personal affinity did not supersede the trade and/or security threat that those leaders' governments represented. Only a few governments, most notably Iran's and Venezuela's, would remain consistently in the administration's "enemy" category. ISIS captured the administration's primary military attention, but it was slowly crushed during this period.

Meanwhile, even though the United States held built-in cooperative structures with a number of governments, particularly democracies, around the world, Trump, and increasingly his administration, treated them as possible trade threats. Indeed, the administration allowed early exceptions on its big push for tariffs in 2018, but it eventually treated even G-7 governments as no different than any other. In sum, the Trump administration's grand strategy consistently displayed a global geographic scope characterized by treating nearly all governments as either potential allies or adversaries depending upon their willingness to deal with Trump's trade and security agenda.

Substance

Core Interests

The administration's underlying theory or ideology evolved around a core set of principles. For the incoming Trump administration, *trade* was the most commonly cited strategic interest for the United States. Trump himself viewed international politics, along with business, as zero-sum. In that environment, whether ally or adversary, any other state gaining wealth or advantage was actively weakening the United States. Minimizing loss in trade, ran this theory, would strengthen the United States in all other domains.

In turn, *projecting strength* was also seen as an early strategic interest, and it persisted throughout these two years. As discussed in "Orientation" and "Maximal Pressure," the specific type of strength projection was only partially direct military deployment. As a strategic interest, even an image or impression of toughness and strength could gain leverage in the bilateral deals that Trump wanted to pursue. By 2018, Pompeo and Bolton in particular actively supported this agenda. Projecting strength in itself was an innate state interest, not simply a strategic tool. Rather than primarily providing deterrence, perceptions of strength could lend leverage to trade and other negotiations.

Sovereign rights and *national identity*, along with *immigration*, also played a consistent role in the administration's stated strategic interests. Previous administrations took sovereignty as given and noncontroversial. For Trump nationalists, however, "globalists" had actively undermined distinctively American prerogatives. International trade and political agreements, in their account, put others' interests before Americans'. Trump and other immigration hawks in his administration often falsely claimed that their political opponents favored "open borders." What they seemed to mean is that migration into the United States felt unchecked to many Americans and posed an existential threat to the country's cultural and demographic identity. If the United States had become great under a certain set of demographic and cultural conditions, undermining those would prove domestically and globally disastrous. Protecting sovereign rights and national identity against outsiders and foreign interests was a pressing national interest. This was classic nationalism.

As budget plans developed, *traditional military power* also emerged as a distinct national interest. Though Trump himself never presented as a militarist *per se*, expanded military spending and investments served useful functions. They signaled toughness and strength, and they fit with both nationalists' and traditional realists' tendency to see a world comprised of state threats. Rather than start wars and interventions, their goal was to maintain America's lead in classic great power politics.

Finally, *enemy governments* remained a core and growing strategic interest. This category is idiosyncratic. It represents Trump's tendency to focus on a few governments, along with ISIS, that he treated as significant threats. Left unchecked, these enemy regimes would do bad things in the world and to the United States. This category is awkward for the Trump administration because Trump himself also emphasized transactionalism: he was willing, in theory, to deal with anyone and set aside traditional values. In practice, which governments were treated with transactional agnosticism and which were treated as menacing enemies depended upon the president's personal preferences. Iran and Venezuela fit here.

North Korea did, as well, but to a far lesser extent once Kim, through the South Koreans, opened a path toward direct talks.

Nature of the System and Role

The administration's core grand strategy interests remained relatively stable; nevertheless, its theory of the international system, and the US role in that system, saw several versions. Each reflected the president's core "America first" instincts. Campaigning and assuming office, Trump brought a set of issues and interests, many based upon perceived grievances and views that he had held for decades, but it was nationalists like Steve Bannon and Stephen Miller who knit all that into a more coherent theory. In his inaugural address, Trump spoke of "American carnage." The United States had been internationally and domestically victimized and had failed real Americans. A strong leader like Trump could push deals and change that trajectory. In practice, this meant bilateral relations rather than multilateral agreements. It also included trade protectionism and demanding "fair" dealing. Still a set of impulses, this vision was fleshed out over the next months. At its core emerged sovereignty. "Free nations," Trump told Congress in early 2017, "are the best vehicle for expressing the will of the people." In a later speech, he also argued that the modern sovereign state had proven to be the most effective tool for protecting human rights and advancing human prosperity. Respecting US and other governments' sovereign prerogatives, then, was the *sine qua non* of an effective grand strategy. Again, in action this meant wielding American power against friends and foes alike in order to renegotiate the United States' relationships around the world. As a theory of international politics, this transactionalism meant that any threatening situation was open to negotiation. It also meant that any given "ally" should be treated as a competitor. When critics raised questions about Trump's unusually friendly relationship with Russia's Vladimir Putin, he could point to this principle.

The United States could be a leader, but it could lead only in the sense of a first among equals. Under Trump, it would not commit to new long-term, internationalist frameworks, and it would seek to shrink the influence of many of the very organizations, like the World Trade Organization and United Nations, that the United States itself had set up after World War II. Perhaps appropriate at that time, reasoned Trump's team, those arrangements had ensnared the United States and compromised its sovereignty.

Still, through most of 2017 and into early 2018, many senior officials in the administration remained skeptical of a thoroughly nationalist, America first grand strategy. James Mattis and H.R. McMaster, for instance, still broadcast the value of diplomacy and internationalism. Such approaches in fact could help share the burden of global security and achieving US national interests. Throughout this period, "principled realism" emerged in speeches and documents, most notably the National Security Strategy (NSS). It could serve as a bridge between these more conventional views and the administration's nationalists. Principled realism seemed to hold that international affairs are inevitably defined by states and their interests, but that did not mean those states cannot cooperate and seek mutual benefit. The United States should invest in remaining economically and militarily competitive. It should also leverage its existing alliance and trade frameworks.

Ultimately, though, principled realism was an unstable hybrid and gave way to "America first" and, in effect, nationalism. The NSS, for instance, highlighted migration; "free, fair, and reciprocal trade;" and overmatch, or an investment in overwhelming, traditional military capabilities. As senior personnel gave way to hardliners like Pompeo and Bolton, nuanced realism disappeared. Throughout 2018, the administration cranked up its trade disputes into "trade war" with a range of governments. Trump met with Kim Jong Un but also suffered criticism for his stands on Russia. The administration also continued to ratchet pressure on military spending and border enforcement. In all these cases, the administration's success record was mixed. For this study, though, its *intention* and its rationale grew more unambiguously nationalist. Indeed, Trump himself was unambiguous: "I'm a nationalist."

In sum, though the specific form of "America first" varied over these two years, it always returned to a few key principles that are most accurately called nationalism. The international system is defined by zero-sum competition among sovereign states. Trade, migration, and, to a lesser extent, other states' military prowess all posed existential threats to US sovereign identity and prerogatives. In that environment, the United States should maintain its lead position, but it should avoid the dangers of *leadership*. In other words, it should avoid all possible entanglements and solely advocate its narrow and immediate interests. This was an explicitly anti-internationalist approach. Still, though the administration did withdraw from several newer and a few older multilateral and bilateral treaties, it did not seek to actively withdraw from or collapse the existing international order. Trade regimes and intergovernmental organizations remained in place. Rather, it sought to transform the US view of the international system from an interconnected community to a field of competition comprised not of teams but of individual players. In that world, the United States did not owe anyone—not even Canada —consistency or support. It only owed itself fair deals and supremacy over threats, both material and cultural.

Assertiveness

Achieving the Trump administration's nationalist vision would require real force, but at any given point in time, that force remained at a relatively moderate level. It proved to be economic and diplomatic— or, if not exactly diplomatic, then rhetorical—as much as military. He and his administration, however, did try to wield the *threat* of force. "Maximum pressure" persisted as a key guiding principle. Not quite a security strategy, maximum pressure remained a simple touchstone across issue areas. On trade, military, and political issues, Trump officials tried to leverage the United States' incredible power to force target states to accept US demands. Often, this meant tariffs and sanctions. Sometimes it meant moving military assets and targeted strikes. Of course, the challenge of maximal pressure is that it may end with achieving very little at high cost or, more dangerously, setting up the conditions for spiraling misperceptions and conflict.

Force Level

Some of the new president's more vocal critics worried that Trump would prove to be a militarist and, through bluster and undisciplined threats, pull the United States into unnecessary wars. As an analogy, they often looked to the neoconservatives in the George W. Bush administration or to the fascist and militarist regimes of the 1930s. Trump certainly liked to deploy the imagery, personnel, and rhetoric of military force. At no point during this period, however, did he indicate that he considered military force the primary tool of US grand strategy, that he was comfortable with ambitious military commitments, or that, like the fascists, he considered military confrontation an inevitable aspect of international relations.

For example, he roundly criticized neoconservatives in the G.W. Bush administration for their calamitous overcommitments. Those policy makers had believed that the United States could and *should* use its vast power to change the world. Trump disagreed. Almost by definition, his nationalism dictated aggressively reducing military commitments. For instance, in May 2019, as tensions with Iran reached another peak after the period studied in this book, observers suspected neoconservative John Bolton was, as National Security Advisor, positioning the United States for a war. Trump lifted the veil on White House debates to contradict this. "He has strong views on things which is OK," he explained, "I'm the one who tempers him, which is OK. I have John Bolton and I have people who are a little more dovish than him."[2] Admittedly, Trump may have underestimated Bolton's bureaucratic prowess and his ability to manipulate both policy and the president. Still, as Trump's rhetoric of force spiraled up and down, his actual commitment to applying violence remained low or moderate.

Several examples illustrate this finding. He discussed but never initiated plans for a military intervention in Venezuela. He preferred one-off strikes and to wind down existing hostilities in places like Syria/Iraq (against ISIS) and Afghanistan. He was happy to sell Saudi Arabia military goods for its war in Yemen, and he was even willing to lend limited direct support; however, he was not interested in opening a wider US campaign. When confronted with a chemical weapons attack in Syria during his first months in office, Trump green lighted limited air strikes. The action was a one-off event. Over that year and into the next, Trump gave Mattis and Joint Chiefs Chairman Dunford leeway to work up a new Afghanistan strategy (dubbed R4+S), but as president, he lent the effort no serious attention or political capital. Indeed, shortly after the midterm election, he abruptly announced that he was done pushing back the US commitment to Afghanistan and would withdraw immediately.

By contrast, Trump seemed comfortable slowly ramping up extensive commitments to "trade war" and sanctions. By middle to late 2018, the administration had imposed high tariffs against friends and adversaries alike. It sought government subsidies for US farmers affected, and it gave no indication that the pressure, particularly toward China, would end soon. Toward Iran, the administration attempted to build up similar "maximum pressure" and laid blame on the regime itself, not just its weapons program. With North Korea, it rapidly built up pressure, reversed course to welcome two summits, and then faced null results.

Security Strategies

Over this period, no single security strategy emerged, though "maximum pressure" seemed to serve that purpose. Concepts like *principled realism*, *peace through strength*, and *overmatch* captured the administration's belief that traditional great power politics required renewed investments. Governments, ran this logic, are basically on their own to achieve security, and, whether they choose it or not, they are locked in competition with other states. As putative security strategies, though, they proved to be rhetorical frameworks rather than active policy. By contrast, throughout this period, Trump emphasized one of the administration's core strategic principles: "maximum pressure" or "maximum leverage." It appeared to be an operating principle, one that fit both Trump's self-image of a hard-charging negotiator and his Republican team's hardline preferences. Under this framework, the United States would use its uniquely vast power to threaten and then ratchet coercive measures. Typically, this meant using economic sanctions, though it might also include cutting military aid, working with Trump's sometimes wildly confrontational rhetoric, or activating—sometimes actually using—military assets. If the target government did not respond favorably, the administration could ratchet further.

Eventually, the target state, as a self-interested actor, would return to the negotiating table and make greater concessions than if the adminis-tration simply started with standard diplomatic talks. That, in any case, appeared to be the operating logic. Officials pointed to trade talks with a number of partners as well as the North Korean summits as successes. Still, maximal pressure as a theory was limited. A target government might dread impending or unpredictable threats from the United States, but it could also game out responses and calculate reciprocal pressure. After all, the administration was setting itself high standards. If negoti-ations failed or slowed, it would own the failure. Both foreign partners and traditional adversaries seemed to find the Trump administration's approach exasperating, but they also knew that the administration needed a deal. Indefinite trade wars would, economic advisor Larry Kudlow admitted at one point, hurt "both sides."

On military confrontations, other great powers knew that violence and war were effectively off the table, and with asymmetrical threats, like Syria or ISIS, US escalation beyond air strikes and special operations was also unlikely. The big question mark remained middle level powers like Iran and North Korea. Again, actual war seemed unlikely for a nationalist administration that vowed to end expensive foreign commitments. On the other hand, ratcheting military threats would be difficult to unwind, and they made misperceptions and conflict spirals more likely. North Korea's solution appeared to be meeting, creating an illusion of agreement, and —having achieved little of substance but easing tensions—returning to business as usual. Iran, by contrast (and for many reasons), could not or would not adopt that approach. Tensions continued to increase.

Empirically, then, the record was mixed. Maximum pressure unsettled many relationships in which US partners, clients and others had taken their relationship with the world's largest power for granted. On the other hand, in nearly every case—trade with North American, Asian, European partners; North Korean nuclear weapons; Syrian chemical weapons; immigration—the progress toward a deal or the final deal itself proved marginal. Further, uncounted in this assessment is reputational and opportunity costs. In other words, were those deals worth the price of unsettling and possibly alienating many governments, or of indicating that US leadership was no longer consistent and reliable?

Table 4. Characteristics of Trump's grand strategy summarized.

Dimensions	Characteristics	Trump, 2017-18
SCOPE	Geographic Extent	Global
	Allies	Traditional partners willing to deal
	Adversaries	Trade, migration, proliferation threats; near-peer competitors
SUBSTANCE	Core Interests	"America first:" trade, immigration, reducing commitments
	Nature of System	Zero-sum, state-centric, transactional
	Role	Lead power, Protect sovereign prerogatives
ASSERTIVENESS	Force Level	Low - Moderate
	Security Strategies	"Principled realism" (abandoned), "Maximum pressure"

Donald Trump's Grand Strategy: *Global Nationalism*

In sum, during these two years, the Trump administration displayed a *nationalist grand strategy*. To be more precise, I will call it *global nationalism*. Nationalism as a grand strategy may take many forms. It might display highly militarist characteristics and minimize trade. It might emphasize relative isolation from the rest of the world. In this case, the administration's nationalism was global, transactional, moderately assertive, focused on trade and, crucially, it was also centered on a single personality, Donald Trump. The president himself brought to the office a set of impulses about America's core interests. Trade and immigration, most prominently. Still, he brought no theory of international relations beyond being tough, getting respect, and striking better deals. In fact, in early 2017, he said he was a "globalist" as much as a nationalist. By mid-2018, however, the administration's theory of international affairs and the US role in the world was clear. Sovereign states are not just the world's essential political units. They are fundamentally good and efficacious for their people, and *only* their people. In that framework, "sovereign rights," rather than, say, human rights or international cooperation, would be the administration's lodestar.[3] In short, the grand strategy approach was clearly nationalist, but it held a global view of US interests as well as a specific theory of how international politics could and should operate around the world.

Calling Trump's grand strategy "global nationalism" may seem misleading. As a title, it does not clearly indicate whether "global nationalism" really drove Trump's approach to grand strategy, or whether the concept is just a convenient title for an unorganized set of policies and impulses. A common critique of grand strategy as an analytical concept is that one almost never observes policy makers directly referencing grand strategy. For example, Trump and his officials during this period rarely, if ever, referred to "nationalism" or "grand strategy" to help them determine a course of action. Many scholars and commentators consistently focused on the president's style. Skeptics always insisted that "there is no Trump Doctrine."[4] In their assessment, Trump's preference for *ad hoc* statements and dramatic policy shifts, short-term wins, and pure transactionalism amounts to a style, not a strategy. Another group of observers saw this approach as an asset. In a media column, for instance, scholar Colin Dueck revived the notion that Trump displayed "strategic unpredictability."[5] A high risk approach, strategic unpredictability can unsettle allies. If managed well, though, it can also advance US interests where prior administrations were paralyzed. Scholars John Bew and David Martin Jones take this a step further. They argue that Trump's early administration stood in a classical lineage with Aristotle, Aquinas, and Burke: "prudence."[6] Here, the leader rejects abstract strategies. Instead, he favors a sensibility that mixes action with caution. Ionut Popescu sees a bit more order to the approach. He characterizes the Trump administration engaged in "emergent strategy."[7] Trump and his team—displaying a largely offensive realist strategy—were learning from and responding to challenges.

Chapter 2 argues that leaders may fail to work up a coherent strategy but can still be enmeshed in existing strategic commitments. These patterns of decision and behavior may not reflect strategic forethought, but they often represent implicit theories about means and ends. In other words, leaders may fall into existing strategic patterns. "Grand behavior," as Silove calls it. If one treats grand strategy as an empirical phenomenon, this is exactly what is expected. *A pattern of thought and policy.* In this framework, policy makers do not need to explicitly invoke or apply a grand strategy for such a strategy to exist. Skeptics of strategy are correct that policy makers must constantly respond to events and lack the time and mental space to maintain and implement big strategies. If anything, though, that insight suggests that policy makers are prone to accepting existing grand strategy frameworks. To draw a metaphor, you may have been a passenger on a bus and could not choose the route, but once you take the driver's seat, you take the lead in choosing the direction from that point forward. In a similar sense, grand strategies are real, and policy makers have real control over them. Nevertheless, like decisions made about a bus route made by previous drivers, they exist outside the full control of any one leader. Highlighting Trump's unique influence is correct; however, focusing on the man alone also risks missing larger strategy patterns.

Other observers—Colin Dueck, most explicitly—are more optimistic that Trump presented a coherent and viable nationalism. As seen in Chapter 1, several scholars and former officials argued in 2017 that despite appearing to be radical, Trump's foreign policy fit a mold forged by earlier Republican administrations. For many, this was *conservative internationalism*: active engagement with the world but with an emphasis on sovereignty, shared values, and traditional national interests. This characterization, however, overemphasizes the administration's internationalism. After serving as Trump's Deputy Assistant to the President for Strategic Communications (until April 2018), Michael Anton argued that "America first" should not be confused with internationalism.[8] In short, he said, the logic is this: "Let's all put our own countries first, and be candid about it ... Putting our interests first will make us all safer and more prosperous." Scholar Barry Posen was more academically precise. Trump had "taken much of the 'liberal' out of 'liberal hegemony.'"[9] The president still sought "to retain the United States' superior economic and military capability and role as security arbiter for most regions of the world, but," Posen explained, Trump chose "to forgo the export of democracy and abstain from many multilateral trade agreements." Andrew Bacevich, scholar and retired Amy officer, agreed that Trump shifted US grand strategy away from overambition.[10] Colin Dueck, however, offered a helpful insight into Republican Party traditions and one of the most well developed accounts of Trump as a nationalist foreign policy president.[11] Here, "conservative nationalism" is a well-established foreign policy approach associated with the Republican Party. In this framework, the nation-state remains the most effective political form to experiment with and implement constitutional democracy (Dueck called this "civic nationalism"). Further, said Dueck, conservatives are skeptical that radical change in international affairs is possible, that baseline social and political order helps preserve freedom, and that self-governance paired with sovereign independence should be prioritized in foreign relations. Speaking extemporaneously, Trump himself never explicitly engaged these concepts, yet his prepared speeches often did. Most likely, thinkers in and around the administration worked out the abstract framework they observed in the president's comments, priorities, and decisions. Unfortunately, for this book's analysis, Dueck's conservative nationalism is at once too broad and too narrow. It is too broad because it defines nationalism as effectively the same as patriotism. For Americans, he said, the real threat to national identity is not an ethnic group or rival nation but "domestic tyranny, corruption, and any foreign adversary who threatens the republic."[12] Few conservatives *or* liberals in the United States would disagree. It is too narrow because it is specifically a US tradition. Dueck did observe parallels in European nationalism and the modern state system; nevertheless, that illustrates the common denominator: nationalism itself is a universal phenomenon.

Overall, this book's findings largely confirm these claims that the Trump strategic approach is largely nationalist and global. It argues that *global nationalism* as a concept is accurate, concise, and generalizable. By contrast, "conservative internationalism" and "conservative nationalism," with their focus on the United States, cannot easily be used to analyze other governments. Still, Trump's approach during these two years was explicitly nationalist. That basic framework *is* a generalizable concept that can be applied in other contexts. China and Russia, for instance, are great powers applying different versions of nationalism. "America first," is a helpful slogan with a history directly tied to nationalist thinking, but it is less precise and less generalizable than calling the approach what it really is: nationalism. In Trump's case, the nationalist vision is global: touting—rather than exporting—it as a global model and, equally, using it to justify dominant military power and organize how the US government should approach its global interests. Administration officials used this framework for interpreting US interests to include the following: revising or dropping a wide range of trade and security agreements; privileging bilateral talks; approaching allies and adversaries as potential partners for mutual transnationalism; slowing as much international migration as possible to protect national identity; projecting an image of national strength; and preparing to compete with other governments in traditional great power politics. Officials' vision was global because they believed US interests spanned the world, and they believed security threats could emerge from many places around the world. Notably, they rejected—in fact, never even considered—isolationism. However, they also defined American national interests narrowly around sovereign rights, so even as American interests were seen as global, the strategy's agenda and ambitions were parochial. The United States, they argued, should maintain its lead position, but it should maintain that role only to the degree that it gained leverage and security. Nationalism, like a number of other grand strategy approaches, can slide toward high levels of force and militarism. On its face, however, it avoids interventionism and major military commitments, which could sully or sap the nation itself. Indeed, Trump's administration over these years proved confrontational, but it focused more on discrete military strikes and winding down existing US wars. On trade, it ramped up tariffs and sanctions. It was, in short, a moderate level of assertiveness.

INDIVIDUAL INFLUENCE

An administration's grand strategy approach is largely set by the president. Officials are typically constrained by his statements and are obliged at some level to follow his orders. Just as importantly, though, the president makes appointments and chooses who will surround him. Grand strategy is bigger than a single individual, but a government's foreign policy executive will have disproportionate effects upon the grand strategy. Recall from Chapter 2 that this study applies a series of questions to probe possible correlations between the executive and other players. Donald Trump is known for heated rhetoric and impulsive commentary. Did that pounding on the bully pulpit prove ineffective? Or did his positions pull the government in his direction? As table 5 shows, Trump's individual impact was limited, but it grew over time.

Table 5. Assessment questions and findings.

Executive vs Other Actors	*Candidacy and Early 2017*	*Spring and Summer 2017*	*Fall 2017 to Spring 2018*	*Summer and Fall 2018*
Consistency between president's statements and administration policy, agency actions?	M	L	M	H
Gap between an official US foreign policies before and after a change?	L	M	M	M
Consistency between president's and principals' statements?	L	L	L	M

Note: A simple Low, Moderate, High scale. L (Low) = little correlation between president and target influence, H (High) = president's position and the target variable appear nearly identical.

In early 2017, for example, tensions with North Korea rose. Kim Jong Un followed a long-standing North Korean pattern: escalate missile tests and rhetoric to establish a strong position and, perhaps, intimidate a new US administration. All prior presidents responded with firm but subdued language paired with calls for multiparty talks. Trump, by contrast, escalated expectations and threats, a familiar piece of his business toolkit. He appeared to score a political coup when the two met in Singapore, a first for leaders of their countries. The summit was followed in February 2019 with another in Vietnam. As many experts predicted, however, the relationship saw few fundamental changes. Statements emerging from the summits proved vague, and the North Koreans used follow-up talks to accuse the United States of bad faith. Indeed, the Vietnam summit ended abruptly when Trump walked away from the table. He realized, he said, that no serious deal was available.[13] After all this, US policy toward the South Korean alliance and toward North Korean human rights and weapons programs remained effectively unchanged from the day before Trump took office.

This basic stability is not surprising. If one looks at grand strategies as an observable phenomenon, as argued in Chapter 2, they represent a *pattern of thought and policy.* From one year to the next and from one administration to the next, there are a host of reasons why an existing grand strategy is likely to impose itself on a leader as much as—or more than—the leader imposes on the grand strategy. In Trump's case, historian Hal Brands argues that Trump's early efforts to radically change US grand strategy were thwarted. Though the new president had captured leadership of the Republican Party, Republicans in Congress more than once sided with Democrats on issues like Russia sanctions or NATO funding.[14] They held long-standing personal preferences and political commitments to those strategic policies. Similarly, in earlier eras, Brands argues that the "foundations of U.S. foreign policy" had been tested, but those waves could not fundamentally alter the tide of American international interests and commitments. In the United States, anyway, leaders change far more frequently than the country's basic priorities and the world's overarching conditions.

President's Statements versus Government Policy, Agency Actions

Over his first two years, Trump was only able to achieve a moderate amount of consistency between his statements and policy action. On the one hand, his aggressive statements, some of his senior appointees (particularly on economics), and his constant focus on a specific set of policy issues, like trade and migration, molded US official policy over time. On the other hand, his constant stream of public statements and tweets, his administration's thin bench of top and mid-level performers, and his chaotic management style limited the president's influence over his own bureaucracy.

Many nationalists and Trump supporters—most prominently Steve Bannon—in the lead up to Trump's election and afterwards complained that a "deep state" of elites in and outside government were the real centers of power. There was, they argued, a conspiracy of "globalists" opposed to nationalist policies and, once elected, Trump himself. Reality, as political scientists and practitioners have found, is far less exciting. Any president must actively wrangle with his own bureaucracy because, at a minimum, organizations tend to favor inertia. They will remain on established trajectories and pursue established policies. Agencies, on balance, will advocate for their slice of budget and policy as much as for the national interest. It is possible, though not inevitable, for a president to make pronouncements and public statements but find only superficial support from government agencies.

President Trump and his appointees certainly encountered skepticism and uncertainty from the government's foreign policy professionals, but Trump's team did little to address that challenge. It was, and remained, thin on experts and appointees who could impose some coherence on various agencies. The president himself remained relatively undisciplined in his messaging and policy pronouncements. Still, Trump enjoyed at least moderate consistency between his stated positions and government policy. He was, after all, able to sign executive orders and his political appointees often did follow his lead.

Through the middle of 2017, consistency between Trump's statements and government policy reached its nadir. Senior officials, from Pence to Mattis to Tillerson, continued to assure the world that the United States' core international commitments, even the Iran nuclear deal, remained steady. Trump, however, was more interested in supporting his personally preferred leaders (such as autocrats in the Middle East) and confronting other democracies, particularly NATO leaders. Trump almost single-handedly escalated tensions with North Korea, and in that case, he was able to pull the government along with him.

Through 2018, Trump replaced personnel and settled on men like Pompeo and Bolton who, whatever their policy differences with the president, were ready to support Trump's tone and rhetoric. On maximal pressure, trade war, "Space Force," Iran relations, North Korea talks, and immigration, the president, his team, and his bureaucracy showed relative consistency. Still, Trump's words regularly ran afoul of typical US messaging. Trump rarely if ever invoked "American values," and when he defended President Putin's view of the 2016 election, he directly contradicted the entire US intelligence apparatus. His impetuous pronouncements and his preference to deal with leaders on a personal level—along with his White House's tendency to botch policy implementation on its first try—meant that consistency between the president and other organs in the executive branch remained, at their highest, moderate.

Official US Foreign Policy Before and After a Change
Changes in specific foreign policies are also a useful dimension to assess the president's individual influence. How much, in other words, did the government's official position change when the president sought and/or implemented a new agenda or a revision to US grand strategy? In short, what is the distance between the old and the new policy? Surprisingly, specific US strategic policies changed only a moderate amount during Trump's first two years.

As Trump assumed office, he and the nationalists on this team were promising a revolution based upon the man himself. Trump immediately withdrew from the Trans-Pacific Partnership and attempted to implement the infamous "Muslim ban" policy to halt all arrivals from a set of Muslim majority countries. During those early days, Trump also talked to a number of foreign leaders and, in so doing, often defied normal expectations about how a new president should interact with allies and adversaries. Still, these positions were symbolic as much as substantive. Trump, in many cases, was simply undoing executive orders handed down by his predecessor. In other cases, like the immigration policy, the administration faced court challenges and had to moderate its initial positions. Similarly, when Trump tried to rearrange personnel and positions on the National Security Council, he faced pushback even from Republicans and eventually returned to a position closer to the median. Indeed, throughout these two years, despite the support of a Republican-led Congress, the administration secured very few unambiguous budgetary or policy wins. Often, administration officials' deliberately extreme positions were rejected, but instead of securing a deal closer to their end of agenda, they had to settle for more mainstream positions. This is why, for example, military spending increased, but only marginally, and why cuts to diplomacy and foreign aid remained relatively small.

Moving into 2018, the United States continued to participate in all the existing international organizations and regimes, albeit with a far more confrontational and skeptical demeanor than during the Obama years. Trump continued to join the G-7 and NATO meetings. He did achieve a five percent cut to the UN budget and did pull the United States out of the United Nations Human Rights Council. In the larger context, though, a five percent cut is symbolic more than substantive, and the United States had only sought membership to the UNHRC in 2009. Trump rejected the Paris climate agreement of 2016, but for decades, the United States, and particularly Republican administrations, had remained officially skeptical of global climate treaties. Trump's own treatment of international organizations and norms, and the White House's stated positions and agendas, theoretically threatened to undermine much of the existing "liberal world order." As implemented, US strategic policy continued to take those organizations and arrangements into account rather than completely withdrawing from them.

On specific issues, as with international commitments, policy movement appeared more dramatic in the headlines than in substance. To be clear, US strategic policies *did* move. Climate policy, the Iran deal, the Trans-Pacific Partnership, trade policy, border security, North Korea talks, and Afghanistan strategy, alongside relations with NATO, Russia, Venezuela all saw distinct impacts from the Trump administration. The substantive gap between policy before and after the Trump administration touched these issues was real. It was also marginal. Actual strategic policy in each of these areas was not revolutionized.

President's Statements versus Those of Principals

This final category seeks to determine the degree of consistency between what the president says and positions adopted by his senior foreign policy officials and, to a lesser extent, party leaders outside the administration; where the first question focuses on official US policy and agency positions, this question focuses on individuals. The trajectory for the Trump administration for these two years is a move from less to more consistency. In concrete terms, over time, Trump enjoyed more agreement from his principals because he drove out a series of early appointees before settling on a team that worked with both his stylistic and his policy preferences. During the transition and the administration's early months, Trump and his team wanted to install a mix of Trump loyalists and, to lend some credibility and gravitas, more experienced hands. Almost immediately, however, two basic wings and a third, rump faction emerged: insurgent nationalists and, for lack of a better term, conventional Republicans. The rump faction comprised some of Trump's closest advisors. People like his daughter Ivanka and her husband Jared Kushner. They were loyal to Trump personally and arrived with relatively few policy commitments.

Due to the formation of these factions, Trump achieved little consistency between these statements and those of the various camps. This persisted into 2018. Notably, Trump himself remained relatively consistent about his tough talking approach. He wanted to bid up tensions and unsettle normal expectations. Unfortunately for productive diplomacy, the content of his statements and their focus—or, rather, their scattershot impact—could vary from one day to the next. Meanwhile, national security principals like Tillerson, Mattis, Pence, and Nikki Haley, UN Ambassador, spent much of 2017 reassuring allies at meetings like the annual Munich Security Conference that US strategic policy had not fundamentally changed. Haley, for instance, consistently confronted

Russia at the United Nations and in the Security Council even as Trump himself consistently insisted that he trusted Putin. Senior Advisor Bannon, meanwhile, saw himself articulating the core strategic vision of a Trump revolution, but even he parted from Trump on North Korea because he saw China as the real threat.

Inside the White House, Bannon was soon marginalized and later drummed out, and in theory, National Security Advisor H.R. McMaster would have more leeway to mold US national security strategy. Holding tough but relatively mainstream views, McMaster would often try to revise Trump's more nationalist policy impulses. He also helped shape the 2017 National Security Strategy. The NSS was designed to bridge the administration's factions, but, in fact, its vision of "principled realism" was never adopted by Trump himself. Through late 2017 and into 2018, Trump's confrontational nationalism, supported by economic hardliners like Peter Navarro, continued to diverge from the internationalism of Mattis and others. Mattis, for instance, emphasized cooperation with allies and even China but worried about Russian strategic threats. Trump, by contrast, was ready for trade war with anyone and continued to insist that Russia was not a threat. Notably, over this first 18 months, Pence seemed to quietly shift his rhetoric to emphasize hardline confrontation, which broadly fit Trump's preferred style, or emphasize issues like religious freedom, for which Trump held little interest. This move increased the consistency between Pence and Trump.

The latter half of 2018 saw Trump finally achieve more consistency—but only *moderate* consistency—between his stated positions and those of his principals. Trump reconsolidated his personnel in late spring. With Pompeo as Secretary of State and Bolton as National Security Advisor, the administration was now set up more favorably for Trump's personal mix of strategic nationalism and temperamental, confrontational nature. Mattis, however, still quietly parted ways with the president, yet even if one sets him aside, Trump's almost manic public commentary meant that achieving high consistency between his statements and those of his principals would always be difficult.

Assessment Questions Overall

In sum, during these two years, Donald Trump never achieved a high degree of personal influence over US grand strategy. His management, his communication, his cognitive, and his policy styles inevitably created distance between himself and the government he was positioned to lead. They also created tensions among his senior foreign policy principals. This result is both surprising and not surprising. It is surprising because Trump seemed like a force of nature. His personality was inescapable for those around him, and his nationalist policy positions seemed to directly contradict long-standing US approaches to grand strategy. Indeed, there is no doubt that the tenor of US grand strategy did change in response to Donald Trump. He, as an individual, did have a real impact. If, for instance, Hillary Clinton had won the Electoral College along with the national popular vote, observers can reasonably assume that her positions on grand strategy issues would largely fit with Obama's. In that context, Trump's impact on US grand strategy is clear. Trump's unique characteristics, however, also appear to hold the seeds of tragic failure: they brought Trump to a position of power, but they often undermined his ability to move something as ponderous as US grand strategy.

SUCCESS OR FAILURE?

Such findings raise a follow-up question: was Trump's grand strategy during these years successful or failing? I argue that by the administration's own standards, its strategic approach was failing. In addition, Trump's personal approach and his nationalism were calibrated to score immediate wins, but, as the findings indicate, they also undermined most long-term strategic agendas. To be clear, these arguments come with an important caveat. This book's frameworks are designed to observe the empirical life of a given grand strategy. Evaluating success and failure are related but different exercises. They require short-, medium-, and long-term time horizons. For instance, a strategy that effectively serves short term goals may actively undermine long-term agendas. More importantly, evaluating success and failure also requires the analyst to set out and defend desired priorities and acceptable tradeoffs for a strategy. In other words, evaluating grand strategic success and failure requires a distinct normative as well as an empirical framework. This study only analyzes the latter. Still, not broaching the question at all would be irresponsible. For many scholars and practitioners, the point of empirical analysis is to determine lessons learned and make policy recommendations. At the very least, this discussion helps set the stage for later studies expressly evaluating success.

Contemporary discussion of Trump's foreign policy and grand strategy diverged along several cleavages. The most skeptical observers argued that, whatever the administration's intentions, Trump's temperament and Trump's ineptitude undermined any hope of strategic success. Already cited throughout this book, these arguments are concisely summarized by journalist Susan Glasser, who surmised, "It's worse than you think."[15] She wrote that foreign leaders found their encounters with Donald Trump "jarring." He questioned shared interests and upended established norms, but they seemed to believe he did so out of ignorance and egotism rather than calibrated nonconformity. Hal Brands was even more unsparing. "Trump's first year," he assessed in January 2018, "has been quite bad."[16] Though some competent officials surround Trump, Brands spoke for many critics who believed that the president's own ignorance reduced the number and quality of strategic options available. Other takes held that the president's main challenge was indeed implementation, but implementation was mixed. For instance, senior fellow at the Council on Foreign Relations Robert Blackwill worked up a report card for Donald Trump's international affairs. "Trump's foreign policies," it declared, "are better than they seem."[17] Along with a 'D' for policy implementation, Trump received failing marks on all procedural and foundational subjects: management of the policy process, "issues of character," promoting US values, as well as managing alliances and deterrence. On substance, he received another 'D' for European security along with 'F' grades for climate policy and Russia relations. In other areas, however, Trump's performance was neither better nor worse than many other administrations': China (B+), North Korea (B), Syria (B +), Saudi Arabia (B+), Israel (B), Iran (C), Afghanistan (B+), India (B+), Venezuela (B+), and trade (C).[18] On these latter issues, the administration at least grappled with "the manifold challenges the president faces in trying to deal with a deteriorating world order that he inherited."[19] In this vein, conservative commentator Yuval Levin commented that senior officials during this period were running US foreign policy while the president spun off unrelated rhetoric and pronouncements.[20] Sokolsky and Miller held that Trump's "strategic impatience" with North Korea looked promising but was completely undermined by the president's temperamental preference for raw reactions and his focus on fighting opposition at home.[21]

The president's supporters, of course, held that his tough talk and aggressive military budget already set the United States on a more successful trajectory. Scholar Randall Schweller even declared "three cheers for Trump's foreign policy."[22] The new president, like Obama, avoided large-scale wars, enforced a redline on chemical weapons against Syria's Bashar al-Assad, and pressured Kim Jong Un to the negotiating table. Conservative publisher Dimitri Simes admitted that Trump's diplomacy could be weak and inconsistent, and that the president tended to pose better questions than answers about US foreign policy. Still, Simes argued that Trump was "poised for success."[23] He leveraged limited but real pressure against his targets, effectively protected US sovereignty, and brought a fresh approach to a stale foreign policy establishment. Dueck, similarly, argues that Trump was hindered by a relative disregard for details and precedents, but that he effectively challenged conventional wisdom, delivered on campaign promises, was adaptive with new circumstances, and brought effective negotiating acumen to diplomacy.[24]

Evaluating Success by the Administration's Own Standards
This book presents a slightly different type of evaluation: was the administration successful over these two years *by its own standards?* Trump's strategic goal as he campaigned was to get better "deals" for the United States. This meant more favorable trade conditions, payment for military support, and less migration into the United States. In his zero-sum view, other governments were prospering off US wealth. He also wanted to restore some sense of "respect" to the United States. This was almost certainly a line developed specifically for campaigning rather than an agenda designed to address a specific international issue. Nevertheless, there is evidence that Trump had felt for decades that the United States was a "loser" in a lot of international relations. Gaining respect was a useful shorthand to communicate two things at once: his appreciation that many Americans felt they were being forgotten and disrespected, and, second, that restoring fear and respect among US interlocutors would, in itself, help the United States achieve better deals and more security without overseas military commitments. Trump said he was also ready to drive negotiations on security threats like Iran and North Korea after decades of failure by the experts and insiders. To these Trumpian impulses, nationalists like Bannon added a larger framework. They wanted to re-center international affairs on the sovereign state rather than the global organization or international business. They were also protective of "Western culture" or "Western civilization," and they believed that the United States was at a pivotal moment to either protect that culture and identity or face decline and implosion.

Of course, strategic agendas evolve as an administration gains experience, but comparing initial goals with subsequent outcomes is a useful inductive exercise. How did the Trump grand strategy in practice compare with its ambitions? Passable, but not well. Following Blackwill, I argue that the effort earned a C-, and much of that grade is based upon effort rather than outcomes. The administration effectively moved against accepted economic wisdom and US policy as it built up threats and then implemented tariffs against a range of governments. Over the two years covered, here, those efforts resulted in some marginal deals, but they did not fundamentally affect the United States' economic growth. The deals themselves, most notably the USMCA, appeared to be updates of existing frameworks. The big target, China, was willing to talk but yielded little and a steady tariff tit-for-tat grew over time.

Assessing respect is inevitably subjective and unsatisfying. With that caveat, there is evidence that many other governments recognized that the Trump administration was different than its predecessors. What they afforded, however, was not the respect Trump sought. They seemed to believe that President Trump was difficult to predict, but they also sought to coopt his displeasure by playing to his ego, tailoring messages (as did Netanyahu of Israel) for his preferences, and even sending delegations to stay at his hotels and properties. At the GOP convention in 2016, Trump told the delegates that "I alone" could fix the United States' problems. By centering so much of the administration on himself, Trump was targeted by foreign governments for personal dealing and, if possible, manipulation.

On overseas military commitments, Trump was, on balance, more successful. His administration and, specifically, the Department of Defense carried forward the Obama-era strategy to destroy ISIS and accelerated it by adding more direct air strikes and Special Forces units. Elsewhere, Trump resisted occasional calls to make new or expanded military commitments in hot spots like Yemen. His administration was also able to secure more military spending. On the other hand, the United States' global military posture, with all the global bases and trigger points that Trump disliked, remained basically the same.

On North Korean and Iranian relations, the performance is middling or worse. Trump landed talks with Kim Jong Un, but US negotiators and Trump himself made no substantive progress. With Iran, Trump and his team argued that simply ending the Obama agreement was a success. What should follow, however, was not clear. By moving first, the administration handed Iran great legitimacy also to stop following the deal, and it was left scrambling to convince other governments to *re*impose sanctions to force Tehran to the negotiating table.

Overall, the administration did achieve significant changes to the tone and focus of US grand strategy; however, its concrete successes were not nearly as radical as promised 2016 and early 2017. For example, when the White House released its list of foreign policy achievements in December 2017, in good bureaucratic fashion, it enumerated actions taken rather than substantive outcomes. Many of the skeptical and mixed reviews of Trump's performance are borne out in this study: the administration's early ambitions were almost all undermined or stymied by the man who made them possible. Even committed nationalists like Bannon quickly grew disillusioned with the administration's performance. For them, the Trump White House was not truly revolutionary and was tinkering at the margins. Whereas their concern for sovereign rights and identity might have been written into officials' speeches, many of the old elites and national interests remained unchanged. Further, observers should consider the cost-benefit analysis of creating instability and turbulence versus wins achieved. Trump's chaotic approach could be seen as a success in itself if it shook up old approaches in favor of new, more successful practices. Clearly, the administration did enjoy success at resetting the US agenda, both at home and abroad. On the other hand, the effort may have proven counterproductive if, like Pyrrhus winning the battle but losing his army, it created instability without achieving commensurate strength.

Evaluating the Strategy Itself
Another way to evaluate a given grand strategy is to assess the quality and prospects of the strategy itself. In other words, did Trump and his administration display a feasible, coherent, and sustainable strategy? Specifically, some scholars argue that Trump displayed an effective *anti-*strategy. Here, Trump was deliberately unpredictable, kept both allies and adversaries off balance, and, in turn, enjoyed strategic leverage. This is "strategic uncertainty" or "strategic ambiguity." Such an approach can

be savvy and effective. Based on this book's findings, however, Trump fostered uncertainty without a matching strategy.

I propose two sets of expectations to determine whether the Trump administration during these two years was driven by calibrated strategic uncertainty or by ad hoc, individual preferences. In the first set of expectations, if the administration displayed deliberate strategic uncertainty, then one would likely observe 1) preparation within the administration (even if within a small cadre of senior officials) to establish groundwork for a given policy decision, 2) deliberate attempts to consolidate seemingly abrupt or ad hoc policy moves, and 3) an emerging pattern of geopolitical or other strategic agendas. In short, strategic uncertainty might seem unpredictable from one announcement to the next, but policy makers would also display patterns of intentionality and efforts to consolidate their moves. In the second set of expectations, if the administration displayed literal uncertainty and impetuous decision-making, then one would likely observe 1) abrupt policy announcements and internal confusion about the administration's strategic priorities, 2) scattered or inconsistent efforts to consolidate unexpected policy announcements, 3) an emerging pattern of decisions that fit the executive's personal interests or prerogatives more consistently than a national strategic agenda. In short, truly *un*strategic decision-making would be both externally unpredictable *and* internally chaotic, and it would show no consistent pattern of national strategic priorities.

For example, President Richard Nixon deliberately fostered uncertainty but was a consistent and self-aware strategist. Most observers agree that Nixon was a calculating but relatively paranoid political operator. These characteristics helped him build a domestic political coalition. They also undermined his presidency as the Watergate scandal unfolded. Privately, Nixon also struggled with depression and substance abuse. Nevertheless, Nixon also built a series of effective—if sometimes amoral—strategic successes. To extract the United States from the Vietnam War, he expanded aerial bombing of North Vietnam and violated Cambodian sovereignty. During his first year in office, he placed the US military on war readiness and had nuclear bombers fly near Soviet air space over several days in order to alarm Soviet leaders. He also surprised the world when he built a wedge between Moscow and Beijing by formally recognizing the Communist People's Republic of China. Nixon admitted to some advisors that he espoused a "madman theory" of diplomatic negotiation and leverage. Projecting fanaticism and unpredictability, he wanted his foreign interlocutors to believe that he might resort to violence or other desperate measures to stop communism. Though seemingly temperamental and ad hoc, much of Nixon's strategic behavior 1) was often supported by groundwork quietly laid by Henry Kissinger or Nixon himself, 2) displayed follow-on publicity and diplomacy, and 3) showed a pattern of strategic support for reducing US costs in its competition with the Soviet Union while containing or marginalizing Soviet influence in key geostrategic regions. Whatever one thinks about the desirability of the Nixon administration's strategy, the fact of its relative coherence and effectiveness is difficult to deny.

Nixon's "madman" precedent of calculated strategic uncertainty is so well-known that both supporters and critics considered it a relevant framework to evaluate Donald Trump.[25] Supporters argued that with allies and adversaries alike, the president was forcing talks and compromises. US negotiators could leverage their status as the biggest power with the most volatile leader. If true, observers might conclude that the Trump administration may indeed have espoused an internally coherent but externally chaotic strategy. Critics, by contrast, considered Trump all madman and no theory. Rather than long term calculations, impulse and short-term wins drove his every decision. As with Nixon, observers can apply those three analytical questions to determine whether Trump and his team were running a deliberate strategy of uncertainty or simply running with a mix of Trump's impulses and nationalist priorities.

First, the Trump administration's approach to strategy was typi-cally characterized less by coherent preparation and more by 1) abrupt policy announcements and internal confusion about the administration's strategic priorities. In some cases, such as North Korea or trade, senior officials did make efforts to sort out specific policies and do early legwork. More often than not, though, the president's unpredictability worked against, or intersected only tangentially with, those plans. This was particularly true in the National Security Council, whose policy processes the Oval Office largely marginalized. Revealingly, no core of advisors or senior officials emerged who seemed to be helping prepare and orchestrate the president's policy decisions. Most often, officials were responding to off-the-cuff statements, tweets, and decisions emanating from the president. The administration also experienced both constant personnel turnover and regular, high-level infighting or confusion about any given policy statement or decision. "Maximal pressure," for example, emerged as a stable guideline, but it was a general concept, not a substantive strategy.

Second, the administration displayed 2) scattered or inconsistent efforts to consolidate unexpected policy announcements. Follow-through on strategic decisions was equally inconsistent or, in some cases, deliberately truncated to avoid the appearance of failure. Trump's surprise decision to meet Kim Jong Un, for instance, did produce a second summit, but in neither meeting was substantive change achieved or pressed forward. Trade is perhaps the strongest area of consistent strategic follow-through. Trump and his senior advisors steadily ratcheted pressure on allies and adversaries alike. Ironically, though, this consistency also undermines the "strategic uncertainty" approach. For the most part, trade negotiations continued at a steady pace rather than emerging in the aftermath of a seemingly abrupt or ad hoc policy move.

Third, and finally, the administration displayed mixed strategic coherence defined by 3) a loose pattern of a geopolitical or other strategic agenda, but one often directly shaped by the executive's personal interests or prerogatives more consistently than a national strategic agenda. Despite its relative chaos, the administration might still have displayed a consistent push toward a clear pattern of geopolitical or other strategic agendas. The record found in this book is mixed. On the one hand, though inconsistent and unpredictable, the administration's basically nationalist view of US strategic interests remained fixed. In that vision, reducing US commitments but maintaining global economic and security interests remained the consistent strategic goal. Trump pushed for "better deals" on trade and declined to expand military commitments. On the other hand, the administration's basically inconsistent prioritization of threats and partnerships often diverged from long-standing Congressional, bureaucratic, and earlier administrations' priorities. In most cases, Trump's personal and shifting priorities were the best framework to understand why one geopolitical or strategic agenda was elevated over another.

Admittedly, two years is insufficient time to truly weigh grand strategy success. Under that note of caution, this brief assessment finds that the Trump administration achieved its goal of changing the tone of US grand strategy but failed to achieve its more substantive, "America first" goals. Even if the administration was consciously applying a version of the "madman theory," such studied unpredictability was not nested within a careful or well developed strategic agenda. Instead, it was guided by a loose set of nationalist priorities and the president's own, often shifting, preferences and instincts. Donald Trump created an environment so focused on short-term wins—and so disinterested in traditional planning—that even short-term strategizing was difficult or impossible. Crucially, Trump's personal approach also slowly circumvented those in his administration—the "principled realism" set—who made efforts to build the foundations of a long-term strategy. Trump clearly held certain strategic goals, but his approach was based in personal intuitions and impulses rather than calculations and long games. It was a series of tactical gambits rather than a coherent strategy.

CONCLUSION

Donald Trump is a nationalist. I name his approach to grand strategy *global nationalism*. He is also brash, bold, inconsistent, uninterested in details, individually charming, and confrontational. Both the president's personal style and his temperament mattered to American grand strategy. Yet despite Trump's unignorable presence and clear impact on the tenor of US grand strategy, neither his policies nor his personality fundamentally changed American grand strategy. This final section summarizes the book's findings.

"An Arch Nationalist"

Most foreign policy public talks are subdued, and Kiron Skinner's appearance at the 2019 Future Security Forum seemed to fit that mold. A conservative academic, Skinner had been appointed to work directly with Secretary of State Pompeo and head the State Department's policy planning office. This is one of the US government's few places specifically devoted to big, strategic thinking. As a woman and an African American, Skinner stood out from the median foreign policy elite. What startled—and alarmed—many observers, however, was her depiction of the administration's "intellectual architecture" for grand strategy.[26] Within 48 hours, academic commentators were raising warning flags about the theory she said would drive the "Pompeo corollary" of the Trump doctrine.

Two years earlier, Trump campaign advisor James Carafino argued that Trump is "no isolationist." There was a "method to the madness" the president instigates. Rather than try to solve the world's intractable problems, Trump was seeking to minimize threats to the United States. He was, in sum, "an arch nationalist in the positive sense of the term." Carafino was trying to bridge the gap between Trump's impulses and formal strategy. What exactly American nationalism might mean, however, was unclear. Indeed, throughout that year, officials attempted to formulate "principled realism," a hybrid of traditional Republican foreign policy and nationalist impulses. Some observers characterized the administration's budget proposals, zero-sum logics, and transactional approach as simple militarism.[27]

Back at that spring event, Skinner provided an insider's take. She set out Trump's strategic priorities and a useful intellectual framework to unite them. It was a cipher. It was also, as Carafino predicted, pure nationalism. As president, she explained, Trump was forcing foreign policy and international relations professionals to reconsider "first principles" when confronted with Trump's strategic "pillars." Though a loose collection of concepts, these effectively summarize much of what this book has uncovered. First, Skinner explained, *national sovereignty* is a priority. Protecting and respecting borders and national prerogatives is the font of national prosperity as well as the most effective way to protect individual rights. In turn, *national interest* based on this elevated understanding of sovereignty should guide all foreign policy. Abroad, *burden sharing* and *reciprocity* should define international relationships. The United States, she explained, "cannot take on the whole globe." NATO, for instance, had seen the United States spending a larger percentage of its budget on the military than any other state despite others' obligations. During Trump's tenure, Germany and others had started to increase their spending. Finally, rather than building international organizations and regimes, the United States would focus on *regional partnerships* to address specific issues.

To apply these principles, Skinner described the State Department's emerging strategy toward China. Her effort spiraled toward notoriety among international relations scholars, who had long rejected race as an analytical category.[28] It was, she explained, "the first time that we will have a great power competitor that is not Caucasian." Beijing rather than Russia represented a true long-term challenge to the United States. Where McMaster, Mattis and others had reframed US national security strategy from unconventional threats to traditional power politics, Skinner argued that the logic of competition was not distrust and balance of power, as described by realists, but culture and history. Trade was important and had been tackled by the administration, but there were deeper, more profound differences. The United States and China see the world in fundamentally different, sometimes incompatible, ways. Human rights, for instance, had been a useful wedge issue to critique the Soviet Union, but "that's not really possible with China."

When pressed, Skinner acknowledged that this theory overlapped with Samuel Huntington's "clash of civilizations" thesis. One of the great American political scientists of the latter twentieth century, Huntington predicted that conflict during the twenty-first century would center on fault lines between the world's cultural and religious zones. Critics immediately pointed out the racialized undertones of this theory and argued that, in any case, most international relations scholars reject Huntington's thesis as analytically and empirically invalid.[29] For Skinner, however, this approach represented a fair characterization of Trump's intuitions on national security strategy.

Trump's Grand Strategy

Nationalism, in other words, perfectly bridged Trump's personal preferences and the need for some larger strategic and intellectual framework. Most observers agree on Trump's personal operating principles. He saw the world, like his real estate business, as full of winners and losers, and he was "perfectly willing to dispense with seemingly core beliefs in return for negotiating advantage."[30] Of course, there exist dozens of other contemporary interpretations and takes seeking to define Trump's grand strategy. As inductive, individual-level assessments, these are valuable. However, these insights also are typically yoked to political or theoretical agendas. They assess what the strategy *is* but do little to separate that from what it *should be*. Again, though valuable, what that type of diagnostic work typically lacks is a standardized framework to compare strategies across eras and cases. Such a framework allows the observer to separate the empirical reality of the grand strategy from ideological and political debates. What studies of grand strategy in general, and Trump's grand strategy in particular, have lacked is this kind of framework.

This book sheds light on Donald Trump's grand strategy using two simple frameworks. The *scope, substance, assertiveness* framework revealed

the parameters of what I have called "global nationalism." The administration, sometimes uneasily, combined a relatively parochial reading of
US strategic goals with a global purview. There was no region irrelevant
to US national interests, but at the same time, the US agenda should
enhance its own sovereign rights. Aside from a few governments that
administration officials singled out as serious enemies, Trump and his
core advisors looked at other governments less as allies and adversaries
and more as clients. Foreign governments posed a threat to the degree
that they benefitted more than the United States from trade relationships
or, though less immediately, to the degree that they posed a long-term
threat to drag the United States into a conflict or pose a threat to the
homeland. It was a transactional and bilateral approach. Migration,
meanwhile, was elevated to the level of grand strategy because, under
this nationalist rubric, foreign identities and cultures could pose as much
danger as trade or security challenges. Trump and his team favored tough
rhetoric and, as an operating principle, adopted "maximal pressure." In
practice, though, Trump veered away from high levels of assertiveness
in favor of limited military threats, hardline policies, tough talk, and
ratcheting economic pressure.

The assessment questions, meanwhile, showed some early insight
into President Trump's individual impact on US grand strategy. Overall,
Trump's influence was real but contained. The study showed moderate
correlations between the president's individual statements and positions,
on the one side, and government policies and foreign policy principals
on the other. That Trump, as opposed to Hillary Clinton, was elected
had a real impact on US grand strategy. As president, however, Trump
during these two years never personally embodied or fundamentally
altered the full nature of US grand strategy. He shaped but failed to
revolutionize grand strategy.

These findings are correlations. They do not show the content of the
relationship between the individual in the Oval Office and the country's
larger approach to the world. Fortunately, the narrative cases offer some

insight into that interaction. On balance, Trump's individual style was both an asset and a liability. It allowed him to directly confront challenges like trade with China, free-riding NATO governments, and North Korean bluster. On the other hand, Trump's inconsistency, inattention, and preference for marketing over substance weakened his control over the foreign policy bureaucracy and regularly left even his closest principals contradicting his positions. In turn, this chapter also ventured a brief estimation of the Trump administration's relative success. It found that Trump and his team were able to radically reset the United States' grand strategy tone. They achieved, however, only modest success toward their goals of revamping US trade relations, reducing military commitments, securing greater respect, and tamping migration. Indeed, future analyses may likely conclude that the administration's chaotic, norm-breaking approach created more harm than benefit.

Both these approaches show the promise of grand strategy analysis (GSA). As developed in Chapter 2, this approach to analyzing grand strategy emphasizes studying the individual in order to identify a pattern of thought and policy. The assumption, here, is that grand strategy is an empirical phenomenon. It can be observed and assessed. Like a social movement or an institution, it can exist outside any one leader's mind. Most studies are, understandably, focused on whether a grand strategy is effective or whether a single person or regime can effectively implement a grand strategy. Though important, such approaches can also be category errors. If a grand strategy is long-lived beyond the control of any one administration, then leaders' ambitions with grand strategy are inherently constrained. The strategy acts on the individuals as much as or more than they act upon it. Following foreign policy analysis, GSA focuses on individuals and groups as the locus of actual behavior to observe grand strategy.

The president's global nationalism may represent a significant change for US grand strategy. It was expressly opposed to internationalism, promised to rearrange how the United States defined its relationship with the world, and in late 2018, it even led Trump to disavow the views of his Secretary of Defense. Trump himself seemed *sui generis*, a category unto himself. Unconcerned with precedent and norms, he roiled the bureaucracy, the media, the public, and other governments. His administration's "maximal pressure" approach threatened to entangle the United States in multiple, simultaneous disputes. The GSA framework helps divide and observe this environment. It introduces a systematic focus on individuals in the context of both ideas and systems. Here, it reveals that Trump's grand strategy was distinct and potent during this period. It also, counterintuitively, reveals that Trump's personal impact was constrained. Do leaders matter? They do. Grand strategies also matter. They may, in fact, carry more influence than the leaders espousing them.

Notes

1. Leslie Stahl, "President Trump on Christine Blasey Ford, His Relationships with Vladimir Putin and Kim Jong Un And More," *60 Minutes*, aired October 15, 2018, https://www.cbsnews.com/news/donald-trump-full-interview-60-minutes-transcript-lesley-stahl-2018-10-14/

2. Staff, "Trump says Bolton doing a good job but has to temper him," *Reuters*, May 9, 2019, https://www.reuters.com/article/us-usa-trump-bolton/trump-says-bolton-doing-a-good-job-but-has-to-temper-him-idUSKCN1SF2AI.

3. Mike Pence often framed guiding principles as "lodestars." Justin L. Mack, "Mike Pence, lodestar and the New York Times op-ed: What we know," *The Indianapolis Star*, September 6, 2018, https://www.indystar.com/story/news/2018/09/06/lodestar-definition-mike-pence-and-anonymous-new-york-times-trump-op-ed/1209714002/.

4. Rebecca Friedman Lissner and Micah Zenko, "There Is No Trump Doctrine, and There Will Never Be One," *Foreign Policy*, July 21, 2017, https://foreignpolicy.com/2017/07/21/there-is-no-trump-doctrine-and-there-will-never-be-one-grand-strategy/. See also Richard Haass, "Donald Trump and the Danger of 'Adhocery,'" *The Atlantic*, July 18, 2017, https://www.theatlantic.com/international/archive/2017/07/donald-trump-adhocracy/533934/; Eliot A. Cohen, "Trump's Lucky Year: Why the Chaos Can't Last," *Foreign Affairs*, Mar/Apr 2018, https://www.foreignaffairs.com/articles/2018-01-20/trumps-lucky-year.

5. Colin Dueck, "Trump's Strategic Unpredictability, Its Pros and Cons," *National Review*, December 28, 2018, https://www.nationalreview.com/2018/12/trump-foreign-policy-strategic-unpredictability-adversaries-allies/

6. John Bew and David Martin Jones, "A Trump Doctrine?" *The National Interest*, Jan/Feb 2018, 43–52.

7. Ionut Popescu, "American Grand Strategy and the Rise of Offensive Realism," *Political Science Quarterly* 134, no. 3 (2019): 375–405.

8. Michael Anton, "The Trump Doctrine," *Foreign Policy*, April 20, 2019, https://foreignpolicy.com/2019/04/20/the-trump-doctrine-big-think-america-first-nationalism/.

9. Barry R. Posen, "The Rise of Illiberal Hegemony: Trump's Surprising Grand Strategy," *Foreign Affairs* 97, no. 2, Mar/Apr 2018, 20–27.

10. Andrew Bacevich, "Saving 'America First': What Responsible National-ism Looks Like," *Foreign Affairs* 96, no. 5, Sep/Oct 2017, 57–67.

11. Colin Dueck, *Age of Iron: On Conservative Nationalism* (New York: Oxford University Press, 2020).

12. Ibid., p. 9

13. Jung H. Pak, "The good, the bad, and the ugly at the US-North Korea summit in Hanoi," Brookings Institution, *Order from Chaos* blog post. Washington, DC, March 4, 2019, https://www.brookings.edu/blog/order-from-chaos/2019/03/04/the-good-the-bad-and-the-ugly-at-the-us-north-korea-summit-in-hanoi/.

14. Hal Brands, "America's Foreign Policy Isn't Dead. Yet," *Bloomberg*, April 22, 2019, https://www.bloomberg.com/opinion/articles/2019-04-2 2/trump-hasn-t-killed-american-foreign-policy-yet.

15. Susan Glasser, "Donald Trump's Year of Living Dangerously," *Politico*, January/February 2018, https://www.politico.com/magazine/story/2018 /01/02/donald-trump-foreign-policy-analysis-dangerous-216202

16. Hal Brands, "If You Thought 2017 was Bad, Just Wait for 2018," *Foreign Policy*, January 8, 2018, https://foreignpolicy.com/2018/01/08/if-you-thought-2017-was-bad-just-wait-for-2018-trump-united-states-foreign-policy/.

17. Robert D. Blackwill, *Trump's Foreign Policies Are Better Than They Seem*, Council of Foreign Relations, New York City, Council Special Report No. 84, April 2019, https://cfrd8-files.cfr.org/sites/default/files/report_pdf/CSR%2084_Blackwill_Trump.pdf.

18. Ibid., p. 67.

19. Ibid., p. 4.

20. Yuval Levin, "Situation Normal..." *National Review*, February 19, 2018, https://www.nationalreview.com/corner/president-trump-tweets-officials-say-ignore/.

21. Aaron David Miller and Richard Sokolsky, "Trump's foreign policy is neither strategic nor competent," Opinions, CNN, October 17, 2017, https://www.cnn.com/2017/10/17/opinions/strategic-competence-opinion-miller-sokolsky/index.html.

22. Randall Schweller, "Three Cheers for Trump's Foreign Policy: What the Establishment Misses," *Foreign Affairs* 97, no. 5, Sep/Oct 2018,133–136, 138–143.

23. Dimitri K. Simes, "A Trump Foreign Policy," *The National Interest*, June 17, 2018.

24. Dueck *Age of Iron*, p. 131.

25. For example,, see Jonathan Stevenson, "The Madness Behind Trump's 'Madman' Strategy," *The New York Times*, October 26, 2017, https://www.nytimes.com/2017/10/26/opinion/the-madness-behind-trumps-madman-strategy.html?action=click&pgtype=Homepage&clickSource=story-heading&module=opinion-c-col-right-region&region=opinion-c-col-right-region&WT.nav=opinion-c-col-right-region; James Hohmann, "The Daily 202: Trump suggests his embrace of the 'madman theory' brought North Korea to the table," *The Washington Post*, February 26, 2019, https://www.washingtonpost.com/news/powerpost/paloma/daily-202/2019/02/26/daily-202-trump-suggests-his-embrace-of-the-madman-theory-brought-north-korea-to-the-table/5c7422741b326b71858c6c33/?utm_term=.6ec7b96da080; and Keith Johnson, "Trump's 'Madman Theory' of Trade with China," *Foreign Policy*, May 10, 2019, https://foreignpolicy.com/2019/05/10/trumps-madman-theory-of-trade-with-china/.

26. Future Security Forum 2019, recorded interview with Kiron Skinner, conference hosted by New America Foundation and Arizona State University, Washington, DC, April 29, 2019, https://www.newamerica.org/conference/future-security-forum-2019/.

27. Eric Gomez, "Trump's First 100 Days and the Deepening Militarization of U.S. Foreign Policy," *Cato at Liberty*, Washington, DC, April 28, 2017, https://www.cato.org/blog/trumps-first-100-days-deepening-militarization-us-foreign-policy

28. Dan Nexon, "Better Reading of Story Must Bring Home The Truth That The Basic Factor in Human Affairs Is Not Politics, But Race," Lawyers, Guns, Money Blog, May 3, 2019, http://www.lawyersgunsmoneyblog.com/2019/05/a-better-reading-of-history-must-bring-home-the-truth-that-the-basic-factor-in-human-affairs-is-not-politics-but-race.

29. Daniel W. Drezner, "Let's grade the State Department's director of policy planning on her grand strategy musings!" *The Washington Post*, May 1, 2019, https://www.washingtonpost.com/outlook/2019/05/02/lets-grade-state-departments-director-policy-planning-her-grand-strategy-musings/?utm_term=.eace3a5c7b01; Paul Musgrave, "The Slip That Revealed the Real Trump Doctrine," *Foreign Policy*, May 2, 2019, https://foreignpolicy.com/2019/05/02/the-slip-that-revealed-the-real-trump-doctrine/; Jessica Chen Weiss, "No, China and the U.S. aren't locked in an ideological battle. Not even close," *The Washington Post*, May 4, 2019, https://www.washingtonpost.com/politics/2019/05/04/no-china-us-arent-locked-an-ideological-battle-not-even-close/?utm_term=

.0f9d5432cf4a; Steven Ward, "Because China isn't 'Caucasian,' the U.S. is planning for a 'clash of civilizations.' That could be dangerous," *The Washington Post*, May 4, 2019, https://www.washingtonpost.com/politics/2019/05/04/because-china-isnt-caucasian-us-is-planning-clash-civilizations-that-could-be-dangerous/?utm_term=.16693388fc3b. For an overview of Huntington's thesis, see Jacob Shively, "Clash of Civilizations" in *SAGE Encyclopedia of War: Social Science Perspectives*, edited by Paul Joseph (Thousand Oaks, CA: SAGE Publications, 2017), 312–314.

30. Maggie Haberman and David Sanger, "Transcript: Donald Trump Expounds on His Foreign Policy Views," *The New York Times*, March 26, 2016, https://www.nytimes.com/2016/03/27/us/politics/donald-trump-transcript.html?_r=0.

INDEX

About the Author

Jacob Shively is an associate professor in the Reubin O'D. Askew Department of Government at the University of West Florida, where he teaches international relations. He holds a PhD from Indiana University, where he completed his dissertation "Lost Ambition: Grand Strategy Stability and Abandoned Change in the Jimmy Carter and George W. Bush Administrations." In addition to *Hope, Change, Pragmatism: Analyzing Obama's Grand Strategy*, Dr. Shively's other work includes academic articles, numerous papers and talks, media appearances, and briefings for national security professionals.

CAMBRIA RAPID COMMUNICATIONS IN CONFLICT AND SECURITY (RCCS) SERIES

General Editor: Geoffrey R. H. Burn

The aim of the RCCS series is to provide policy makers, practitioners, analysts, and academics with in-depth analysis of fast-moving topics that require urgent yet informed debate. Since its launch in October 2015, the RCCS series has the following book publications:

- *A New Strategy for Complex Warfare: Combined Effects in East Asia* by Thomas A. Drohan
- *US National Security: New Threats, Old Realities* by Paul R. Viotti
- *Security Forces in African States: Cases and Assessment* edited by Paul Shemella and Nicholas Tomb
- *Trust and Distrust in Sino-American Relations: Challenge and Opportunity* by Steve Chan
- *The Gathering Pacific Storm: Emerging US-China Strategic Competition in Defense Technological and Industrial Development* edited by Tai Ming Cheung and Thomas G. Mahnken
- *Military Strategy for the 21st Century: People, Connectivity, and Competitipauon* by Charles Cleveland, Benjamin Jensen, Susan Bryant, and Arnel David
- *Ensuring National Government Stability After US Counterinsurgency Operations: The Critical Measure of Success* by Dallas E. Shaw Jr.
- *Reassessing U.S. Nuclear Strategy* by David W. Kearn, Jr.
- *Deglobalization and International Security* by T. X. Hammes
- *American Foreign Policy and National Security* by Paul R. Viotti

- *Make America First Again: Grand Strategy Analysis and the Trump Administration* by Jacob Shively
- *Learning from Russia's Recent Wars: Why, Where, and When Russia Might Strike Next* by Neal G. Jesse
- *Restoring Thucydides: Testing Familiar Lessons and Deriving New Ones* by Andrew R. Novo and Jay M. Parker
- *Net Assessment and Military Strategy: Retrospective and Prospective Essays* edited by Thomas G. Mahnken, with an introduction by Andrew W. Marshall

For more information, visit www.cambriapress.com.

www.ingramcontent.com/pod-product-compliance
Lightning Source LLC
Chambersburg PA
CBHW031416270326
41929CB00010BA/1478